The Speaking All-Unity
The Word of the Universal Creator-Spirit

THE SPEAKING ALL-UNITY

The Word of the Universal
Creator-Spirit

*A Cosmic Work of Teaching and Learning
From the School of Divine Wisdom*

*Taken from conversations
with Gabriele
and compiled by
Martin Kübli and Ulrich Seifert*

THE WORD
THE UNIVERSAL SPIRIT

The free universal Spirit is the teaching
of love for God and neighbor
toward man, nature and animals

First Edition – June 2014

Published by:
© Universal Life
The Inner Religion
P.O. Box 3549
Woodbridge, CT 06525
U S A
www.Universal-Spirit.org
1-800-846-2691

Licensed Edition
translated from the original German title:
"Die Redende All-Einheit.
Das Wort des Universalen Schöpfergeistes"
with the consent of
© Gabriele-Verlag Das Wort GmbH
Max-Braun-Str. 2, 97828 Marktheidenfeld
Germany

Order No. S 173en
The German edition is the work of reference for all
questions regarding the meaning of the content.

All rights reserved

Printer: KlarDruck GmbH, Marktheidenfeld

Photo Credits: Cover Earthball © freshidea/fotolia.com.
p. 326: © Per-Anders Pettersson/Corbis.
p. 327 and 333: © Jenny Matthews/In Pictures/Corbis.
p. 328 above: © Viviane Moos/Corbis. p. 328 below: © Les Stone/Sygma/Corbis
p. 329: © Karen Kasmauski/Corbis. p. 330: © Bettmann/Corbis.
p. 331 above: © Peter Turnley/Corbis. p. 331 below: © David Turnley/Corbis.
p. 332: © Alison Wright/Corbis.

ISBN: 978-1-890841-33-1

Table of Contents

*Foreword
A Divine-Prophetic Vision, Conveyed in the Simple Words of Our Three-dimensional World* 15

Preface 23

The Make-up of the Core of Being in the Eternal's Cradle of Drawing and Creating 38

The spiritual birth of filiation – The developing spirit child is taken into a spirit family 41

The paramount primordial power – God – The cosmic Law-word of the All in all beings and all things 44

*The steps to life.
The bridge to the core of being* 47

*The sons and daughters of God –
Heirs to infinity* 51

The Kingdom of God and the Life of the Divine Beings in the Eternal Being 54

The primordial image of the creation of Being 54

The Workings of the Four Primordial Powers in the Condensed Being 61

A scientist reports 67
   The Big Bang 69
   What was before the Big Bang? 73
   The four quantum numbers 74
   Four bases determine the genetic code 75
   The concept of the four elements 76
   Important biomolecules have a
   four-part structure 76

The All-Harmony of the Eternal Being 78

Every heavenly plane has its specific color
and its design 79

The meaning of our life on Earth –
Becoming aware of our true origin 81

The Five Components in the Life of Man that Become Warfare Agents 83

In order to learn, we could ask ourselves:
Who are we and what do we emit? 83

The primary warfare agent – Our thoughts 86

Our life film – We human beings live in pictures ... 89

Why the weapons arsenals of this world? 91

Combat and warfare weapons against
God's creation 94

The five warfare agents of the vandal "man" 97

The five warfare agents from a physician's point of view 106

The path of recognition for the liberation of the soul. We can put a stop to the thought disaster 112

The Human Being, the Core of Being and the Spirit Being 115

A comparison: Communication technology on Earth and the All-communication principle 120

What exactly is love? 126

The Breath of God – The All-Law, the Light-Ether 131

The breath of God is the "Let There Be," which continues up to the spiritual filiation. 134

How can we imagine the birth of a spirit? 136

The Fall of the Spiritual Beings Down to the Coarse-Materialness of the Human Being 139

The Fall-law: "divide, bind and rule." The demon aspires to destroy the divine core of being. 141

*Loss of energy and the loss of freedom
lead to addictions and other excesses* *143*

*The "murder machinery" man on behalf of
the pagan god Baal and his adherents* *146*

*Man destroyed the original, harmonious
symbiosis between animals and nature.
The maltreated Earth is rebelling* *149*

*The estrangement from the All-Unity
is the spiritual poverty of egomania.
The hellish brandmark: "Everything is mine!"* *152*

Your Consciousness Lies in You – Faith Cannot Be Proven *154*

*The law of love for God and neighbor:
"Link and be"* *156*

We Learn – Learn Along with Us! "Sending and Receiving" and the All-Communication that Makes You Free *159*

*Particularly the present situation in the world
makes it blatantly obvious what "divide, bind
and rule" means* *161*

Man – An image of God? *165*

*We Learn to First Fashion the Great
Garden of Eden in Ourselves* 168

*All living beings and life forms from God's
creation are beings of the All-Unity* 172

*Again and again, the question comes up:
Dual pairs, dual parents, and children from
the duality – How can that be? In the temporal,
an analogy to the Kingdom of God* 174

*What separates us from the All-Unity, the
communication with the eternal Creator-God?
We learn on ourselves* 176

*Everything is consciousness – Even in our sleep
we experience our consciousness* 178

*True humility is freeing, caring and
uplifting. Egoism is contemptuous of life
and destructive* 183

*Animals want to be taken seriously
and treated with care* 185

*Our aura reflects our behavior patterns –
The animals perceive our radiation* 187

*An interjected question from the conversations.
To understand the animals, we have to become
permeable* 191

Learning from animals 194

Experiences of the viewers of the program series "The Speaking All-Unity – The Word of the Universal Creator-Spirit" and of the participants of the conversations 198

Animals want to make themselves understood – They have their "language" 211

Several statements about animals from "great minds" 213

When walking in woods and fields, man seeks a respite – While doing so, he enters the dwelling places of his fellow creatures 215

Animals take flight; plants tremble – What does this want to tell us? 219

We learn and practice, to become aware of what precious creatures live among us. We practice watching our animal fellow creatures 224

Sensory perception is important for the development of awareness 226

Together We Experience a Virtual Walk! *230*

*During a virtual walk, many a thing can be figured out more easily and deeply.
We learn and practice* *230*

*Everything bears within the melodies of the All; everything is part of the All-symphony.
We take in a bird's body of sound* *231*

To what extent has our sounding box become more light-filled and brighter? Our virtual walk leads us to a clearing – We take in another animal's body of sound *237*

We take the life form of a flower into our body of sound *241*

The report of an experience *243*

Practice makes perfect! *245*

The Earth is a living organism *250*

*In the very basis of our soul, we are unendingly rich. The inner wealth is decisive -
The eternal life* *254*

*Let Us Continue Learning to Fathom
What We Heard and Read* 255

*How can we respond to the great suffering of
the animals, the plants, of all of Mother Earth?* 255

*There is still much to do, to achieve
the cosmic All-communication, and this means:
Learn, learn, and learn again!
Shall we dare to do this?* 256

*The Covenant of the Eternal
with the Animals* 259

The Earth-killer man 264

*The Principle of All-Communication –
Without Technology.
Man's Worldly Communication Aids* 266

*The All-Communication Network Goes
with the Approaching Earth Citizen* 271

The life cycle of a human being on Earth 271

*Via the core of being, the new person remains
connected to the All-communication* 272

*The soul prepares the person
for his passing* 277

*The Incorruptible Core of Being –
Hope Leads to Eternal Life* 281
*The seat of the maturing core of being
in animals, plants and minerals* 281
*Man's idolatry mania. The manipulation
of animals, plants and nature* 283
Why doesn't God intervene? The law of freedom 285

*Epilogue
The Unending, Inexhaustible Light-Ether,
the Primordial Substance from which the
Infinite, the Eternal, the Primordial God,
Creates and Forms* 289
The Light-Ether 292

*The Emergence of the Earth According
to the Present Position of Science* 308
  The primeval time of the Earth.........................310
  The Paleozoic Era 316
  The Mesozoic Era (251-65 million years ago) ...316
  *The Cenozoic Era (65 million years ago
  until today)* 319

An Appeal 321
We Are All Children of God 325
*I Am in Your Soul as Strength and Light.
For Virtual Observation* 335

Foreword

A Divine Prophetic Vision, Conveyed in the Simple Words of Our Three-dimensional World

Dear fellow people, in the cosmic work of teaching and learning "The Speaking All-Unity – The Word of the Universal Creator-Spirit," you will read words of truth, given from the eternal truth, from the eternal life, which is seven-dimensional.
The word of truth encompasses dimensions that usually remain closed to our largely materially shaped way of thinking.

Jesus, the Christ, made true what He promised mankind 2000 years ago, when He said: *I still have many things to say to you, but you cannot bear them now. When the Spirit of truth comes, he will guide you into all the truth.*
In roundtable discussions with Gabriele, the prophetess and emissary of God in our time, we have recorded the descriptions of her inner vision and her word. Insofar as it was possible for us, we pass on the content of these conversations here in the book "The Speaking All-Unity – The Word

of the Universal Creator-Spirit. A Cosmic Work of Teaching and Learning from the School of Divine Wisdom." It sheds light on the make-up and the works of the all-encompassing mighty event of creation, from the Light-Ether to the make-up of the core of being of all beings of creation and God's perfect form of Being.

We human beings live in the three dimensions, which for us usually is the measure of all things. This is why our language is also shaped by the three dimensions. We fill words with the most diverse content. This is also true of the word "God," with which far more disaster has been wreaked in the history of the world than blessing was brought. When God is mentioned in this book, then the content of this word is not the institutionally shaped image of a punishing God who envelops Himself in mysteries, but rather the all-encompassing primordial intelligence, the Creator-power of the Eternal, which, in universal, inherent laws, is effective in all of infinity.

During the conversations about His work – "The Speaking All-Unity – The Word of the Universal Creator-Spirit" – we received previously unknown insights, which, in this unique work of cosmic teaching and learning merely convey "a glance through a crack in the door."

Expressed in our words, God's truth comes alive only when we do not dismiss everything right away, but learn to understand it step by step through spiritual exercises that bring self-recognition, so that we comprehend that God is the truth in us and that our words are merely shells into which the Eternal pours the truth.

Among other things, we will frequently read about the divine core of being, which is the primordial heart in the very basis of our soul. In all these elucidations, we are encouraged to learn to grasp and fathom the Eternal Being in us. We ourselves are called upon to intuit the spaceless and timeless eternity in the very basis of our soul, and to recognize who or what truly pulsates in the depths of our soul, namely, the primordial heart of eternity, the essence of the Kingdom of God, of which Jesus of Nazareth essentially said: *The Kingdom of God is within, in you.*

The word of truth leads us into the dimensions of the All-communication of all Being, so that it becomes possible for us to sense for ourselves in what mighty cosmic All-life – permeated by the Spirit – we are embedded, from which cradle all life went forth and in which the smallest component is part of the all-encompassing creation.

Step by step, a fundamentally different approach to life in all Being is opened to us. We become aware of where we and all beings of creation come from and to where we will ultimately go. It is an all-encompassing vision, the content of which opens up for the one who opens himself to the omnipresent Spirit of life.

Anyone who, based on this work of teaching and learning, walks the path himself, in order to experience the unity of all life in himself more and more, often stands bewildered, yes, helpless, before the brutal ignorance toward all life, which for the majority of people has become commonplace, if not even an elixir of life, because with their world of thoughts and senses they have closed themselves off from the All-life, the speaking All-Unity, the Universal Creator-Spirit.

Someone who does not merely read the schooling text, but works with the cosmic work of teaching and learning, by including himself in the elucidations on the speaking All-Unity, will realize ever more how shockingly far we human beings have removed ourselves from the All-Unity, culminating in the manipulated artificial creations by human hand in the animal and plant worlds, which do not originate from the breath of God. Man behaves in nature like a stranger; he has turned away from the life in all Being.

Because this unity of all life has become so foreign to us, the elucidation of the many facets is necessary, which for this reason are also conveyed to us in repetitions and deepening explanations. Thus, the questions and answers that arose during the discussions on the subject are included in the text. In this cosmic work of teaching and learning, explanatory repetitions thus serve to deepen and better understand the subject matter on the speaking All-Unity of the Universal Creator-Spirit, which humiliatingly, first has to again be brought home to us human beings.

But anyone who attentively follows the text is overcome with awe before the unceasingly flowing law of God, which contains the All-Unity of all Being. It is the beauty and perfection of the All-Intelligence of God, which, in being aware of the speaking All-Unity of the Universal Creator-Spirit, also becomes recognizable to us in the material Being. The person who walks the path of learning will be richly rewarded through the refinement of his sensibility toward creation, through the increasing perception of life in all Being. He will also find himself, and live more and more in the awareness that his life, too, is part of the speaking All-Unity, of the word of the Universal Creator-Spirit. Through this, it will gradually become a matter of course for him to no longer harm, use, exploit or enslave other beings. The Golden Rule for life of Jesus of Nazareth: *Do to others as you would have them do to you* – spoken differently for the present time: *Do not do to another what you do not want to have done to you* – will be filled with life by him, which incorporates all forms of Being.

To experience the unity of creation and to comprehend that everything, from the smallest to the largest, originates from a cosmic order, which has its origin in the All-Intelligence God, is the greatest evolutionary step that man is capable of. This is the foundation for all peaceful development in the life of the individual, as well as in that of the whole family of mankind, in the life with animals and plants, with all of nature and in the relationship to all Being. For this reason, the cognizance of the speaking All-Unity, the word of the Universal Creator-Spirit, is also the hope for the Earth, on which a humankind will grow that, in awareness of the cosmic unity, will have left behind exploitation, hatred, violence, war, murder and manslaughter, because it will have grasped that life is limitless and that all Being – also that in the mineral kingdoms, in the plants and animals – comes from the one eternal source: from God, the Creator of all Being.

In conversation, Gabriele encouraged us: "Let us learn, so that we gradually immerse in the ocean of life, because ultimately, we come from the ocean of life and are called by the Eternal to return to the eternal homeland; for each of us bears within the essence of the eternal homeland, the eternal home, the eternal Being, the core of being, the primordial heart, which we people are given an understanding of step by step in this book. Then we will understand that no person can lead us there, but solely the eternal Spirit, God in us all.

Join us! Go with us into the cosmic school, to learn, to grasp what true life means, in order to eventually experience for yourself that there is no death, only a changing over into another aggregate state that is of finer material."

The content of this great work of creation, "The Speaking All-Unity – The Word of the Universal Creator-Spirit. A Cosmic Work of Teaching and Learning from the School of Divine Wisdom," is given by the mighty Spirit of God, the universal, highest Intelligence.

We will also read about the experiences of several participants in the roundtable discussions – particularly with the five components in relation to the laws of God – and about the insights from the viewpoint of today's science, explained by a scientist.

The authors have compiled the cosmic content of teaching and learning in this book.

Martin Kübli, Ulrich Seifert

Preface

Dear fellow people, in this book, the spiritual terms and words are adapted to present-day understanding, such as the words eternity, All-Unity, God, eternal law, universal life, eternal Being, spiritual life forms, divine beings or even God-Father and Kingdom of God.

We human beings are shaped by three-dimensional terms. All earthly terms have a content that needs to be understood, by thinking about it and analyzing it.

Science has its coined words, that is, they are also terms, which – like all words – are shaped three-dimensionally. The word "God" is also a term. Behind it are words like primordial Spirit, All-Spirit, primordial stream, Creator, eternal life, cosmic unending power of love or even Father-Mother-God.

Only we ourselves can answer what is to be understood in the words, or terms, by taking the steps that God, the Eternal, taught us through Moses – in the Ten Commandments – and Jesus, the Christ, in His Sermon on the Mount.

There is no other way to be able to grasp what speaks, or talks, in the very basis of our soul, and that, only by way of inner perception.

Many people ask themselves and also ask their fellowman: "Where does God come from?" This question can be answered by us only with the smallest word "is": HE IS.

Anyone who asks further, for instance, "What is He?" receives the answer: The eternal "now," which has no beginning, no past and no future. IT is present, eternally. If there were a beginning, then God would not be eternal. If there were a past, then God would also cease to be. God was and is eternally present.

However, in the word usage of man, the word "present" has nothing in common with the word "omnipresent." Nor does the eternal "now" have anything to do with the "now" commonly used by man, just as the word "love" commonly used by man has nothing in common with the love for God and neighbor.

The Eternal, the eternal Spirit, the eternal Creator, the Father-Mother-God of all His children gives people the answer from His omnipresence, which is:

> I AM THE I AM, the God of Abraham, Isaac and Jacob.
> I AM THE I AM, the God of all true prophets.
> I AM the life, the Creator, the Being, and for you, My child, the Father-Mother-God, eternally.

If we human beings could ask the princes of heaven, the cherubs before His throne, where God comes from – they would answer: The coming of God would be a beginning, and thus, God, too, would have an end. But He is eternal and is eternity, everlasting.
That He is, is omnipresence. What He is like, each one may experience in himself.

All the spiritual terms and words in this book are based on the foundation of the all-permeating, all-encompassing Light-Ether.

The Light-Ether is the inexhaustible primordial source of eternity. It is the drawing and creating All-principle of the Father-Mother-God, from which the ethereal forms emerge.

The Light-Ether, which we will read about in more detail in the epilogue, is the highest, inexhaustible energy, in which the Kingdom of God, all pure life forms and all divine beings are embedded. The finer-material realms, that is, cosmoses, and the material cosmos are also surrounded by the Light-Ether.

The finer-material realms, as well as the material cosmos, were formed through the Fall-concepts of rebellious divine beings, who, despite everything, remain divine in the very basis of their being. However, in the spirit of the Fall, they wanted to create their own realm.

Their goal, their desire, was primarily the dissolution of the divine creation, of all divine forms and divine beings. According to their ideal, everything was to go back into the eternal stream, from which they themselves wanted to draw, create and form, according to their ideal.

In the eternal law, free will is decisive. For their purposes, the once divine beings took with themselves a volume of creative energy approximately equal to a handful of Light-Ether, predominantly from the Center of Being – we also call it the Sanctum of God-Father – in order to bring about the dissolution of all divine forms with this.

The infinite, inexhaustible Light-Ether is the Eternal's spiritual energy of drawing and creating.
As stated, the Fall-thought of the Fall-beings was to found a realm according to their ideas, following the dissolution of the divine creation.

We have to consider what energetic wealth approximately one handful of Light-Ether contains, with which the pugnacious beings surrounded themselves. Although they became more light-poor, they continued to fight against God and His creation. We can only vaguely appreciate what energy volume the Light-Ether must contain.

With the already transformed-down state of consciousness, with the one handful of Light-Ether, the rebellious beings created stations, finer-material realms, suns and planets, which corresponded to their desire, to their Fall-picture. According to their consciousness, which became ever narrower, condensing more and more, the finer-material, that is, the transformed-down ether, just like the Fall-beings, also became denser substance, that is, it was no longer fine-material.

Through their intentions, they became ever more material, ever denser, so that their plans also featured ever coarser structures. From the ether-mass, that is, the energy volume that became increasingly denser according to their state of consciousness, it could be recognized that their plan to dissolve the divine creation was failing.

Despite all this, they hope to defeat the Eternal from a stronghold in the All.

The Fall continued over unimaginable periods of time – we can talk about windows of time. According to their transformed-down energy volume, formless masses of ever denser energy developed in regions of the All. Over further periods of time, that is, over windows of time, the transformed-down Light-Ether began to change into a shapeless, ever denser mass, from which the material cosmos with the stronghold Earth emerged.

As the planet Earth solidified, coarser structures developed according to the rebels' state of consciousness. They were shapeless structures that constantly changed. Very gradually, cell-like structures developed. On page 308 of this book, you can find a description of the processes leading to the emergence of the Earth from a scientific point of view.

As the dense form-giving Earth energy provided the magnet for Fall-beings, again, in long periods of time, in windows of time – the development of

man began on the planet, which the Fall-beings had foreseen as a stronghold against God.
A so-called handful of highest Light-Ether, which surrounded the Fall-beings, brought about what we human beings see and do not behold. From this, we can recognize, or realize, what inexhaustible wealth is the Light-Ether.

The Fall-thought, the dissolution of the eternal Being, of divine creation, has failed.
Today, the Fall-thought is the destruction of that which the Earth bears. But the human excesses and the destructive frenzy has already been arrested. The Eternal fetches the life back into the All-Eternity. The overthrow, which the Fall-thought itself has now introduced, is succinctly called: climate change.

The infinite is and remains the All-Creation. As stated: Everything, absolutely everything, is surrounded by the infinite, inexhaustible flowing Light-Ether.
Science talks about unexplored in-between spaces, from solar system to solar system, from Milky Way to Milky Way. Everything that cannot be penetrated and researched is described as dark matter or dark energy. But it is nothing other

than the inexhaustible Light-Ether, the eternal All-Law of infinity, the All-communication-network of the All-One.

As stated, the Fall-thought, the dissolution of divine creation, has failed. Over windows of time, the Eternal leads everything back. Everything goes back into the Light-Ether and the ethereal forms into the Kingdom of God.

If possible, in this book, "The Speaking All-Unity – The Word of the Universal Creator-Spirit. A Cosmic Work of Teaching and Learning from the School of Divine Wisdom," read the elucidations that are given with our three-dimensional terms and words, under the premise that everything, but absolutely everything, is Light-Ether raised to the highest power.

The All-One, the infinite All-God, the paramount Intelligence, the free Spirit, draws from the never-failing Light-Ether and creates pure ethereal forms. The Kingdom of God, too, is ethereal Light-Ether that has taken on form. All the ethereal suns and planets in the Eternal Being are compressed Light-Ether. All divine life forms, all pure beings, spirit beings, are ethereal light forms and figures of light.

God Himself gave form to Himself from His primordial source, the Light-Ether. It is as we already heard, the Father-Mother-God, the noble light-figure of love for His creation.

Please read in the awareness that all pure Being has ethereal forms and that the Fall-thought never could, or can, withstand what flows and streams in the All: It is the light, the Light-Ether, the Eternal, the All-One, the work of creation of God-Father, who is also Mother to His own.

Dear fellow people, the goal of our subject, "The Speaking All-Unity – The Word of the Universal Creator-Spirit," is that – if we want to – we orient our life to the highest in us, and this, step by step, in order to learn and experience ourselves what All-Unity means.

We ourselves should have our own experiences.

And so, let us begin – as well as it is possible for us as human beings, and even though much still remains incomprehensible to us – to walk the path, in order to have a glimpse through the aforementioned crack in the door, behind which we can surmise what we will experience as divine beings upon having returned home. Then the door will open like a mighty gateway, and we will behold our homeland, the eternal Kingdom of God, our true, eternal Being.

Although many a person lets himself be described as a genius – the sole genius, the sole genius in all of infinity, is the Infinite One, the highest Intelligence of Being. In all of infinity, the highest principle of Being, the love, the All-One, draws, creates and fashions by way of His four primordial powers. Whether it is in God's Creator cradle, whether it is the Primordial Central Sun with its prism suns, it is always the four nature powers, the primordial powers in infinity.

In the material cosmos, too, the one principle prevails, the four primordial powers, which bear latent within the three attribute powers of God – Kindness, Love and Gentleness – whereby the highest power of the Being is Love. It is the All-Spirit of the Being in all things. No matter what we call the Spirit of infinity – for instance, primordial power, God, All-Spirit, eternal intelligence, All-One – it is always the Infinite One; it is always the highest Intelligence; it is always the All-Genius and the All-Ingeniousness, God, the Spirit.
No matter what one may call the Being, it is always the four nature powers of God, the primor-

dial powers, and the three attribute powers, the filiation attributes.

Everything is of a spiritual-atomic structure, pure spiritual, eternal substance, the principle of infinity. The glimpse through the spiritual crack in the door is merely an attempt to explain the make-up of the Kingdom of God. Therefore, please understand when different words are used for the seven powers of the Being. With this, each of us human beings, according to his state of consciousness, should be given an understanding of the all-one great event.
Freedom is given to each one of us.
May the one who can grasp it, grasp it. May the one who wants to leave it, leave it. No one is compelled to believe or to accept the spiritual wealth. But each one himself can learn about it and grasp it, if he walks the path that God, the Eternal, gave us through Moses in the Ten Commandments and Jesus of Nazareth in the highest teaching, His Sermon on the Mount.

We people speak so often of our life and with this, we mean our earthly existence.
The true life is from God and is endless, unalterable unity, the All-communication, the language

of the eternal Creator-Spirit, who is the love, and whom we in the western world call God.

The Spirit of infinity, God, is the word of infinity in all Being, in all life forms and in all divine beings, the spirit beings. He, the All-Life, is in the very basis of the soul of every human being and also in every discarnate soul. The visible and invisible cosmoses, all heavenly bodies, stones and minerals are directed and guided by the All-Law of the Eternal. Everything is embedded in the eternal law of life, the Light-Ether. All heavenly bodies, all the plant and animal species created by the Eternal live in the great All-Unity of the Creator-Spirit. Everything, but absolutely everything, is in the All-communication with everything and with the omnipresent Spirit, God.
The Light-Ether, from which the Eternal draws, creates and forms, is the carrier substance of the All-communication.
In infinity, there is no separation and thus, no being separate from the eternal Spirit, who is the eternal life. All divine beings, all life forms and living beings respirated by the Eternal are linked in the All-One through the All-principle, the All-Law of "sending and receiving." The word of the Creator-Spirit is in all beings and in all things.

God emits. He gives – and all Being, everything pure, receives His word, the All-Law of infinity. Nothing and no one is excluded from the infinite All-communication, nor the universes with their suns and planets.

Everything is based on communication. According to their consciousness, that is, their state of development, all animal and plant species perceive their Creator's word of creation. Every stone and every mineral contains the All-Law, which is communication. All life forms created by the Eternal answer their Creator through communication.

The eternal Spirit, God, is thus constantly with His All-community, which we also call All-Unity. And so, God is present, eternal life, which is inseparable and indivisible.

All universes are suffused with His Law-word. The Eternal is the All-One, the All-Spirit and the All-Law of infinity.

Even though, as human beings, we are the material microcosm in the material macrocosm, and God, the Eternal, gave us the Earth with its plants and herbs as the provider – and that, for all human beings and animals – we can hardly perceive God, the eternal Creator-Spirit, in the very basis of our soul, which is likewise cosmic, however, still finer-material. The question arises: Why is it so difficult for us human beings to perceive the word of the All, the Eternal's Law-word, also in the animals and plants, but also as the power of law in minerals and stones? The word "why" is also part of our subject "The Speaking All-Unity – The Word of the Universal Creator-Spirit."

We, who are human beings today, presently live – let us emphasize presently! – in time and space. In this limitation of time and space, we think, speak and act. But the divine, incorruptible core of being, of which we will frequently read, is the primordial heart in the All-communication, which is the "link and be" also in us, in the very basis of our soul.

We repeat: The true, eternal life is seven dimensional. When we return to our eternal homeland, to our origin, as pure, divine beings, as spirit beings, we will again consciously live in the eternal stream of creation, in the seven-dimensional Being. As pure beings, we are not only knowing; we live eternally in our homeland, which is our eternal home, the Kingdom of God, that unceasingly expands – and that, eternally. Eternal life is the awareness and the life in the All-Unity.

With our limited three-dimensional words, with our human understanding, what has been briefly indicated here is hardly comprehensible, but in the very basis of our soul, in the fully developed primordial heart, in the core of being, everything, absolutely everything, is alive.

In the core of being, in our soul, the Eternal speaks the word of Being, the All-Law.

The core of being is the All-Unity in all beings and in all things. God, the Creator of life, is the communication principle of infinity: "sending and receiving." All living beings and life forms are included in this cosmic All-communication.

A completed core of being is ethereal light. It can be compared to a cut and polished diamond.

The Make-up of the Core of Being in the Eternal's Cradle of Drawing and Creating

We human beings are still far behind in our understanding and perception of these divine-spiritual correlations. No one is born a master. We are all learning. If you like – learn along with us!

The eternal core of being develops in God's cradle of drawing, that is, of creating. For better understanding, we could say that the cradle of drawing and creating is the divine "birth body," in which the fine-material, ethereal-spiritual body of the divine beings develops.
In the first basic power of the principle of drawing and creating, Order, also called the primordial power, the Eternal, the Father-Mother principle, the Love, respirates a certain fine-material kind of atom, in which the complete development to the filiation of God, to a matured spirit being, is inherent: the mentality of the developing spirit child, the spirit being, its name and in which spirit family the spirit child will be born. All colors, forms and fragrances of the Being are also active in His "Let There Be." The process of becoming

and maturing into a spiritual child takes place in rhythms, which are set in cycles.

In the first basic power, also called the primordial power, the Order, minerals, viewed energetically, begin to form, which continue to develop in rhythms until they have developed, that is, opened up, all spiritual mineral forms within themselves. In each matured mineral substance, a spiritual germination takes place, which, in rhythms of evolution, forms into spiritual particles.

Once all the spiritual mineral forms have completed their development, respirated by God, the germinating life begins to take on more and more form. In a mighty energetic surge of Light-Ether, the All-Spirit, the Creator-Spirit, carries the completed mineral forms to the next higher formation in the plant kingdom, to the second basic, or primordial, power of the Creator, to that of Will. In the second basic power in God's cradle of drawing, that is, of creation, the plant kingdom develops plant consciousness by plant consciousness, again, in rhythms; this is growth, that is, evolution and maturity.
When in all plant species, in which the mineral substances are present, the entire cosmic power

of Will, the second primordial power, has developed, then these are, in turn, set in further spiritual particles and, as before in the mineral kingdoms, raised by an energetic surge of Light-Ether, by the All-Spirit, into the realm of the animal world. The energetic development continues in the third basic power, the primordial power of divine Wisdom.

Very gradually, likewise in rhythms that are set in cycles, all the ethereal substances and powers of the total animal world develop. Once the animal species, respirated by the Creator-God, the All-Spirit, and which, of course, are ethereal, have completely gone through the animal kingdom and have absorbed all substances and powers of the third primordial power, then the particles of all animal substances are lined up with the existing spiritual particles of the minerals and plants.

In this way, very gradually and in unimaginable cycles, the divine ethereal core of being develops, which we have been, and will still be, reading about – it is the All-essence of the eternal Being. On the last step of evolution, the fourth basic power, that is, the primordial power, that of the divine Earnestness, begins the development, or formation, into a nature form, a nature being.

Once all the steps of evolution have been completed, then the filiation of God begins to take effect in the fully developed nature being.

The spiritual birth of filiation –
The developing spirit child is taken
into a spirit family

At the end of the last step of evolution, the level of divine Earnestness, the fourth basic power, or primordial power, the small being imprinted by nature is led to the spiritual birth of filiation, Kindness, Love and Gentleness, to the Father-Mother principle. It is then raised by a spiritual dual pair to a divine child. How does this take place?
Predetermined by the Father-Mother-God, a divine dual pair, the giving and receiving principle – we would say, the male and female principle – together form a mighty magnetic cocoon of energy. It is the cocoon for receiving a matured nature being from God's cradle of creation, that corresponds to the mentality of the dual pair.

The ethereal-magnetic cocoon of the dual pair attracts that being that corresponds to its men-

tality, receiving it into its magnetic cocoon of energy. Very gradually, the energetic aura, or radiation, flows into the small being.
The radiation of the cocoon, Kindness, Love and Gentleness, brings about the transformation of the nature being to a spirit child. Once it has absorbed the total energetic radiation, then it has matured into the spirit child. The dual pair – we would say the parent couple – is totally and completely one with its spirit child, and the spirit child is one with the dual pair, its spiritual parents, as well as with the entire extended family in God, the Father-Mother-God.

The spirit child of the dual pair now bears within the pulsating divine primordial heart of all four basic powers, all four primordial powers, and the three attribute powers, the filiation attributes of Kindness, Love and Gentleness – all in all, the core of being of the Being.
In the spiritual family, the spirit child matures into the completed spirit being, by once more activating, bit by bit – as spirit child – all four natures of the four divine planes of development and, at the same time, bringing to completion the three attributes of Kindness, Love and Gentleness as the All-communication.

Once the spirit child has attained the maturity of the completed, fully formed spirit being, then all energetic powers are active in it. They are the completed basic powers, the nature powers, the primordial powers of the Being, and the completed attribute powers, the filiation attributes. This means the activated All-communication of infinity to all beings and life forms, to all suns and planets. All in all, it is the eternal Spirit, the creating, drawing and inexhaustible Light-Ether.

As in all divine beings, the completed basic powers in the now matured spirit being form the cosmic primordial heart – it is the core of being of infinity. Once the spirit child has matured into the completed spirit being, then the core of being and the spirit being is cosmically light-perfect, like a perfectly cut and polished diamond.

*The paramount primordial power – God –
The cosmic Law-word of the All
in all beings and in all things*

The core of being is thus the cosmic primordial heart of each divine being.
God is the paramount primordial power, the Love in the Kindness and Gentleness, whereby Love is the highest source of light of the Being. The love and humility in the Love, Kindness and Gentleness are the highest pulsating energy in the atoms of the Light-Ether, which, through His four powers of drawing and creating, draws from the Light-Ether and creates formative life.

The paramount primordial power is the All-Law, which consists of the seven basic pillars that, in all atoms of Light-Ether, are set in five powers. The highest pulsating primordial nucleus of each spiritual atom is the Love, Kindness and Gentleness. The four elemental powers, Order, Will, Wisdom and Earnestness, revolve around the primordial All-power, the primordial nucleus.
Without the highest power of light, the Love, which is effective in all things, there is no life and no spiritual formation.

The love for God and neighbor is the key to eternal life, to peace, to harmony and to the consonance of all universal powers.

Thus, in the whole of infinity the paramount primordial power, the All-Spirit, is active in all His creation powers, for instance, in the mineral, plant and animal kingdoms, and, via the three filiation attributes, Kindness, Love and Gentleness, in every divine being. He is the All-principle, "sending and receiving."

The incorruptible core of being, the essence of the seven basic powers, that is, the Law-powers of God, is also in the very basis of the discarnate souls and in the soul of every human being. As already mentioned, it is the four nature powers, that is, the drawing and creating powers, Order, Will, Wisdom, Earnestness, and the three filiation powers, Kindness, Love and Gentleness. It is the All-Law of the Being. God, the Eternal, the All-Intelligence, is thus in all beings and in all things, as well as in all suns, in all planets. In all the powers of infinity is the life, God. And so, the eternal Creator is omnipresent in His creation.

God, the Eternal, the All-Spirit of infinity, is the word of the All in all beings and in all things. All life forms and all divine beings, spirit beings, are in constant communication with their Creator-God in all beings and in all things, and the Creator-God is in communication with His All-creation. All divine beings, all pure life forms are linked with their Creator and hear His word, the life, which is the All-Law.

The human being could likewise hear the word of the Creator-God, just as all other forms of Being in infinity hear the word of the God-Father-Mother, because in its very basis, the soul is a spirit being from God, the Father-Mother-God. However, the human being receives the word of the All-Unity solely from the All-heart, the primordial heart, the core of being in the very basis of his soul.

How often we hear: God in us. The communicative bridge to all life forms, up to the Kingdom of God and ultimately to the Father-Mother-God in us, is and remains the core of being, set in the three filiation attributes and the four primordial powers.

If, in his life of feelings, sensations and thoughts, in all his behavior patterns, the person has built the bridge to God in himself, to the core of being, to the primordial heart, to the law of the universal Being, then he hears the Father-Mother-God, who is the life of His child, and he also hears the divine life forms, the All-Law, in all beings and in all things, the cosmic Being. That is All-Unity; that is community; that is true community spirit and true community life.

The steps to life.
The bridge to the core of being

Let it be repeated, for repetitions are given for learning; they serve to make it easier to remember. When a person fulfills the principles of the laws of inner life step by step, he matures toward the pure community of life. Only then, is it possible for him to receive the word of the Creator, of the All-Spirit, the All-Unity, in his mother tongue, which, even though it is three-dimensionally shaped, conveys the word in pictures and thoughts.

Via the soul's core of being, that is, God in us, we human beings can hear the word of the All-One, who, in all of infinity, in the smallest particle of the Being, is the Law-word.

God is love and humility. He is in the tiniest and the tiniest in the All is in the great whole. His All-word, the Law-word, is always presence. Solely through selflessly serving love for God and neighbor, by helping and serving in devotion to God, do we human beings experience what All-Unity means.

Deep in the very basis of our soul, we human beings bear the sonship and daughtership of God. For the individual, this raises the question: Where do I, the person, stand?
How often we say, "I want to grow closer to God" or, "I would like to experience the light of love in me!"? But it is not about thinking, "I want!" or, "I would like to!" For us human beings to again become what we are in the very basis of our soul – beings in God – we would have to set out on the path to live the All-Law, the All-Unity of the Being, step by step, and to fulfill it in daily life.
The first step to life would be, and is, to build the bridge to our true being, which means to fulfill the Ten Commandments of God.
The second step, to draw closer to the core of being, God in us, is to live the Sermon on the Mount of Jesus.
The third step is: Respect, cherish and love the innermost of the soul of every person, for he is your brother, your sister, from the eternal homeland, from the divine community; and love the life in the mineral, in every plant, in every animal.

Love the All-life, just as you want to be loved, yourself.

Learn to perceive all life forms, the whole Mother Earth, as a part of you, because God's word is the word of creation, which says: "I AM THE I AM, the love for God and neighbor." All life forms, including Mother Earth, as well as the ethereal power in the four elements, fire, water, earth and air, are part of the love for neighbor.

As stated: The person thinks and says, "If God is the Creator of all Being, in all beings and in all things, in the whole of infinity, the Law-word, then I want to hear Him, the Creator!" But the inner wisdom, the All-Being, the I AM THE I AM, has never revealed itself with, "I want"! Only when we put the principles of the laws, which are found in the Ten Commandments of God and in the Sermon on the Mount of Jesus, into practice step by stcp, do we gradually begin to understand what love for God and neighbor means.

It is not in talking about what should be done that the Spirit of God works; but instead, through the just deed, we create the bridge to the All-word, to the All-Unity of life, which is love.

God, the All-Spirit, the drawing and creating All-Law, does not sit back and do nothing and with this mean, "Go ahead!" God, the Father-Mother-God, is the power of the deed, in all beings and in all things. Through Him and in Him, the creation of Being is in unstoppable motion.

Only when we human beings have found the root of the true life and have become humble, without the echo of the ego, which says, "I am my own best friend," do we experience what it means that God is close to us and His word is omnipresent. Only then, do we grasp and experience in ourselves that everything, absolutely everything, is contained in the divine core of being, in the primordial heart of the Being, and that solely by way of the core of being is the true, communicative All-life possible, the All-Unity, the word of infinity and of the infinite.

How did the little prince say it? "One sees clearly only with the heart." But one also hears clearly only with the heart. One hears clearly through the heart of life, through the incorruptible core of being, God, for in Him and out of Him speaks the community of all life forms and of all divine beings. All of infinity is suffused with His word, for God, the Eternal, is in all beings and in all things.

*The sons and daughters of God –
Heirs to infinity*

Why have most people lost respect and appreciation for life? Because man thinks too little about life after this life.
Let's think about this now: We human beings are merely temporary wayfarers on this Earth. When the time has come for us, we then discard our physical body – but our life goes on. After the death of our body, we have a finer-material body, which we call soul. The soul is also on a journey, until it again lives and is active as a divine being, a spirit being in the Kingdom of God, in the eternal homeland, in its original being.

In the Kingdom of God, we are fine-material beings, spirit beings from the primordial substance, the Light-Ether, the eternal law, God, the All-One.
God is our eternal Father, who, in the eternal core of being, in our primordial heart, is also Mother to us. The inextinguishable core of being is the All-Law of love for God and neighbor.
For better understanding: The physical body is coarse-material, transformed-down and reversed Light-Ether, that is, Light-Ether that is drawn into the negative. The soul is finer-material Light-Ether.

As long as the soul is burdened, it may very well be finer material, but not fine-material.
The divine beings, the spirit beings, all divine life forms, all suns and planets of the eternal Kingdom of God are fine-material; they are pure exponentiated Light-Ether.

God, our heavenly Father, made His sons and daughters heirs to infinity. Every spirit being is an equal heir to the eternal Being, to the cosmic ethereal energies of the Kingdom of God. This is why the spiritual body of every divine being is compressed, eternal ethereal law, that is, Light-Ether. The spirit being is not God, thus, not omnipresent; however, as spirit being it can be present in all of infinity through the All-heritage.
With His Spirit, God, the Eternal, the Father of all His children, remains the all-streaming ethereal Law-power, the omnipresence, which means that His Spirit is the life in all beings and in all things.

The homeland of the divine beings is the Kingdom of God, infinity, by virtue of the core of being, of the law of love for God and neighbor, which is cosmic freedom.

Jesus of Nazareth essentially taught us: *The Kingdom of God is within, in you.*
With cosmic freedom is not meant the freedom that people advocate, when they say, "I want to be free" or, "I am free!" – Divine beings are free because they are heirs to infinity and are one with infinity, the Kingdom of God.

The divine principle of inheritance, the All-Unity, is, "Link and be!" which means to be linked with everything pure and with all beings and all Being. Through this, they, the spirit beings, are present, but not omnipresent. This is the all-encompassing heritage of every divine being.

The Kingdom of God and the Life of the Divine Beings in the Eternal Being

The primordial image of the creation of Being

Dear fellow people, people ask and seek proof of whether there actually is a God. This book "The Speaking All-Unity – The Word of the Universal Creator-Spirit" is a cosmic teaching and learning work from the school of divine Wisdom. In this, we want to become aware of the statement of Jesus: *The Kingdom of God is within, in you.* With this, is certainly meant the essence of the Kingdom of God in us, in the very basis of our soul.

The foundation of the Kingdom of God is the All-Law, the unity. The love for God and neighbor is the basis of eternal life. Divine beings, spirit beings, are at home in the eternal Being.
They live and dwell in spiritual structures. Animals live with the divine beings and plant species adorn the gardens of the Being.
The life is love; it is light, form, color, sound and fragrance. Every heavenly plane has its characteristics in terms of sound, color and form.

In pre-creations, the Kingdom of God, the heavenly planes with the divine beings and the seven-dimensional gardens and life forms, was the vision in the four primordial powers, the primordial image for the creation of Being. According to iron laws – we call them the inner clock – a certain movement began in the four primordial powers, which, before the creation of Being, also called themselves gods. The primordial image came into action. A clockwork, that is, a primordial stroke, stimulated the primordial image for the creation of the Being.

Before we come to the subject – God, also in matter – just a brief indication of what pre-creation and creation of Being mean. It is merely a teeny, tiny glimpse into the seven-dimensional Kingdom of God, which is the homeland of the divine beings and which we are, as essence, in the very basis of our soul. There were several pre-creations. In "The Speaking All-Unity – The Word of the Universal Creator-Spirit," we predominantly read about the completed creation of Being, the Kingdom of God.

In the pre-creations to the eternal creation of Being, four God-conscious primordial powers radiated into the still unformed All, into the inexhaustible

Light-Ether. In accordance with the inner clock, the primordial image, the creation of Being, unfolded itself in unimaginable cycles of eons. From the four primordial powers, the one All-Godhead unfolded, the paramount primordial power, the Kindness, Love and Gentleness, whereby the Love is the highest power, the one drawing and creating primordial power, the All-God, the All-Spirit.

At first, the paramount primordial power was one particle, which radiated and moved in itself. From this developed two equally radiating particles, which, in accordance with the inner clock, came more and more into movement and divided into approximately two-thirds giving and one-third receiving. The paramount primordial power – it is the All-Godhead, the Eternal – drew the four powers to Himself, in order to make them into His four powers of drawing and creating, which are still His four primordial powers.
The Eternal's four drawing and creating powers, also called four primordial powers, have a deep significance, for after the completion of the first creation of Being, the paramount sovereignty, the All-Godhead, the All-Spirit, will, in further universes, raise the four primordial powers to their primordial purpose.

The paramount primordial power – approximately two-thirds giving, one-third receiving – now began His work of creation. In a mighty course of eons, the All-One, the drawing and creating One, the All-light of Being, the Eternal, created an ethereal Primordial Central Star, also called Primordial Central Sun. In the same course of eons, the One, the Infinite, the Eternal, whom we in the western world call God, created from the Light-Ether seven ethereal prism suns, which refracted, and refract, the white-gold primordial light of the central star into color spectrums and radiate them into the All.

In each of the prism suns, the light of the other prism suns is active because the All-Unity consciousness is the infinitely eternal law that is equally active in infinity and is contained in all things.

In this mighty first course of eons of His creation, God gave Himself form. He, the All-One, the Spirit of infinity, took the substance for an ethereal embodiment from the four drawing and creating powers, whereby the three powers primarily became active in its shaping – the three filiation attributes Kindness, Love and Gentleness – so that all divine beings, His sons and daughters, can behold God-Father, who is also Mother to them, face to face.

During this eon cycle, the All-One created His first light-beings, the archangels. First, He created the first four beings, which, spiritually, that is, ethereally, embody the four primordial powers, the drawing and creating powers. Then, from the Light-Ether, He created the three other archangels that embody His three attribute powers, the Father-Mother principle. The seven archangels are the cherubs of the eternal Being, which intrinsically represent the eternal law in all of infinity. This is why they are also called the law angels. From His paramount primordial power – approximately two-thirds giving, one-third receiving – He created the seraphs. In human language, this means that He created seven male and seven female principles.

In this cycle of drawing and creating, the Eternal, the All-Spirit, the paramount primordial power, began to create four planes of development, in which He, the All-One, is active through His four primordial powers to create formative ethereal life, step by step. In the divine planes of development, which can also be called the divine body of birth, fine-material spiritual life forms develop.

The Eternal beheld the beginning of His first work of creation, and it was good.

By way of His four primordial powers, the powers for shaping the filiation of God, He now began to draw and to create. Via the prism suns, the primordial light, the Light-Ether, likewise flooded into the All, where gigantic heavenly planes were formed and emerging spiritual heavenly bodies followed their pathways.

This gigantic communication network of the Being developed from the principle of All-Unity: Everything is Light-Ether, all is contained in everything, and all beings and all things are in communication with all forms of Being and with all powers. He saw, and it was good.

During further creative courses of eons, the first ethereal life forms developed, the life that forms in cycles and rhythms. The All-Unity consciousness, the Kingdom of God, developed from the All-drawing and All-creating principle, of which we will read more. From His All-principle of drawing and creating, the primordial heart gradually developed, the core of being, the essence of the All-Law and the essential powers of all life forms, the All-life as son and daughter of God.

No matter how one wants to describe the eternal Being, it remains a distorted picture, which can hardly be conveyed in three-dimensional words and terms. One tries to find words for a seven-dimensional event, and ultimately realizes that one goes in circles around the same words, even though one has put a different vision into the same words.

In this cosmic work of teaching and learning, we very gradually learn about and understand our divine heritage, the essence of all Being, which is alive in the very basis of our soul, the core of being, the primordial heart of eternal life. Yes, in you, in all of us, in the very basis of our soul, beats the primordial heart of Being, the power and the life of our eternal homeland.

May what follows stimulate the reader to reflect how God works in matter, in His four drawing and creating powers, so that the attentive reader may, perhaps, be able to grasp the nearness of God, the omnipresent Spirit in matter.

The four eternal drawing and creating powers, also called primordial powers, merely have different names in matter and are given corresponding terms that want to make comprehensible for us human beings, the fact that the primordial Eternal One is effective in the various materials and substances of matter, as well as in the body of each human being.

The Workings of the Four Primordial Powers in the Condensed Being

In the following inserts (pages 61 to 77) a well-read citizen and a scientist will try to convey information to us about the four primordial powers in matter. But, as stated, it is all merely an attempt to unveil the work of the Spirit of God in matter.

We heard about the drawing and creating powers, the four primordial powers, which bear within the three attribute powers of the Father-Mother-God. Since everything is contained in everything, the Law-powers of the Spirit are also contained in matter as energetic basic powers.
Due to the Fall-thought on the one hand and the three dimensions on the other, the four drawing and creating powers, including the three attribute powers, are viewed differently in matter and are poured into other forms than in the pure Being.
Considering the great cosmic correlations, all efforts of science are merely a search for traces, even when ever so many means and so much

energy are used to gain information on the origin of the material universe.

When modern physics presents the Big Bang theory with complex models, many a one embraces the conventional scientific explanation of the material universe. The Big Bang theory states that approximately 14 billion years ago, from an unimaginably energy-rich starting point, the birth of the material cosmos was initiated with the so-called Big Bang. Everything that is at work visibly and invisibly in the whole material cosmos with its billions of solar systems is said to have gone forth from it. Many accept this process – which is unimaginable to us human beings – as a given, simply because science explains it that way today.

On the subject of "The Speaking All-Unity – The Word of the Universal Creator-Spirit," there is often mention of the "four nature powers and the three attribute powers of God." When we look at these somewhat more closely, we conclude that in all the processes taking place on matter, but also in all life forms, we can recognize the four nature powers of God, which manifest themselves as the four powers of development, that is, the basic powers in all Being, thus, also in matter, in the most varying forms of appearance.

Scientific models of explanation, as certain as they appear at the respective time, are usually merely attempts at clarification, which correspond to the state of the respective scientific research. They are based on observation, experimentation and the theories that build on them. Often, this knowledge is certain only until it is overtaken by new knowledge. However, the latest position in physics, mathematics, astronomy, biology and other branches of science lets us recognize many parallels to the overall picture that is conveyed to us from the spiritual world. Of particular interest concerning this is the way the described primordial powers of the All work in the material cosmos.

Wherever natural scientists, philosophers and humanists occupied themselves with an explanation of the harmony of the All, the "Tetractys" (group of four) played a central role. The discovery of world harmony is attributed to Pythagoras of Samos (570-510 BC). The Pythagoreans assumed a harmony of the spheres, in which each heavenly body produces a certain sound according to its size, speed and distance from other heavenly bodies, which leads to the music of the spheres. They assumed a congruence of mathematical, musical and cosmic harmonies. The basis and key of their world knowledge was the group of four (Tetractys).

The Pythagoreans had a form of oath, in which it was said: "... by the one who gave our soul the Tetractys, which contains the source and root of the eternally flowing nature." They spoke of "God, who entrusted the holy Tetractys to our being, implanted in the divine being." In music they concluded that the harmonious basic consonants could be expressed with the four numbers of the Tetractys.

According to the Pythagoreans, the Tetractys also forms the basis of geometry. The one stands for the point, the two for the line, the three for the surface and the four for the body volume. And Giordano Bruno, who referred to the Pythagoreans, wrote: "The Tetractys is the first thing to be found in the nature of space bodies ..." (Giordano Bruno, "Über die Monas, die Zahl und die Figur der Elemente")

But modern physics also knows four basic powers, to which all physical processes can be traced back. Why exactly four?

It is the phenomena of four basic powers observed in the physical world that are effective in matter. These powers, which are also called fundamental interactions, have the effect that certain particles attract, repel or come into interaction with each other in other ways. They form the energetic framework of visible matter.

One of the goals of modern physics is to conceive of an overall concept, the so-called "Theory of Everything," which combines the four basic powers or interactions in such a way that it becomes possible to trace back the four basic powers and all their forms of appearance to one basic power.

The life forms in the pure spiritual Being have a different structure than the life forms in matter.

The spirit body of the beings in the Kingdom of God is built in a particle structure that is respirated by the primordial light via the prism suns. The life forms in the coarse-material existence are also respirated by the breath of God.

However, on Earth, the cells form the basic component of life. The four powers of God's drawing and creating power are also active in these cells, but in the material form, in structures and density forms, unlike in the eternal Being, in the Kingdom of God.

We find the efficacy of the four drawing and creating powers, which are reflected in the body cells, in the basic genetic components of DNA. They are the four nucleobases, which, in their various combinations, form the basis for all organic life forms. From their various combinations, develop the unimaginable diversity of all life forms in the material Being.

Let us consider that everything is energy, vibration. The four spiritual drawing and creating powers radiate into coarse materiality and, within the spiritual principles that are valid in matter, bring forth the corresponding life forms. Interestingly, the formation of sperm cells in a man is also based on one original sperm cell that, through division, causes four original sperms to develop. These four original sperms develop to four typical sperms capable of fertilization. And so, from one original sperm cell develop four original sperms respectively – here, too, a distant echo of the creation event.
Likewise, the phenomena of light in the material Being bear within the principles of the primordial light; however, they are adapted to the principles of densification in matter. We see this especially clearly when we refract white light through prisms into seven spectral colors. Isaac Newton (1643-1727) determined the seven spectral colors

as red, orange, yellow, green, blue, indigo and violet. According to the concept of color by Johann Wolfgang von Goethe (1749-1832), white light is the causative light in which the seven spectral colors are contained.

A scientist reports

Four basic powers, in other words, four fundamental interactions, underlie all physical phenomena in nature. These basic powers are: gravity, electromagnetic force, weak nuclear force and strong nuclear force.

Of the basic powers, man can perceive gravity and electromagnetic force in daily life. Gravity ensures the weight of all living beings and objects and is responsible for the fact that the planets revolve around the sun in designated orbits. The electromagnetic force is responsible for most everyday phenomena such as light, electricity and magnetism, chemistry and much more.

Gravity and the electromagnetic force have a large range and are effective in the entire universe, while the weak and the strong nuclear forces have an extremely small range and are effective only within the scope of an atomic nucleus. Weak nuclear force is responsible for certain radioactive decay processes, among others, also for the atomic processes in the sun (nuclear fusion), with the help of which the sun produces its energy. The fourth force is the strong nuclear force, which is responsible for the cohesion of protons and neutrons. The strong nuclear force holds the innermost part of the world together.

Of the particle energies prevailing in the universe today, the electromagnetic force, the weak and the strong nuclear forces have very different characteristics. At short distances, the strong nuclear force is approximately 100 times stronger than the other forces. In experiments in particle accelerators, it can be verified that the intensity of the three forces increasingly match each other the higher the particle energies are, and thus, the temperatures as well. Above a certain temperature, a unification of the electromagnetic and weak nuclear forces occurs, which is then described as electro-weak force. The standard model of particle physics assumes that above a certain temperature and energy, a merging of the strong nuclear force with the electro-weak force occurs, as well. At even much higher temperatures and energies, a uniform "super force" could then form from all four nature powers.

Such extreme physical conditions can only have occurred with the Big Bang.

The Big Bang

The Big Bang does not describe an explosion in an existing space; rather, in the physical sense, we understand the Big Bang as the starting point of matter, space and time.
Most astronomers assume that the material universe began with the Big Bang about 13.7 billion years ago. The immediate Big Bang event itself cannot be described physically and mathematically with the formulas known to us.
Astronomers surmise that at the beginning of the visible universe there was a very small area of space (smaller than the head of pin) consisting of space-time-quantum-foam.
Presumably within a minimalist fragment of a second after the Big Bang event, this teeny area of space expanded into huge dimensions. The inflation of the universe was gigantic. We can imagine it somewhat, as if one atom were to expand to about 10,000 light years. Mind you, a light year is 9.5 billion kilometers.

Of course, science has sought explanations for how it came to this inflation of the universe. Today, most astronomers assume that a very strong energy field, the so-called inflation field, caused the expansion. This energy field most likely had a repelling gravitational effect that increased ever more with the growing volume of space.

At the end of this inflation, there was a very hot particle mixture with temperatures of around 10^{29} (10 with 29 zeros) Kelvin – that is, unimaginably high temperatures. The following era is called the electro-weak era. During this phase, the fundamental particles appeared. The universe slowly cooled more and more. After 380,000 years, the universe became permeable to light. The cosmic background radiation, presently measured by satellites, stemmed from this time.

While the universe was still very, very tiny, quanta fluctuations must have occurred, which, through the expansion of the universe, inflated to huge magnitudes. Regions developed in the All with more particles and other regions with fewer particles than on the average. Within a billion years after the Big Bang, gravitation began to build up the first complex and massive structures.

The most recent measurement results indicate that there are 100 to 200 billion galaxies in the universe, all of which are more or less similar to our Milky Way. Every galaxy consists of up to 200 billion stars; the total number of stars in the universe could be given in words as 20 sextillion stars; that is a number with 22 zeros.

If each star in the universe were to correspond to a fine grain of sand, then we could cover the entire surface of Germany with half a meter of sand.

For a long time it was believed that with the model of the Big Bang, the key to understanding the universe, as it were, had been found. But during recent years, it has become increasingly clear that many of the phenomena in the universe are neither properly researched nor understood. One example is that of dark matter. Over the course of the 20th century, while observing galaxies and galaxy clusters, astronomers discovered that their dynamism cannot be explained from the amount of visible matter. There must definitely be more matter in the universe than assumed. Because this matter does not radiate any light, it was called dark matter. As we know today, around the galaxies there is a corona of dark matter that is at least 10 times as large as the region in which the stars are revolving.

It has been known only for a few years now that our universe is developing totally differently than was previously assumed. Contrary to former concepts, since ca. 5 billion years, the universe has been expanding ever faster; this is called cosmic acceleration.

The volume of space in the All must have a kind of internal energy, which is constantly pressing outward and attempting to make the universe grow larger. What is extraordinary about this is that this energy also increases with increasing volume. There is no scientific explanation at all for this energy, which is called dark energy.

Today, it is assumed that the universe consists of only 4.6 percent atomic matter that is also visible to us. Approximately 23 percent is dark matter and about 73 percent is accounted for by dark energy.

If dark energy keeps the upper hand in the universe, which astronomers assume, it will come to a total dissolution of all material components. Even the black holes will then presumably be annihilated; then there will be only a minimal radiation.

If for some reason or other, gravitation should gain the upper hand in the All, the universe would contract and at some time or other, totally disappear.

What was before the Big Bang?

The general theory of relativity states that the world had its beginning at one point in the cosmic past. Questions regarding what "came before" would make no sense. The Big Bang model deals with the question of how the Big Bang took place. But it does not ask about the reason for the Big Bang, let alone ask what was before. Some astronomers and physicists are not satisfied with the Big Bang model and have developed totally different ideas.
For example, there is the model of a Big Bounce. Before our universe, there was another universe that was filled with quanta fields and consisted of pure energy. Other mathematical-physical models presume cyclical universes. The final state of a universe automatically leads to a new beginning in the form of a Big Bang.
Physicists have frequently been amazed that of the four fundamental forces in physics, gravitation is by far the weakest of all the forces. One

hypothesis is that gravitation seeps, so to speak, into a parallel universe, thus thinning out in our universe.

In summary, we can say the following: According to the present state of scientific knowledge, directly at the time of the Big Bang a uniform force must have existed, from which gravitation split off first and then in the further course of development, the other basic powers.

The four quantum numbers

Just as the four nature powers play a prominent role in physics, so do the four quantum numbers have a central meaning in chemistry.

At the time the make-up of an atom was being researched, it soon became known that the atomic nucleus consists of protons and neutrons. Electrons revolve around the nucleus. The electron shells of atoms play a central role in chemical reactions and compounds. It took many years until the state of the atomic shell could be satisfactorily described.

To correctly describe an electron, four quantum numbers are needed: the principal quantum number, the angular quantum number, the mag-

netic quantum number and the spin projection quantum number.

An important principle in chemistry and physics states that two electrons that match in all four quantum numbers can never appear in one atom. And so, each electron has its own character, that is, its own independent pattern of quantum numbers.

Four bases determine the genetic code

Deoxyribonucleic acid, or DNA, is the carrier of the genetic information in nearly all life forms. Only very few kinds of virus use ribonucleic acid, or RNA, to store information. Only four molecules are necessary for storing and coding genetic information; they are called nucleotide bases: adenine, guanine, cytosine and thymine. A group of three consecutive nucleotides is the code for an amino acid. As we know, amino acids are the components of all proteins. Thus, nature needs only four different molecules to decode the information of the genetic make-up, or genome. Remarkably, with just a few exceptions, the genetic code for all living beings is the same. And so, all living beings make use of the same genetic language.

The concept of the four elements

The so-called "four humors" theory was developed in the medicine of antiquity; it remained predominant for natural scientists and medicine until the end of the 19th century. The four humors were: blood, yellow bile, black bile and phlegm. Corresponding temperaments were also attributed to these fluids: sanguine, choleric, melancholy and phlegmatic types of people.
The doctrine of the four temperaments inspired personality psychology even into the 20th century. The physicians of antiquity, (for example, Hippocrates of Kos, Galen of Pergamon), viewed health as a harmonious mixture of the bodily fluids. According to their understanding, illnesses developed from an incorrect mixture of these four substances.

*Important biomolecules
have a four-part structure*

There is a group of natural substances that have a pronounced four-part (Tetractys) structure. These substances are called porphyrins; they consist of four symmetrically arranged ring molecules. Very important molecules belong to the group of porphyrins, for instance, the blood pigment hemoglobin, the red muscle pigment myoglobin, electron-transferring proteins in the power plants of the cells and enzymes to detoxify free radicals. On Earth, the most prevalent compound of this kind is the chlorophyll in plants. With the help of this green pigment, plants can use sunlight as a source of energy for the formation of glucose. Vitamin B12 also has a similar molecular make-up as hemoglobin. Of interest concerning porphyrins is that in the inner part of the molecule, enveloped by the four ring molecules, various metals can be found, for example, iron with hemoglobin, magnesium with chlorophyll and cobalt with the vitamin B12 molecule. The most important molecules for generating energy have a similar make-up in all living beings.

The All-Harmony of the Eternal Being

Dear fellow people, many words about the prevailing four primordial powers in matter turn into a distorted picture once again. In the end, they are assumptions and hypotheses; it is the effort and the attempt to want to express in many words something over which, after all, the veil of the three dimensions remains.

Let us turn back from the scientific presentations to the explanations about the true Being – "The Speaking All-Unity – The Word of the Universal Creator-Spirit," from the vision of the spiritual All-workings of the Eternal, just as Gabriele described it in conversations.
The eternal Being is the All-harmony. It is the music of the spheres of the eternal Being. All suns and planets in all heavenly planes of the Kingdom of God are in constant harmonious movement. The movement of the heavenly bodies and their sounds are in complete accord with the sounds of all life forms and with the spirit beings that live on the respective heavenly planes and have their spiritual structures on the various dwelling

planets, where the spiritual families dwell and live. That is the true life; that is All-communication.

This statement about the heavenly structures and the families in the Kingdom of God cannot be compared with the houses and palaces on this Earth, nor with the families of this world.
The buildings in the eternal Being are not built, but are, instead, created by the spirit beings, and at that, from the ethereal primordial substance of the respective dwelling planet. The ethereal substance of the dwelling planet is raised, so that the created edifice is in absolute harmony with the planet.

Every heavenly plane has its specific color and its design

Depending on their mentality, the spirit beings in all heavenly planes are corresponding bodies of sound. Their garments also correspond to the color of the respective heavenly plane. Likewise, all life forms, from the mineral to the fully matured nature being, have, depending on their state of consciousness, the corresponding form and appearance, which is reflected in their color nuances.

Every color has its fragrance and, according to its state of development, the corresponding sound. All color schemes come from the primordial light, the Primordial Central Sun, by way of the prism suns, which, as stated, refract the white-golden light of the Primordial Central Sun into spectrums of light and radiate it into infinity.

Form, color, fragrance and sound reflect the unity in all facets, also with the sounds of all the heavenly bodies in all heavenly planes. For example, when spirit beings change from one heavenly plane to another, the basic color of their garment assumes the color of the corresponding heavenly plane. Why? Because all colors are contained in the garments of the divine beings and thus, also in all powers of the Being. The form, the color, the fragrance and the sound are predefined in all life forms as well, no matter their state of development.

Form, color, fragrance and sound are a part of the All-Unity, just as in all heavenly planes, all suns and planets, are part of the divine unity. This results in the harmony of the spheres, the music of the spheres of the eternal Being.

*The meaning of our life on Earth –
Becoming aware of our true origin*

Everything that is conveyed here in words, which correspond to the three dimensions, is not even a breath from the eternal Being. Presently, we are human beings on this Earth, so that we may become aware again of our origin by walking the path within, to our true being, which throbs and knocks in the very basis of our soul, repeatedly calling and admonishing us to walk the path that makes us free and happy, and that lets us sense that we truly are not from this world, but are sons and daughters of the Eternal, of the Father-Mother-God.

Each one of us has accepted the human existence, the one more, the other less, so that we again find ourselves as a divine being in the very basis of our soul, so that we become aware of the unity with all positive powers and unite with all living beings, also with the innermost part of each person. This means to examine our feelings, sensations, thoughts, words and actions day in and day out, and give an account to ourselves as to whether what we feel, sense, think, say and do corresponds to the eternal laws of the Kingdom of God. Through the content of the Ten

Commandments of God and the teachings of the Sermon on the Mount of Jesus of Nazareth, we are called upon to examine ourselves every day and to reflect that everything that is to the right, left, above and below us has a purpose in life, which, as divine essence, is part of the life of the All-Unity.

To become sensitive means to understand that everything lives and that all things are in a communicative connection with one another and with the All-Unity.

The Five Components in the Life of Man that Become Warfare Agents

Over and over again, we hear and read that we should think about the way we feel, sense, think, speak and act. In connection with our senses, these five components can turn into explosives, because they are energies that we emit and, ultimately, their effects unfailingly hit the one who emitted them.

In order to learn, we could ask ourselves: Who are we and what do we emit?

A person's five components, with which he works, day in, day out, are the content of his feeling, sensing, thinking, speaking and acting. When we analyze the present time and this generation more closely, then we realize that these five components have become warfare agents, weapons, which are directed against the sender. Few people think about the five components, above all, about their content, because these are the projectiles that the person fires day in and day out and that come exclusively from his weapons arsenal.

For example, every person puts his personal warfare agent into his feelings, sensations and particularly into his thoughts.

It can definitely be said that every single person has set up his special, specific arsenal of warfare agents in his five components. Every day, from the arsenal of "feelings" or the arsenal of "thoughts," "words" or even "actions," projectiles are fired off against people, animals and nature, which, however, also hit people and stimulate them to think the same or similar things, or even to command someone to do something bad, for example, to maltreat animal species or to practice predatory exploitation on the planet Earth.

The projectiles that strike can be initial sparks that stir up the same or similar things in a number of people. The majority of the swirling mass, the splinters, comes back to the sender, who unceasingly emits his negative messages, his warfare agents. They hit the sender right on the mark. The consequences are blows of fate, hardships, worries, accidents, illnesses, even premature death, depending on what the projectiles contain. As stated, the impact of the projectiles, the splinters, primarily hits the sender, but those people are also on the receiving end of it who fire off the same and similar things with the content of their feeling, thinking, speaking and acting. However, the initiator is always the emitter.

Since in all of infinity, including matter, everything is based on "sending and receiving," the catalog of sins says: What you sow, that is, send, you will reap, that is, receive.

Man poisons himself and his environment through his five components, which turn into warfare agents.

But the five components of feeling, sensing, thinking, speaking and acting can also be positive companions, above all, when they are applied according to the eternal law of love for God and neighbor. This would then be the path to higher ethics and morals, up to the life, the primordial heart of the Being. Of course, the cleansing of the five components involves working on oneself. This means that caution is necessary whenever associations come up from one of the five components, for example, from thoughts, that lead to actions that harm others. For instance, this is the case when with nice words a fellowman is made to do something that he wasn't planning to do, but we influence him so that he is at our service.

The primary warfare agent –
Our thoughts

There are many such contents in our five components, for instance, in our thoughts, and each person has different ones.

We human beings think unceasingly. Our thoughts are the primary warfare agent in our "weapons arsenal." With their content, which often builds up in pictorial sequences, we fabricate the warfare agent, which is ultimately directed against ourselves.

Man thinks, thinks and thinks unceasingly, without realizing that every thought is energy and presses to be actualized. Negative contents of thoughts that are harbored against our neighbor can consist of expectations, envy or hostility, including rejection and hatred; they energetically form and are applied at some point, be it through words or actions.

The thought is the leadman that processes everything that romps around as the content of our world of desires and thoughts. One day, the stored energy of thought urges us to actualize what we imagined and worked out in thoughts. The insidious build-up of the warfare agents in our weapons arsenal of thoughts can come to an explosive discharge, be it against our neighbor, or also against nature, the animals and plants, or through the fact that the explosive force of the negative content strikes our organs and body cells. The negative stored data of our thought-content lead to reticence, secrets, intellectual saber-rattling and finally, to brutality against life. In thoughts, we set up what becomes manifest in our words and actions. The content of the five components is the blacksmith's tools of our fate; with them, we forge the causes which, at some point in time, become effects.

Even our desires in terms of our diet are shaped by the content of the five components, which simultaneously affect our sensory perception. This leads to the fact that for certain celebrations, animals that are bred and raised solely for this purpose and have to carve out their existence confined under the most unworthy conditions, are slaughtered, only so that people consume them for the pleasure and delight of the palate, all the while extolling the taste of the tormented animal's meat.

Other victims, our fellow creatures, are hunted, chased and shot for this purpose. Often, they die only after hours filled with agony and fear. The fatal warfare agents, which also have their origin in the five components, are manifested, for example, through the contract killers in Germany, where hunters are paid for their "services."

The same is true of the exploitation of the soil. The soil gives its richness; but that is not enough for man. Driven by the content of the five components, he uses artificial fertilizers and kills the life in the soil with poisons, merely to squeeze the utmost from the soil. It is the various associations from the five components that move us to use our warfare agents against the life. This is always the case when we plan something that harms our fellow people or the animals in and on the fields, in the woods, in the rivers, lakes and oceans, which consequently lose their life in gruesome ways and means, and so on.

Our life film –
We human beings live in pictures

Many people know that everything is energy and that no energy is lost, and that energy is transmittable, also through our thoughts, words and behavior patterns.

We human beings live in pictures. All the behavior patterns of every individual consist of countless picture sequences. We could say that they consist of a film that we reel off over and over again through the content of the five components – feeling, sensing, thinking, speaking and acting – but which we also unceasingly activate, whereby ever new picture sequences are added.

If you do not believe what was just explained, then just try to think slowly and consciously! With these exercises, you will soon realize that a picture or even several pictures want to develop. Do not interrupt; try to look at what you are thinking. What comes from our personal past is what we experience in pictures. This is because no energy is lost. In the process, we simultaneously think and talk, or even talk about what we see in us.

As stated, our behavior patterns are also part of our picture sequences.

What we have not experienced ourselves, that is, what we know only from hearsay, but which we think or talk about, may also develop into a picture. Whether this picture, which developed based on conversations, corresponds to us or to others does not matter. We cannot control what another person says, because his statements are not recorded on our film reel. In case we believe what was said and affirm it, we automatically include on our film reel the picture that we made during the conversation.

This means that we are producers. We produced our past on our film reel – what we ourselves created through the content of our five components – and may likewise cause what we heard from others to come alive in pictures on our film reel.

Everything, but absolutely everything is pictures, and these run in picture sequences. The details of all our manifestations of life as well as what we heard by way of second or third parties and of which we make a picture for ourselves, we include in our life film, but also what we acquire, what we purchase, what we consume, what we move are picture sequences, which show up again in our life film, on our film reel.

Why the weapons arsenals of this world?

If we grasp that we build up weapons arsenals with our feelings, sensations, thoughts and words and if we realize that everything is energy and no energy is lost, we will also understand how things can go so far that our planet Earth is armed everywhere with weapon systems of every kind.

Seven billion people feel, sense, think, speak and act every day, every hour, every minute, every second, yes, every instant. According to the content of the five components, corresponding energies are released. If they are negative, then they form the energetic building materials, not only for weapons arsenals in a figurative sense, but they are also actually the basis upon which people are stimulated to develop weapons, to produce weapons, to deploy weapons, to practice with weapons, in order to ultimately use them against their neighbor.

The negative contents of the five components scatter the splinters of warfare agents and give the impulse for more negativity, when they meet a similar content in individuals or groups of people.

They can also have entirely concrete effects in concentrations of negative energy, by which the negative energy potential, which is created by the feeling, sensing, thinking, speaking and acting at every moment of seven billion people, becomes visible as material manifestations in the weapons arsenals of this world.

The most varying contents of this negative energy stimulate the corresponding people who develop weapons; then new ideas again develop for ever more developed lethal weapon systems. Through this, they become even more sophisticated, their effect ever more destructive, to the point of developing autonomous weapon systems, which, by their programming alone, can ultimately execute their destructive effects on their predetermined targets.

Where does the energy to invent such things come from? Where does the possibility come from, with much effort and energy, to plan, construct and deploy such weapon systems?

As multifaceted as the negative content of the five components is – the energetically formed weapons arsenals in the feeling, sensing, thinking, speaking and acting of the person – just as sophisticated and versatile is the lethal machinery on water, on land and in the air: warships, aircarft carriers, nuclear-powered submarines and sea mines in the ocean, combat helicopters, fighter jets and missiles, fully automated, deadly drones in the air and tanks and missile systems on land, right up to atomic bombs that destroy everything.

All these weapon systems are the product of thoughts, feelings and the systematic actions of human beings, fed by the sum of the negative energy of all warfare agents that romp about as a murderous content in the five components of all of mankind. Often hardly perceivable and inconspicuous, mostly dismissed as harmless, they form energetically, to stimulate people to produce the aggression, brutality and violence, which emerge in the weapons factory of our five components as real weapons arsenals in the weapons factories of this world. As with a magnifying glass, the various warfare agents are concentrated, so that their deadly energy can find expression in the life-destroying machinery of the war industry.

Combat and warfare weapons against God's creation

If we look at the combat mission against God, against His All-love, from a different viewpoint, then we can recognize today that the cancer of demonic machinations has changed its tune: once, dissolution of divine creation – today, destruction.

Many people have subjugated themselves to the demonic dictate to destroy everything that cannot be brought into line, whether friend or "enemy." People kill disagreeable enemies, their neighbors. They devise and produce ever more atrocious, sophisticated combat weapons.

Combat weapons are killing machines against people, animals and nature. People act unscrupulously against their neighbor, and hardly anyone thinks about the fact that the willful killing of our neighbor is fratricide.

German weapon technology in particular is in great demand by those governing many a country. German arms exports are among the highest. Long since, the government of a country that refers to Jesus, the Christ, and produces war weapons has thrown down the gauntlet to the Nazarene, who taught the people: *All who take up the sword will perish by the sword,* or, *Whatever you have done to one of these the least of my brothers, you have done to me.*

Vast sums of money, the same as energy, are required for the sophisticated war weapons. This means that no money is available for starving people and children. At arm's length, they are knowingly allowed to go hungry and starve. People are deliberately sacrificed for the weapons arsenals. This is the murder of children, thus, fratricide.

The effort to dissolve God's creation has failed. Now people destroy and kill all the more. They literally rage and rampage, each one against the other and against God's creation, against God's unity, against love for God and neighbor.
Among other things, the fight against God also means torturing the animals, killing and murdering our fellow creatures, destroying nature and exploiting the planet Earth.
People rage and fight against God's creation, against the commandment of love for God and neighbor and against the law of freedom.
Anyone who keeps animals cooped up as mass-produced commodities, as animals for slaughter, and hands them over to the butcher at a given

time is no better than the one who kills them. Anyone who consumes the meat of the tortured and executed animals is no better than the one who keeps them to be executed and leads them to execution.

All this is against God's love, against His creation, against the life, which is unity.

Nature, too, deserves respect and appreciation, because it also bears the life from the power of God. Anyone who violates nature is against God, against God's love. Anyone who exploits the Earth and brings the planet Earth to the tipping point is no better than the one who kills people or has them killed, who tortures and kills animals or takes them to be killed. Anyone who violates the dwelling planet, seen as a whole, acts against the life, against God's love and His creation.

So-called "Christianity" has thrown down the gauntlet to the Nazarene, and the Earth, which is part of God's creation, has taken it up and thrown it back to the people.

Man has turned his provider, the Mother Earth, into an enemy. The Earth will vanquish the enemy; this is already indicated with the term "climate change."

The five warfare agents of the vandal "man"

A participant of the roundtable discussions with Gabriele noticed how she struggled for the words to explain to us how God, the Eternal, meets His creation in love and humility. He reported:

I realized that even today the cruel vandal man bows down before the god Baal, who, in our time, merely adorns himself with other names. But his cruelty of yesterday is also his cruelty of today. As an immigrant on God's Earth, man wreaks havoc unrestrained, like a vandal, destroying everything that belongs to God, the Eternal.

Science teaches that no energy is lost and that thoughts are also energies that do not miss their mark.

At every moment, seven billion people are sending and sending and sending thought energies with the most varying contents to their fellow people, to the animals, to nature and into the Earth's atmosphere, giving off their personal thought-war-agent to the environment, which joins with similar contents of thought energies there and intensifies. In most cases the content of people's sensing, feeling, thinking, speaking and acting is

against the Ten Commandments of God and the Sermon on the Mount of Jesus of Nazareth and is thus, viewed energetically, negative radiation patterns, that is, negative radiation energies, which are being unceasingly emitted.
If this were not so, why, then, is the Earth with all its life forms in such bad shape, even though the illusion managers from politics, economy and mainstream churches try to whitewash the relatively short-term and unavoidable end to present human civilization?

Who shaped, and shapes, the people of the nations in their ethical and moral thinking and behavioral patterns and teaches them to perceive and imitate as positive conduct the often negative behavior, which is against all life?

Who teaches, schools and educates people in the values or non-values that they ultimately represent and that they continuously emit in the content of their radiation energies of feeling, sensing, thinking, speaking and acting?

When we observe the state of our world and environment, then the question arises:

Where does the widespread unscrupulousness and irresponsibility toward people, nature and animals come from?
Where does this indifference come from, which ultimately leads to the self-destruction of human civilization?
Who put on airs, and has been doing so for 1700 years, as the ethical-moral authority, upholding this claim as highly praised tradition up until today? And who, year after year, in Germany alone, gets paid tens of billions of Euros from general tax monies for this claim? Who?

Anyone who goes through life with open and alert senses will conclude the following, stated the committed participant of the roundtable discussion group:

The warfare agents of our five components, as applied to the level of church traditions, become apparent as follows:
Year after year, the so-called Christian holidays are preceded by huge slaughter feasts, in which millions and millions of liters of blood are shed.

Large parts of the population think nothing of it when millions and millions of animals are slaughtered.

Especially the traditional "Martin goose" is one of the animals to suffer under the killing machinery. Martin of Tours is mentioned in history for his mercy, because he allegedly shared his coat with a freezing beggar.
That's the whole story. Now, what do the millions of murdered geese have to do with the Catholic Feast of St. Martin?
Nothing, absolutely nothing! At some point, with the blessing of the church leaders, people ate the carcass of a goose on this St. Martin's Day and this carcass meal spread ever more in the heads of the people by way of the energies of thought, and not lastly, through the blessings of the caste of priests, until it became a so-called custom that many lemmings simply follow without listening to their conscience.

God, the Eternal, does not bless the murder of His creatures.
Whose blessing lies on all the randomly massacred animal carcasses?
The following, too, is part of the traditional slaughter feast: Millions and millions of turkeys have to

lose their lives at Christmastime, the celebration of love, because ecclesiastical masterminds bless the carcass meal for the "holy night" and thus, more and more people emit the same radiation frequencies and become imitators of a ritual of blood and killing that stems from paganism. The result is a bloodbath among the animals, which has assumed unimaginable dimensions and becomes greater year after year. For the animal torturers who specialize in animal suffering, it is a profitable business on Earth. However, in the beyond, the acquired pieces of silver will be recorded on the debit side of the person's life account in an overriding bookkeeping system.

Preceding the church feast days, the horror also haunts the woods and fields. Every year, tens of thousands of deer and other free-living animals such as hares and wild pigs are sneakily, stealthily and brutally killed by hunters, whereby many, very many animals are merely wounded or their legs are shot off, so that the severely wounded animals hide from the predator man and die an endlessly long and miserable death.

The animals that had a shorter death struggle are called the "bag" in hunter jargon and are often blessed by priests who call themselves Christian. For the "Feast of Love," a finely prepared venison

roast is on the table, of an animal that often died miserably under drawn-out agony – this is then the "blessed" "Silent Night, Holy Night."
In this way, the "holy night," in which true Christians, who follow Jesus of Nazareth, should experience the Christ of God in the stillness of profound prayer in their inner being, is turned into a bloodbath and a carcass meal of an externalized Christianity, which is an abomination to God and closes the gates to heaven.
With the churches' blessing, many people thoughtlessly and indifferently while away the hours of celebration in a befogged night marked by perdition, which the incense in the churches cannot brighten either, for the blind guides of religion, as Jesus of Nazareth called them, can merely point the way into the pit.

The calamitous disaster continues:
The Christmas trees have a similar fate as the animals. Christmas trees came into general use in the 19th century. But it was only after the beginning of the 20th century, that it became a massacre of young trees, which is in no way secondary to the massacre of the animals. The indifferent and negative thoughts of many people disdainful of life combine into massacre energies, which finish

off the young, living trees by the millions. Young plant life with strong roots, filled with sap and strength – filled with joy over the coming spring, in order to continue growing and to give food and protection to the multifaceted life from God, to blossom and flourish, to bear fruit and give shade – is simply felled, chopped down, slaughtered, so that misled people can decorate a room for a few short weeks. Or a magnificent tree is also sacrificed to the pagan cult on a church square.
All this, again with the blessing of the church masterminds, who call themselves priests and who often understand little about the life, which God is, in all beings and in all things.

Many people are aware that trees and plants are living beings. Scientific studies of the interrelationships in woods and fields have verified that trees and plants communicate with each other over great distances. It has become known that trees and plants respond to being addressed by people and that they love classical music. It has become known that plants bear especially nice fruit when harmonious classical music is played to them. It has become known that trees and plants can experience joy and stress, all of it very similar to people and animals.

The participant in the roundtable discussion group requested that he might clearly speak out about what really happens with animals and nature on so-called feast holidays. We want to pass it on here. Why hide the truth?

The killing rituals at the so-called church feast holidays, no matter whether the killed victim is a turkey, a goose, a deer or a Christmas tree, or whatever else takes place the whole year round, are against the law of life, which is God, and come under the fifth commandment: "You shall not kill!"

Particularly at Christmastime, we hear the ritual carol: "O you joyful, O you blessed, O you merciful Christmas time!" But millions of animals are sacrificed without mercy to the god Baal and millions of hectoliters of blood are left to the allegedly Christian sewer systems. Millions of trees are mercilessly chopped down, soon to land in the "Christian trash." One could think that most people are subject to a demonic mass hypnosis, so that they have lost all sensation, feeling and thought and positive support for the life, as well as the decisive action for all life forms. Does this terrible bloodshed have anything at all to do with ethics and morals?

What is given here as examples holds equally true for all animals and plants all over the Earth.
The warfare agents of the five components do not stop before anything, whether duck or goose or sheep, whether pig or chicken, whether cow, carp or salmon, whether trees or flowers – it is always the life that has to lose its life. Even today, this frequently still takes place under the premise: Render homage to "Baal" – whereby today he is equipped with several magic hoods.
Through His prophet Isaiah, God, the Eternal, revealed:
"Woe to those who call evil good and good evil, who put darkness for light and light for darkness, who put bitter for sweet and sweet for bitter!
Woe to those who are wise in their own eyes, and shrewd in their own sight!"
The climate collapse will teach people more. The limits that the species man does not set for himself are his downfall. Even in Paul, who is so esteemed by the Church, it says unmistakably: "Whatever a person sows that will he also reap."

*The five warfare agents
from a physician's point of view*

The central control and organizing organ of our human body is the brain. It consists of three main areas, which are different from an evolutionary point of view: the reptilian brain, the old (paleo) and new (neo) mammalian brain. The reptilian brain is the oldest part of our brain. It controls all vital functions of the body, such as breathing, digestion, heartbeat, etc., that is, our instinctive behavior. The paleomammalian brain houses our feelings and emotions; the neomammalian brain, the neocortex, with its two brain halves that are linked by the so-called corpus callosum, is responsible for our cognitive, analytical thinking. Likewise, our entire body is depicted in the neocortex.

At every moment, all information, which enters the brain from the body and from the "outside world" via our senses, is processed by all the areas of the brain, so that in the end, an individual picture develops in the person, shaped by all the data ever stored in the brain.
The smallest cell unit in the brain is called a neuron. There are 100 billion neurons in the brain.

The contact points, with which neurons communicate with other cells, are called synapses. Every nerve cell comes into contact with other nerve cells via up to 10,000 synapses. The sum of these connections is unimaginably huge. The number of synapses is estimated at more than 50,000 billion. The brain is the switchboard of this huge network, to which each individual cell, each organ is connected – a network that is subject to constant change. There is a constant activity of waves on the synapses, up to 20 impulses per second. Even the slightest changes on the synaptic cleft can greatly affect the entire neural network. This means that each small change in our network has an effect on our whole person.

The communication of the nerve cells with thousands of other cells, with nerve cells in the brain and in the body as well as with other cells in muscles or organs takes place by way of electrophysiological or biochemical processes. Within the nerve cell, this occurs primarily electrophysiologically; the bridging of the synapic cleft between one cell and the other occurs biochemically via nerve messenger substances, so-called neurotransmitters, which are formed in the nerve cell itself. In order to work, a certain neurotrans-

mitter needs a receptor, a docking site, which fits very precisely to this one neurotransmitter.
These receptors exist not only in the brain, but everywhere in the body. There, the neurotransmitters have a hormone-like effect, for instance. Thus, a change in our thinking and feeling brings about a reaction, a change, not only in the brain, but in our whole body. This change in the body is always connected with the complex of thinking and feeling that led to this change.

Psychoneuroimmunology is a science that deals with the connections between the brain and the immune system.
Among other things, nervous system and immune system communicate with each other via said neurotransmitters. It is assumed that thoughts and feelings cause the brain to release certain neurotransmitters, which then influence the immune system. Such neurotransmitters can also become active in the cell directly on the DNA, the genetic make-up. Some researchers even describe illnesses such as cancer as faulty information diseases.
Genes consist of nucleic acids. The activity of the genes requires regulation, a control system. This takes place, for example, through the fact that

certain gene sectors are switched on and off, thus acquiring other functions. This regulation is dependent on an information exchange, which changes constantly. The genetic products are proteins. Which proteins are developed depends on which gene sectors are switched on or off. Proteins form the structure of the body's cells and organs. Most cells of the body renew themselves within 7-10 years, so that after this time the body has totally changed.

In summary, we can say that the nervous system, the immune system and signal molecules are closely connected. Today we know that there is a vast number of signal molecules that are, for instance, called neurotransmitters in the nervous system and cytokines in the immune system.
Today, it has been convincingly verified that messenger molecules of the nervous system also influence immune cells and conversely, immune cells influence the messenger molecules of the nervous system. Thus, illnesses always develop through an interaction of nervous, genetic, immunological and psychological factors.

In this, our thoughts and the emotions connected with them are the strongest creative force. One example of this is the placebo effect. Just the thought and the idea that a medication will relieve pain, for instance, brings pain relief.

That this is not merely "imagination," but that a biochemical effect is actually triggered in our body through our mental image, has been scientifically verified today.

Now we can understand how the content of our sensations, feelings, thoughts, words and actions, which does not correspond to the harmony of life, becomes warfare agents and ultimately, changes our body toward illness or disease.

The primary warfare agent with which we change our body is our thoughts. A word or a deed is always preceded by thoughts. Feelings and sensations are not specific for us; they aren't tangible. Only when they form into thought pictures do they become real and tangible for us.

While "thinking about something," the picture develops more and more, as with an ever more realistic film. For example, if we had a quarrel that has not yet been resolved, and if we think about this quarrel again and again, more and more details are added to this picture of the quarrel, more and more feelings. The inner dialogues, for instance, become ever more realistic and in-

creasingly become our reality. Our emotions also change continuously and adapt to our own developing inner film, until in the end we talk and act accordingly. In the chemical factory of our brain, every thought brings about a release of neuropeptides, which constantly, every second, change our body – with negative thoughts toward illness. Illnesses are faulty information diseases.

Brain research also calls this autocatalysis, which means that parts of the brain begin a cycle that reinforces itself. Among other things, this happens when a person, as in the above-mentioned example, produces thoughts and feelings that become ever more powerful by way of the autocatalysis, until they gain control. This autocatalytically reinforced flow of energy and information then also shapes the body.
In his book "The New Brain," Johannes Holler writes, "In this way, software becomes hardware!" In a positive sense, this leads to more health and joy in life, in a negative sense, to illness, worry, depression, perhaps to hurtful words and acts of violence.
Well-known neuroscientists, such as Prof. Gerald Hüther, at the Universities of Göttingen, Mannheim und Heidelberg, investigate the power of

these inner pictures. Gerald Hüther concludes that a person acts based on the pictures that he has in his head and not on the basis of reality. We human beings are prisoners of our inner pictures. As one of few scientists, he says that a person can change himself, if he changes the pictures in his inner being.

So, with the five warfare agents, the negative sensations, feelings, thoughts, words and actions, we harm ourselves the most, since each of these warfare agents develops its destructive effect directly in our brain and in our body before it strikes anywhere else. This is equivalent to a slow, but certain, suicide.

*The path of recognition for
the liberation of the soul.
We can put a stop to the thought disaster*

As already explained: Everyone has different warfare agents in his five components, which should be worked on in good time, before they become missiles, firearms, and hit others, through which a causality can develop and everyone who is hit binds himself to those of his kind.

We should immediately put a stop to such and similar associations, because anyone who is alert and monitors himself can call himself to order and grasp what may underlie the content of the thought disaster. For example, what can be cleared up? What has already been emitted? Or what has to be set up against the base mindset, the warfare agents in our five components, or what can be remedied right away and what do we have to clear up with people?

Ultimately, the contents of the five components that are in order should be the path to liberation from wrong behavior patterns. They should also be the path of recognition to the liberation of the soul, which ultimately stores our causalities, and is strongly burdened by them.

Anyone who loves true freedom, also well-being, health and peace, should transform his warfare agents against people, animals and nature into light-filled forces, into peace-loving feelings, sensations, and thoughts and into honest, upright words; and in all five components, his actions should be what Jesus of Nazareth taught us: *Do to others as you would have them do to you.* Or spoken differently: *Do not do to another what you do not want to have done to you.*

With this, the life in the All-One would begin.

This would be the way to uncover our core of being step-by-step, and would do justice to the indwelling spirit being that we are in the very basis of our soul.

The Human Being, the Core of Being and the Spirit Being

To understand how human being, core of being and spirit being interact, let us first look at the human being. We think we know a person close to us. His name and appearance are not unfamiliar to us. We say, for instance, "This is Martin." – Do we know the "person Martin"? In reality, we know him only by name. His identity is the inputs in his brain.

In each of us, the brain stores as picture sequences the entire contents of our feelings, sensations, thoughts and words, as well as our actions. In time, our brain transmits this information to the body cells and to the entire body. Our physical body is in constant communication with the brain, and the brain, with all body cells and bodily functions, with all the components of our physical body. This means that the inputs in the brain are in communication with all the components of our body. And so, our brain releases only what we have input into our brain cells.
And what about the core of being? Spoken with our three-dimensionally shaped words: The divine

core of being is the compressed Being, the sending and receiving source of the divine being. The core of being is compressed Light-Ether, as is the spiritual body. By way of the core of being, the particle structure of the spirit being is suffused with Light-Ether, the law of infinity.

The particle structure of the soul and the cell structure of the physical body are suffused with Light-Ether to the extent that the soul particles and the cell structure of the physical body are not burdened. God is omnipresent – even if the make-up of the physical body is structured totally differently.

A human being has organs, bones, tendons, ligaments, muscles, nerves, blood and lymph vessels, etc. – all the components that comprise the physical body.

In contrast, the body of the divine being consists of a particle structure. In a rough analogy, we could imagine the divine body like the scales of a fish, for example. However, the particles do not lie next to each other, but over each other and are set into each other.

The entire body of a spirit being consists solely of the particle structure that is set, fanlike, into itself. In this finest, imbricate, or fanlike, entity, all the spiritual atoms of eternity are arranged, which receive the cosmic energy of the All-Unity from the core of being, the primordial heart.

A rose can also convey a wonderful image to us. When a rose unfolds, there are petals that are folded into each other, which reveal the core of the rose. The flower petals are like fans, similar to an imbricate entity that moves in itself.

And so, the spiritual body has no cell structure, or any organs, bones, tendons, ligaments, muscles, etc. It is absolute spiritual-ethereal substance, that is, fine-material, weightless and thoroughly flexible.

Ultimately, we cannot describe the word "weightless" either. For when we speak of "weightless," we say, for example, "That is more than 'light'." But what we describe with "light" or even "weightless," relates already to weight. The spiritual body has no heaviness, no weight.
It is similar for us when we want to grasp the true reality of the word "eternity." The eternity is the All, the Light-Ether, which continuously expands and moves, and the Eternal One, the omnipresent Spirit, God, is in everything and all beings.

Can we describe eternity with the concept "time"? – No, we cannot. In eternity, there is neither time nor space. Nor can we describe an eon or an eon cycle with our concept of time and space.

Please, let us not forget that everything that we hear or read about the Kingdom of God is not even a wisp of eternity.

Through the increasing density, the transformed-down energy, the Light-Ether, developed a framework of time and space; as a result, man moves in time and space and is marked accordingly. His body has weight, heaviness. And yet, he receives spiritual energy from the primordial power via the core of being, which in the human being is located near the pituitary gland.

Starting from the primordial power, spiritual energies flow via the soul to the spiritual centers that are located in the physical body, and ultimately, to all the components of the body.

In the body of a human being, seven spiritual centers are laid out, through which the Spirit flows into the person. These seven consciousness centers correspond to the natures and attributes of God. They are the distribution sites for the inflowing ether forces. Every organ in the physical body is connected with one of these power centers, and in this way, receives the energy necessary for life.

In contrast, in its particle structure, the spirit being is what the core of being is, the universal life, the All-Unity.
Compared to this, the human being is what he has input, that is, stored, in his brain cells. The human brain is the transformer to all the cells and components of the body and to what the person believes he feels, senses, thinks, says and does.
What the human brain emits, that is the person, that is his imprinting; his five components reflect the same and similar aspects.

The particles of the divine body, that is, the spirit being, are one with the primordial heart – the core of being, God, the Eternal – in the core of being.
God, the Eternal, speaks in the core of being, and the spirit being is His word and is the divine body, one with God-Father, who is also Mother.
All life forms also receive His All-word, depending on their state of consciousness. And the human being, who is able to hear His All-word, receives this via the core of being.

*A comparison:
Communication technology on Earth and
the All-communication principle*

For many a reader, the mobile telephone may be the solution to the puzzle. A lame comparison could help us to better understand the All-word.
Why do we human beings have a mobile phone, for instance?
Stepped down to the lowest level, we could compare the core of being with the mobile phone. The number of the person we are calling is nothing more than a frequency that is dialed in a network that contains all potential frequencies. With the number in his mobile phone, the caller dials the frequency of the person he is calling, thus establishing communication to this one specific network subscriber from the network of all mobile phone subscribers.
To stay with our picture: If the network user does not have the number, that is, the dialing frequency of the mobile phone subscriber whom he wants to reach, then he cannot reach him. It's true that the other subscriber is in the same communication network, but he cannot communicate with him, because he cannot establish a connection to him – he has no access.

To be able to use the mobile phone, I, the caller, need the number of the person I am calling.

The spirit being does not need a mobile phone number of this or that life form, of this or that spirit being, because it has everything within itself and communicates with everything.

Figuratively speaking, in terms of the universal speaking All-Unity, we could say, by way of example, that the person is a number. If his number is not in the human communication network, it seems as though he doesn't exist.

Human perception is more than limited. For instance, an animal can emit to us via picture sequences – but we do not understand it, because we human beings do not communicate via the core of being, but only through the external senses with our fellow humans. And when distances are involved, if possible, we communicate per mobile phone, Internet, E-mail or the like, and that, only if we have the appropriate number or address. So the "number human being" has to somehow be clicked on or dialed.

Even though we human beings also think and talk in picture sequences, we seldom understand one another and hardly understand the animals. The communication connections of the plant and mineral worlds are also foreign to most people, and even more so, the all-connecting communication. This lame comparison shows that we could describe human communication as limitation and spiritual poverty.

Animals, on the other hand, are not numbers, but the life in the ethereal communication network of the love for God and neighbor.

The opposition, the adversary of God, knows about the all-encompassing source of creation, the All-communication of the All-Being. For this reason, he tries to transform the knowledge about it down into the temporal, of the earth. This also takes place, for instance, through radio and television waves, and so on.
As stated: The All-communication of the All-Being was transformed down, and based on matter.
Nevertheless, this transformed-down All-Wisdom, which is fascinating to many people, could be a help to roughly understand what really takes place in the All in terms of communication. For the All-communication is the source of communication to all pure Being.
Our physical mobile phone is a primitive communication source that is relevant solely to human beings.

Man doesn't even have a relationship to the planet Earth, let alone to the All-cosmos, from which the life comes.

In contrast, all spirit beings are in communication with each and every planet, with each sun, with the eternal Being, because they are compressed ethereal All-Law and heirs to infinity.

Over the course of their spiritual development on the planes of development and by way of duality, the children of the Kingdom of God have totally accepted and received the All-communication principle. Thus, all divine beings are heirs to infinity, and that, equally.

Everything is connected to each other through the All-communication, despite the differing degrees of maturity in the plants and animals.

As already stated, plant and animal species have differing degrees of consciousness, depending on their spiritual development. The spirit filiation-link to the Father-Mother-God is still dormant in them. As a seed, plants are still assigned to a spiritual collective. But depending on its state of consciousness, even the seed, that is, the sprouting, forming plant life already has corresponding spiritual-divine particles. Despite the differing degrees of maturity, everything is connected to each other via communication and to the All-One, the Creator-Spirit, who is in His creatures as light and power.

If we could ask an animal, irrespective of its degree of maturity, "Are you burdened?" – then the animal, if we could hear it, would answer us, "What do you mean by burden?"
If we ask further, "Well, are you in constant communication with your Creator?" – if we could understand it, the animal would answer, "What do you want to tell me with your words, 'in communication'? – I am in His law."
The animal will not know what we mean when we ask, "What is communication?" It simply declares, "I am."
And if we ask the plant, "How do you understand communication?" – the plant would say, "I don't know what you mean."
And if we question further, "Well, you have that with your Creator!" – the plant would counter, "But I am in Him!"
And so, that would be the answer of the animals, the plants, yes, even the minerals, the stones, "I don't know what you mean. I am in the stream of life. I live from and in God, the Eternal. I am in His Spirit."

From ancient scriptures, the following parable has been passed down for our existence:

And some who were full of doubt came to Jesus, saying, "You told us that our life and being are from God, but we have never seen God, nor do we know of any God. Can You show us the One whom You call the Father and the only God? We do not know whether there is a God."

Jesus answered them, saying, "Hear this parable about the fishes. The fishes of a river spoke with one another and said: They tell us that our life and being comes from water, but we have never seen water, we do not know what it is. Then some of them, who were wiser than the others, said: We have heard that a wise and learned fish who knows all things lives in the sea. Let us go to him and ask him to show us the water.

And so, some of them set out to search for the great and wise fish, and they finally came to the sea where the fish lived, and they asked him.

And when he heard them, he said to them: Oh, you foolish fish, that you do not think. Yet wise are the few of you who seek. You live and move in water and have your existence in the water; you have come from the water and you will return to the water. You live in the water, but you do not know it. In the same way, you live in God and yet you ask Me: Show us God. God is in all things and everything is in God." (This Is My Word 57:6-9)

All pure beings from God are in the All-ocean, the Light-Ether, that is, in the All-Being. The majority of people hardly have a relationship with the "All-ocean," because the majority of people have been washed ashore, as it were. Now, many are looking for seashells, to hear from the shell who or what they are.

Over and over again, the question arises: What has man wrought with his ego, with his narcissism, that is, his self-love?

What exactly is love?

The largest part of mankind has turned away from the almighty unity, from the speaking All-Unity, the word of the universal Creator-Spirit. The people's world of programs is against the law of unity, against the love for God and neighbor. Many are romping about in these wrong attitudes, which are an egocentric fundamental attitude, based on self-love that says, "I am my own best friend." Again and again, we hear the excuse: We human beings have simply distanced ourselves from the love for God and neighbor. So the question often arises: What exactly is love?

Love is the law of infinity. It is the all-flowing Light-Ether. Love is the love for God and neighbor; it is the Father-Mother-God; it is the eternal All-One, the power, the light and the law in all His creatures and ultimately, also in man, in the very basis of the soul.

If we do not hear Him, the All-One, then we can assume that we have programmed ourselves in accordance with, "I am my own best friend," and in the broadest sense, this means, "I myself am God! – at least God-like!" Many people act like higher gods, particularly in the spheres of science, theology, etc. With the human explosive of "I am my own best friend," with narcissism, that is, self-love, we put ourselves above the truth, which is God.

What does it mean to put yourself above God? – In the last analysis, it is the Fall. The Fall-thought is, "I don't believe in God" or, "I have turned away from Him, because I want to be greater than God." And what is the consequence of the estrangement, the turning away from God, the true life? Illness, hardship, infirmity, loneliness and many more maladies, and not lastly, death, often an anguished struggle until the demise of our physical body.

In reality, only the material form of existence, the physical body, dies – and not even that, because it belongs to the Earth, to which it is given for transformation. Earth to earth – but not our soul, not our true being, not the core of being.

By turning away from the divine, man has terminated the true, deep communication with the All, with all the beings of the Being and with God, by denying – the one more, the other less – everything higher, which ultimately is in the person, in us, in the very basis of our soul. Through this, man has shadowed, that is, burdened, a part of his soul, a part of the spiritual particle structure, and many a one has delivered himself up to the opposition – if not to say, he has sold himself to it – through the "I want."

What you want you do not have, and what you do not have you do not grasp, and what you do not grasp, with this you enslave yourself and sell yourself to others.

Day by day, we should reflect more about who we are in the Spirit of God, our heavenly Father, and should also act accordingly.

In God, our heavenly Father, we are flawless sons and daughters of God. Our divine body is enveloped with our wrong thinking, speaking and acting that are turned away from God, through the five components, which, as we have read, can be the explosives that hit us.

Because this is the way it is, we should hasten to take the path back and cleanse ourselves of the vileness we have inflicted upon ourselves and possibly even on others. Every day, we could give an account to ourselves of our still existing small and large transgressions, in terms of our behavior and what this might trigger. Often they are familiar bad habits and vices, to the point of wickedness.

And so, let us discard what ultimately enslaves us and literally drives us into the arms of the adversary!

With everything that moves us, we should, yes, we ought to, pose the question every day: Is this the will of God?

In the end, the question needs to be dealt with every day: So, do I actually want to fulfill what God wants? – If yes, then cleansing, through self-recognition and clearing up, is on the agenda.

Again and again, we hear the decisive question: Who or what am I if I rectify and no longer do the unlawful, the not good, which is frequently my incentive? What do I resolve for instead? – I can resolve, for instance, to become freer and be happier. I can concentrate better; my work gets done much easier. I learn to listen, so that I better understand my fellow people. I draw closer to the animal and plant worlds, and so on.

Jesus, the Christ, essentially said: *Become perfect, as your heavenly Father is perfect.* And so, it is solely about returning to the origin in us. In time, we will also better understand other words of Jesus of Nazareth, who taught us: *The Kingdom of God is within, in you.* The Kingdom of God is, as essence, the core of being in the divine-spiritual body.
When the core of being has been uncovered, then we also have "clean," willed-by-God feelings, sensations, thoughts and willed-by-God words that link, and accordingly, also lawful actions. If the physical body has cleansed itself from all the egocentric toxins, then our brain has also benefited from this. Our soul also cleanses itself according to the cleansing of the unlawful aspects. This then means a very gradual contact with the higher life.

The Breath of God – The All-Law, the Light-Ether

The breath of life, the eternal omnipresent life, is God, the All-Law, the All-life-force. It is the Light-Ether, in which all divine Being that has taken on form is imbedded.

The Light-Ether is the All-life, the breath of God, which we human beings, too, breathe, as well as all animals and plants, according to the life in the density of matter. When, at this moment, we close our mouth and simultaneously hold our nose, we no longer breathe. Why not? – Because the life force, the breath of life, no longer reaches our body.

Man calls the intake of air or oxygen breath. But in everything is the breath of God, the life, the life force. The life force, the breath of life, supplies, on the one hand, all the components of the physical body via the breath; on the other hand, the eternal Creator-God gives us human beings, as well as the animals and plants, nourishment via the Mother Earth. The omnipresent life, which flows to all creatures on Earth, is always God's love.

In all infinity, including matter, the infinite One is active by way of His four primordial powers and His three attributes, which people seldom mention.

From the Spirit of unity, we hear again and again that the four primordial powers are infinity's powers of drawing and creating. Science has names for the four primordial powers of the eternal Being, which correspond to their value and to the volume of energy they are suited for. And yet, it is always the All-Spirit, the working of the All-One God for His children, for Mother Earth, for the world of minerals, plants and animals.

We human beings have become accustomed to talking in general terms and, as a matter of course, about the breath, the air, about oxygen, about everything that man needs to be able to live on Earth – and yet, it is always the one Spirit, the All-One, the love of God, our heavenly Father, that makes life in the temporal possible for us, so that we recognize the All-life, and again find our true consciousness and return to eternity.

The breath of God is the inexhaustible Light-Ether; it is the life, eternally. In His cradle of drawing and creating, the breath of God stimulates the spiritual formation all the way to the spiritual filiation, the Father-Mother-Principle.

When the Eternal, the paramount primordial power, the All-One, respirates, that is, stimulates the evolution of a spiritual atom in the cradle of drawing and creating, in the four planes of development, to the filiation of God, then formation begins in the mineral kingdom.

The first mineral powers, which are stimulated by the breath of God to the filiation of God, contain all powers of infinity, the name of the developing child, the dual pair, that is, the dual parents, the mentality of the child, as well as the symphonies of the All, such as color, fragrance and sound. All the powers of the All are arranged in each developing mineral form.

*The breath of God is the "Let There Be,"
which continues up to the spiritual filiation*

Let us get back to the breath of God, which we human beings, but also animals, breathe and which flows to the plants; yes, all of infinity is suffused with His breath.

Everything is energy. The carrier substance of the eternal Being consists of the inexhaustible atoms of Light-Ether.
The nucleus of all the types of atoms found in infinity consists of the highest pulsating Light-Ether of Kindness, Love and Gentleness. These three attribute powers are set in the Love, which is the All-One's highest power of drawing and creating.

The nucleus, also called primordial core, is circled by the four primordial powers, the powers of drawing and creating of the divine Order, His Will, His Wisdom and His Earnestness, the same as Justice.

How the energies of drawing and creating function in the ether atoms is very difficult to express with our words.

Because everything is contained in all things, the three attribute powers of God are also respectively contained in the four atomic creating powers; it is the germinating life in the nucleus and in all the creating powers.

Here, the essential ether atoms are only briefly named. With our words, they are: fertility atoms – also called collective atoms – carrier atoms – also called stabilizing atoms – creating atoms or formation atoms, and development atoms, the same as unifying atoms.

The impulse giver for all Being, also for the divinely forming life, is always the spiritual atomic nucleus of Kindness, Love and Gentleness, set in the All-love, the Father-Mother-God.

The infinite One is active in infinity by way of the four primordial powers. But, as stated, in all powers, the highest pulsating primordial core, the Love, is the measure and the efficacy in all of infinity.

The "Let There Be," the breath of God, is the power of the love for God and neighbor, which extends to the spirit filiation. The spiritual child, which develops into a matured spirit being, matures in the duality of the spirit parents, in the extended family of the Father-Mother-God.

How can we imagine the birth of a spirit?

A comparison could give us an understanding of the spiritual-divine "Let There Be."
What is contained in the unfertilized ovum of a human mother? – the mother's predispositions, her genetic make-up. Through procreation by the man, the father's genetic make-up is added. Both merge into one cell, whereby it becomes active. We could say that it starts its path of evolution.

Let us return to the divine: giving and receiving. It is the one power, the Love, which, in a specific spiritual atom, stimulates the "Let There Be" to the filiation of God. The predispositions of the spirit child are already contained in the "Let There Be," the specific respirated spiritual type of atom, because, as stated, everything is in all things.
In the fertilized human ovum, the predispositions for the human child are also already present. The fertilized ovum develops into an embryo and, in the mother's body, gradually matures into a child.
In the divine development planes, in the spiritual birth body, ethereal, that is, fine-material, life

forms develop up to a nature being, which initiates the spirit birth of the spirit child through a dual pair.

The tiny look through a spiritual crack in the door can tell us so much when we bring to mind the development of a human child in its mother's body.
For example, on an ultrasound picture, what can be recognized in the womb? We see that the ovum has divided, and that through further cell division an embryo developed, which, in its outer appearance, is similar to an embryo form as we also know it from the animal world. The embryo continues to develop into a fetus, which then increasingly assumes human features, until the developing being can be recognized as a human being.

And how is it with a developing spirit being? After a being has gone through the development planes, it is raised to a spirit child, to then – as a spirit child – again activate everything that is already inherent in it.
Spoken in our words: The spirit child goes to the divine-cosmic school in the four planes of development to activate, as a spirit child, the powers

of evolution, so that as a spirit being it has communication with all life forms in infinity and with all heavenly planes, with all heavenly bodies of the Being. From this, the picture develops that then opens in the core of being, through which it becomes possible to behold all details of infinity.

Then, everything is present in the core of being, in the primordial heart, the entire radiation volume of the Kingdom of God.

The life in the Spirit of God, of the eternal Being, is a universal All-communication that is unimaginable to us human beings. And so, the spirit child learns to completely internalize the principle of All-communication, in the core of being as picture, color, form and sound. In this way, the spirit child enters into the heritage of infinity and matures into a perfect spirit being.

The Fall of the Spiritual Beings Down to the Coarse-Materialness of the Human Being

Many people live in the Fall-thought that led to becoming human. It is: "Divide, bind and rule!" Anyone who separates himself from the All-Unity, the divine heritage, the eternal law of love for God and neighbor, from the "link and be" cannot exist in the Kingdom of God. For anyone who divides and does not link, who is against the eternal law of All-Unity, falls out of the All-Unity as if automatically, because he divides, binds and tries to rule. That brings a lack of freedom!
Perhaps the repetition of the remarks about the Fall-thought reminds many a reader of the five components, above all of the "thought," which, as we read, is the greatest and most powerful splitter bomb and can unleash devastating actions.

Several divine beings in the eternal Being began to rebel against God's law of unity, the love for God and neighbor; they began to create their ego-law in tendencies of "divide, bind and rule." As a result, they could no longer stay in the All-Unity, in the Kingdom of God. These tendencies developed ever more into the Fall-thought: "divide, bind and rule."

Many, very many divine beings gradually joined this thought of wishing and wanting, "divide, bind and rule." It has been passed down that the archangel Michael led them out of the Kingdom of God. Because of their intransigence to turn back and change their ways, they fell ever deeper, so that their bodies became darker, heavier, and thus, condensed more and more in accordance with their Fall-thought "divide, bind and rule."

During unimaginably long periods of time, that is, windows of time, the planet Earth developed with corresponding plant and animal species. Later, came the beings that had now become coarse material, and which, over the course of countless thrusts of condensation in the finer-material realms, condensed into humanlike beings and then, into human beings.

The law of "divide, bind and rule" is the Fall-law, the law of "cause and effect" – also called "sowing and reaping" or "action equals reaction."

According to the divine inheritance law of freedom, every being is responsible for itself, as are we human beings in terms of our feeling, sensing, thinking, speaking and acting.

By origin we are pure beings, spirit beings, which came from the Kingdom of God, but the Kingdom of God is, and remains, in the very basis of each soul as essence, just as Jesus of Nazareth taught us: *The Kingdom of God is within, in you.*

God, the Eternal, the All-One, is, and remains, the life with His children, in the very basis of each soul, in the core of being, the primordial heart, which beats in soul and person. The unlawful existence of man, the law of "divide, bind and rule," or cause and effect, envelops the soul and person as energy. These are so-called soul garments, burdens of the individual, which are mirrored in the aura.

*The Fall-law "divide, bind and rule."
The demon aspires to destroy
the divine core of being*

Since the Fall from the eternal Kingdom of God, the All-One has sent divine beings over and over again. The All-One gave clarification and showed His fallen sons and daughters – later human beings – the path back to the eternal homeland. Thereupon, many Fall-beings returned; others, in turn, went on to become human beings over unimaginable periods of time, that is, windows of time. Bit by bit, they built up a structure of domination, which in the finer-material realms operates as the "demonic power."

The demonic "divide, bind and rule" influenced the first Fall-beings that had become human beings ever more, and made them dependent. During the further course of increasing condensation, which today we call matter, human beings created external religions and disastrous power structures.

Since the dissolution of the eternal Being failed, the demons' objective today is to destroy everything that bears the existence of God, above all, the core of being that is inherent in all living beings, in each life form, in each animal, in the plant and mineral kingdoms. From the very beginning until today, their striving is to make the Kingdom of God subject to them and it is still their desire to dissolve it, if possible.

Anyone who joins with the Fall-law of the demonic power, "divide, bind and rule," loses more and more energy and ultimately, his freedom. Through the loss of energy, people bind themselves to deceptive power structures, which want to convey to them the idea and certainty that they are on the right path or are already gods, not to say, God Himself.

Here we immediately think of idolatry cults, of statues of clay and bronze, of the idol Baal. The ritual idol and his priests today rule in a similar way to ancient times; it's just that they have different names, faces and titles. Right from the beginning, the knaves "from below" were liars and murderers, who wanted, and today still want, to destroy everything that, in truth, belongs to God, the Eternal.

If you like, reflect on the five components, to figure out what it means to relinquish to others the reins of your own life.

Loss of energy and the loss of freedom lead to addictions and other excesses

When people commit themselves to the law of "divide, bind and rule," and follow similar patterns of thinking and acting, they lose more and more energy in soul and body. This means that because of this, they can hardly find their way to God in the very basis of their soul. Then doubt in the Eternal sets in and, in many cases, addiction.

In the last analysis, addiction means that a person is looking for a hold – but where?

If an addiction gets out of hand, because it causes the person to lose more and more energy, then in many ways the person presumes to be the ruler over life, which ultimately means, "I am God! I am more intelligent than the animal, the plant and the stone and not lastly, more intelligent than many a person – everything is mine!"

Among other things, this leads to loss of freedom, to countless addictions, even to so-called fits of raving madness, which are encountered in people everywhere these days. Because the lapse from higher ethics and morals is gaining the upper hand and becoming the norm, most people think only of themselves and unscrupulously use people, animals and Mother Earth for their own base purposes. The spiritual poverty, the energy descent through the distance from God, is the outcry, "I want! I want!"

At some point in time, the outcry "I want!" becomes the deed. People make people dependent; they treat animals in the cruelest ways, killing and murdering them. They keep animals in animal ghettos as so-called slaughter animals, and the animal-ghetto wardens hand them over to the butcher who slaughters them, cuts and portions their flesh into pieces, which then lands in the frying pans of the animal cannibals.

Among other things, people also keep animals imprisoned, to live out their drives on them or for personal entertainment. And so, people influence animals, to train them for their human purposes and needs. People turn animals into livestock, and so on.

Much, if not to say, everything, originates from the contents of the five components.

The just way of feeling and sensing has become lost to many people. They have dedicated these two components to the ruling structure of Baal.

Dear fellow people, animals are sentient beings, which, like us human beings, feel suffering and pain, and sense what man, the cruel fellow, is up to. As a result of man's turning away from the divine, from the origin of his true being, which is unity, he hardly has a way to reach his neighbor anymore, much less the animal, which is in communication with its animal brothers and sisters of the same species and with the All-One.

Through the loss of energy, most people have become hangers-on and imitators. They submissively joined what "god Baal" and his entourage have established. From the component "thought," developed the base mindset that makes you unfree. By sacrificing freedom, the way of thinking in terms of castes and external religions with cult priests and pastors, power structures and belief systems, as well as purposeful "traditions" spread. Depending on the epoch, the power structures and their manifestations change, but the animal murder of our fellow creatures remains.

The "murder machinery" man on behalf of the pagan god Baal and his adherents

When cultists teach that animals do not have souls, that nature is likewise inanimate and that man is allowed to make the animals and nature subservient and available for his use – then people who are still alert and who believe in the one God, who is the All-Unity, should actually sit up and take notice.

Anyone who is servile to external compulsions, as it applies to the madhouse "divide, bind and rule," on the one hand, brutally violates the provider of mankind, the Mother Earth, and, on the other hand, violates the animal world by torturing animals, massacring and murdering animals and by animal cannibalism.

During the Middle Ages, people treated people as they do animals today, only back then, they did not slit human bodies open in order to consume them. Today, the pagan terrorism, the tradition of destruction and slaughter, is particularly going after Mother Earth, her animal and plant species as well as the mineral kingdoms. Today, animal cannibalism is the order of the day; man consumes the flesh of his fellow creatures, his little animal brothers and sisters, and robs them of their means of subsistence on Earth.

Everything, but absolutely everything, is subject to the "murder machinery" man: the torture of animals, the extermination of the animal and plant beings, the manipulation and modification of the genetic material and much more. Through genetic engineering of animals, but also through artificial insemination of animals, people produce "fake animal creatures." Note well, these are not animals from God's cradle of creation, but beings that do indeed suffer and feel pain, too, but are on the drip feed of the life of those people who cause and affirm such things and profit from them, and those who consume the meat of all tortured and cruelly killed animal bodies.

All this is by order of the pagan god, who comes "from below" and who, from the very beginning, was a liar, a torturer, a slaughterer and murderer. The validity of the statement by Jesus of Nazareth concerning this can be seen everywhere today. He said:

You are of your father the devil, and your will is to do your father's desires. He was a murderer from the beginning, and does not stand in the truth, because there is no truth in him. When he lies, he speaks out of his own character, for he is a liar and the father of lies!

A very direct question to our readers: Do you also belong to the pagan guild?

Are you, too, a terrorist, as far as the Earth, with its animals, plants and minerals, is concerned? If yes, then you will not understand us, we who are for the one Creator-God, who is the All-Unity, the love for God and neighbor.

*Man destroyed the
original, harmonious symbiosis
between animals and nature.
The maltreated Earth is rebelling*

Countless people in all generations adhered, and today still adhere, to the dominion of the cult "Baal," which, however, expresses itself today under various names.

As already stated, the pagan cult traditions of the underworld claim that animals do not have souls and plants do not have sensations; they claim that we human beings may use and also abuse these living beings and life forms at will.

People in all generations were infested, that is, marked, by this idolatry, this idolatrous mania. For this reason, animals in general bear the stamp, "intended for use, that is, for consumption." Because of this, our animal brothers and sisters suffer tortures; they are abused as livestock, chained up, maltreated, cruelly and brutally killed, kept in prisons and animal ghettos, until they are murdered by the butcher, to finally be consumed by human beings, animal cannibals.

Everything, but absolutely everything, is based on energy. Since no energy is lost, any brutal act whatsoever – the abuse of animals and nature and the predatory exploitation of Mother Earth in equal measure – is stored in the aura of the planet Earth, and likewise on the film reel of the soul garments of those people who are addicted to the idolatrous mania.

This negative energy radiates back to the Earth, with the result that animals, filled with fear and terror, avoid the originators, the human beings, and run away from them, that is, they take flight. People, who are, after all, their big brothers and sisters, should offer their fellow creatures protection and support instead of being a terrifying image. Because many animals imitate the behavior of their big brothers and sisters, they hunt their small fellow brothers and sisters – just as people demonstrate. They kill and eat them. – Who taught the animals this?

Ultimately, man, who serves the cult of tradition, the god of the underworld, who, as stated, was a liar and murderer right from the beginning and still is up until today.

The maltreated Earth rebels and many ask why God allows such things – when storms and tornadoes destroy houses, when floods break in over the countryside, when entire areas become infertile through aridness and drought. All this and much more is caused by man, according to the law that man inflicted upon himself, which says, "You will reap what you sow." In the end, it is the principle "divide, bind and rule."

When, according to the law of free will, the Eternal, whom we in the western world call "God," let the Earth develop for human beings, for His fallen children, animal and plant species were there first. At the beginning of the formation of the Earth for people, the animals did not eat each other. They took what nature provided them with. They did not pull up plants by their roots, as people do today. They took the leaves; they took the herbs, the seeds and fruits and then let the plants and trees continue to grow, so that they flourished through the power from above. This was the harmonious symbiosis between animals and nature. And what is it like today?

Today, what happens corresponds to how people are. They have transmitted their behavior to the world of animals and plants, to the whole planet Earth: plundering, robbing and murdering. And yet, the original order remains the eternal divine principle: The creatures from God, the animals, plants, stones and minerals are part of the great All-Unity, God, because God is the All-life and thus, all His living beings and life forms carry His breath, the life. That is, and will be, eternally.

The estrangement from the All-Unity is the spiritual poverty of egomania. The hellish brandmark: "Everything is mine!"

The estrangement from the All-Being, the All-Unity, is the egocentricity, which exhibits its spiritual poverty in "divide, bind and rule" – as a claim to power, which means, "I am my own best friend."

This is the spiritual imbalance, the disinterest in true values, in higher ethics and morals; it shows itself in intolerance, striving for power and claims to possession, with the greed for money and goods in tow. The proof that this is so is becoming ever more evident, because present-day society is a society of egomaniacs, with the corresponding all-too-human state of consciousness.

Most people do as the masses do and, as egomaniacs, no matter of what degree, trot along the same beaten track, with no regard for what perishes in the process. When someone with a higher attitude attempts to cross this beaten track of the ego, then right away the egocentric hellish roaring comes from below, from the system of Baal, the demand to ostracize and exclude and perhaps even to butcher the dissenter who is dangerous to the prevailing system.

For today's cult of Baal and its adherents, any ember from hell is fine, which it tries to lay on God's creation, so as to stoke up the fires of hell more and more, to afflict the creatures of God, including the Earth, with the hellish brand mark, that implies, "Everything is mine!"

People who are in on this hellish game were, and are, symbolically inflicted with an "ear tag" by the pagan system, the program of insinuation to influence from "below." It's possible that the "ear tag" also bears as identification the base consciousness, which is marked by the proviso, the concept, that faith alone is enough.

Your Consciousness Lies In You – Faith Cannot Be Proven

No matter how a person thinks about his day: Each day is the day of each individual and lies in his responsibility. Each day decisions need to be dealt with and, at the same time, corresponding challenges, which want to stimulate self-recognition – if a person is alert and does not blindly swim with the masses of humanity, with the current of indifference, in the opinion that it is sufficient to say, "I believe in God" or, "The belief in God, by itself, is enough." Or the person simply leaves the responsibility to others, by stating, "I believe what the priests and pastors preach." Or he remains undecided, in the sense, "It's all the same to me. Belief here, belief there; what are we supposed to believe anyway?"

In the end, many a one says, "I don't believe in anything at all, not even in myself – or perhaps in myself, after all?" And he rigorously rejects dealing with questions of belief, "Be it as it may, leave me in peace as far as belief is concerned!" The statement "...or perhaps in myself, after all?"

may cause many a one who thinks similarly to take heed. Passive faith simply cannot be verified, not even the individual can verify it for himself. Why not? Because a passive faith is something static, something inflexible. Nothing that leads to more can come of passive faith; it is incapable of developing. In this passive principle, "I believe or I don't believe," the days ripple by, without people seriously asking themselves whether this is truly the life.

Dear fellow people, neither passive faith nor what is explained here can be verified. No one can prove it to you – it is totally up to you and your consciousness for this, and this lies in you.

If you like, think along with us: In all of the universal infinity, there is nothing static. Only in the ecclesiastical denominational sector, where it essentially says, "Faith alone is enough," everything is supposed to remain as fixed as possible. The child baptized into the church simply has to believe what the church prescribes for it. This is the passive ecclesiastical faith.
Faith is a matter of belief. To prove to oneself what one believes in leads to self-recognition and nearness to God – when one experiences the

belief in God in oneself through what Jesus of Nazareth taught us: *Do to others as you would have them do to you.*

The law of love for God and neighbor: "Link and be"

If you believe in the Eternal, in the true, All-One God, in the Creator of infinity, in an absolute intelligence, then let your belief in the All-One become active, for the eternal law of love for God and neighbor is "sending and receiving," "link and be!" This is All-communication, this is the true life.

You, yourself, are consciousness; in the very basis of your soul, you bear the incorruptible core of being, the All-life.

So, you, yourself, are called upon to verify for yourself that God, the Spirit of infinity, exists, and that in the very basis of your soul, He, the All-One, is the eternal life, the I AM THE I AM.

The Eternal is the Omnipresence, the All-Law. The All-Law is effective in all of infinity – and who can receive it in tone and sound? All beings – including human beings – who are in communication with the All-One, the Spirit of infinity. Man cannot perceive the pulsating life with the mere words, "I believe," but with deeds of true love for neighbor, for the Eternal is the love.

In comparison to many people, the animal, plant and mineral kingdoms are in constant communication with their Creator, the Eternal. People who pay honor to the I AM THE I AM, to the omnipresent Spirit, by walking the path that the Eternal pointed out to us in the Ten Commandments through Moses and Jesus of Nazareth in His Sermon on the Mount, are, in the very basis of their soul, close to the primordial light, God in us. They experience what "link and be" means.

Let us realize once more that in all of infinity, there is nothing static, nothing fixed. Something fixed cannot bring forth anything inventive, anything creative and cosmic. God, the Eternal, is always movement, always the drawing and creating life, always omnipresent evolution.

No person can prove God to you. We frequently hear and read about "consciousness." The consciousness of man – note well, of man – consists of what he feels, senses, thinks, speaks and how he acts. Each day, among other things, the person works with these five components, which, in turn, affect his sensory organs. With these five active agents of feeling, sensing, thinking, speaking and acting, which can also be explosives, and with his senses, he creates his consciousness. Sheet by sheet, that is, layer by layer, he builds upon it, and that, day after day, hour after hour, minute by minute.

Every single one of us creates the content of these consciousness layers ourselves, through the five components. And so, they are your personal human consciousness. And only you, yourself, can probe into what you have stored in your consciousness sheets, that is, consciousness layers.

We have created our consciousness layers – we, all by ourselves. Before this background, we could ask and also answer for ourselves: What good is it to us then, and to our state of human consciousness, when we cling to the rigid faith that requires no deeds?

We Learn – Learn Along With Us!
"Sending and Receiving"
and the All-Communication
that Makes You Free

Dear fellow people, if you love God's creation, the animals, nature, the mineral world, then break with the Baal system and let your seal of value, which says, "I believe in God," become active! If you like, learn along with us to strive toward the free Spirit. Learn with us what love for God and neighbor means. Learn with us what "sending and receiving" means, that is, the All-communication, which makes you free! And remember: No one is born a master.

Again and again, we should renew our awareness that all living beings and all life forms created by the Eternal belong to the All-community of God, to the cosmic All-Unity, to the family of God, our heavenly Father.

We human beings, every single one of us, live in this divine All-principle of "sending and receiving," because of the incorruptible core of being in the very basis of our soul. Depending on their state of consciousness, which, of course, is divine, God's creatures, the animals, plants, stones and minerals are in communication with their Creator, because cosmic "sending and receiving" knows no time and thus, no emitting time and no limitation of space, either.

We are learning! Will you learn with us? – All living beings and all life forms that bear the seed of being and the core of being – animals, plants, stones and minerals – breathe the breath of their Creator, who is the life. Note well: They breathe the breath of their Creator, who is the life!
Everything is respirated by the eternal Creator-God. Every animal, every plant and every stone in the Creator's stream of life is a divine fellow creature in the great All-family of God. The animals from the breath of God, but also the plant beings are the little brothers and sisters of man. The state of consciousness of the mineral kingdom also belongs to the eternal Creator-God, who created the minerals in His cradle of drawing, that is, of creating, toward the formation and further evolution of consciousness and who accompanies and cares for them all-encompassingly on their path of evolution.
He, the great All-One, is by and with His Creation – note well: He is by and with His Creation. The

same also holds true for us human beings. God is with us in the very basis of our soul. Can He, the All-One, be with us in our thoughts, in everything that we say and do? If yes, then we will become sensitive, feeling people, in whom the All-Unity is effective, the All-community.

The life of All-Unity is the Being. It is the creatures from God, the All-One, the world of animals, plants and minerals, the divine beings, the spirit beings. In the origin of our soul, we human beings also belong to the eternal Father-Mother-God, to the extended family of God. All things and all beings are linked with one another and, via the core of being, the primordial heart of Being, they are in communication with the All-One, the Creator-God, the Father-Mother-God.

Particularly the present situation in the world makes it blatantly obvious what "divide, bind and rule" means

Many people have lost their belief in God, because He, God, does not do what they expect, even demand, of Him. They separate themselves from the All-power of God and bind themselves to so-called gods, to people who let themselves be idolized by people.

Even though many a one calls on God in hardship, suffering and fear, most people have forgotten the true meaning of the existence and the workings of God.

Everything from the works of God that we human beings see, and don't see, bears the life, which is God. If we turn away from the All-Giver, we separate ourselves from the All-communication with the positive forces; we more or less break with God, the Creator of life, the All-life. The person then just barely believes in what corresponds to his opinions and ideas.

To "divide" means nothing more than, "I'm a human being. I create for myself what I assume is right and good for me. I primarily believe in what I see and possess; I consider this to be my property."

What developed, and develops, from being tied to self-glorification, to the power of money and goods, perhaps even to sizable inheritances? Claims of power and possession and self-glorification let us recognize the principle of "divide, bind and rule," whereby each one is against every one. This satanic principle reveals the state of being separated from the All-Unity, from the

All-life, the universal Spirit. The insinuations from below, from the adversary of life, say, "Don't believe in the eternal existence; believe solely in yourself, then you believe in me."

From the greed for power and prestige, develops the drive to be a ruler, of which the driving force is wealth. From these components of power, which often have their root in the most trivial incidents, grow discord, fighting and murder, even war. This is the demonic influence; this is the negative force that comes from below. From this so-called "warfare agent," the negative powers, the demonic, the demon draws his energy to fight against God's creation and affects people negatively. The demonic power structure, the principle of "divide, bind and rule," exists on the negative energies of people. Through this, people not only become unfree, but are often pressed into a militant straitjacket.

The divine "link and be," on the other hand, brings freedom, because the person binds himself to nothing and no one; for he is aware that when his journey over the Earth as a human being comes to an end, he cannot take anything with him, only the burdens in his soul by way of the principle of "divide, bind and rule." Despite all this, the power of the Christ of God remains in his soul, so that he may overcome and discard the demonic aspects he has inflicted upon himself.

For each one of us, the actualization of "link and be" can be seen as follows:
I, the person, learn to establish the link, that is, the communication, to the smallest components of matter, by making myself aware over and over again of the following:
In all beings and in all things is the positive, the Spirit, God.
I learn and work to establish a positive relationship to nature and to the animal world, also to the Earth with all its life forms.
I learn to grasp that my life on Earth is an invaluable gift from the Eternal.
I learn to embrace the connection to the innermost being in my fellow humans, for in the very basis of each soul is the law of brotherliness and sisterliness that connects us to every brother, every sister.
I learn to make peace and to keep peace.

From the learning steps toward the cosmic principle of "link and be," gradually develops the living belief in God, who gave us the commandments through Moses, excerpts from the All-Law, and the Sermon on the Mount through Jesus of Nazareth, which explains life in the Spirit of the All-One.

Man – An image of God?

To pass on the seven-dimensional life of the law with our three-dimensionally shaped words, always remains a balancing act. When we read or hear that we human beings should be images of God, this does not directly mean the sinful human being, but the unalterably pure being, the spirit being.

Everything simply is energy. The human body is also energy, even though we talk about bones, tendons, ligaments, blood vessels, nerves, hormones, glands, organs, etc. This fact is very normal for many people. But when it is said that all these components of the body are nothing other than energy and carriers of energy with varying degrees of vibration, because they correspond to the content of our five components, which are also energy, then this is often questioned with a shaking head.

Whether we want to accept or reject it: The content of our five components determines our earthly existence, including the structure and radiation of our physical body. In time, the five components – positive or negative – enter the cell structure of our body and mark our physical body as well as our soul. From this imprinting of the person, his character and appearance develop.

In summary, we can say that each person is his personal energy body, which radiates his individual frequencies according to his inputs of energy, which correspond to the person. Figuratively speaking, this is the individual's person-law.

Often we hear that we human beings are shaped by the genes that we have inherited from our ancestors, for example, by those of our grandparents or great grandparents. That's possible. It can be that we actually do resemble our grandfather or grandmother in several aspects – but do we also think like our forefathers? The person today thinks and acts according to his present situation in life and not according to that of his ancestors.

Just as the person thinks, feels, senses, speaks and acts now, that is what shapes him today.

Each person – then and today – shapes his earthly existence himself, including his genes.

We human beings are, after all, garbed divine beings. However, our energy body is shaped, that is, marked, by our present behavior patterns; but viewed in terms of energy, as a figure, a well-proportioned person resembles a divine being. The divine being is well-proportioned, eternally beautiful, eternally young, pure. It is a cosmic ethereal being of the Being through and through; it is fine-material.

When we hear about the "resurrection of the flesh," which is taught in many an external religion, then we have to bear in mind that the following holds true for us human beings: earth to earth. Our physical body is from the Earth and belongs to the Earth. In contrast, our finer-material soul bears the resurrection to the eternal life as a process of becoming. This means that the soul takes its path to the eternal life. How long it takes and how often it incarnates till then, is up to the person himself, who, as stated, marks his soul. But unalterably inherent in the soul is the resurrection to the eternal life, to the divine being, to the ethereal spirit being in us.

We Learn to First Fashion the Great Garden of Eden in Ourselves

Dear fellow people, join us, in fashioning the great Garden of Eden in ourselves first! The world of animals and plants and the entire world of minerals belong to us, and are, as stated, as essence, as the source of life, in the very basis of our soul.

Let us allow it to become in us – on Earth as it is in heaven!
All of God's creatures, all living beings, all animals, the nature kingdoms, all Being, want to live in harmony with us human beings.
They are in the All-stream, in the mighty workings of creation of their Creator, in the further development of God's all-wise cradle of drawing, that is, of creating.

Join us in respecting and cherishing the life!
Join us in growing closer to the core of being in our soul, in the awareness that the All-One is in us and in all living beings and life forms of nature.

A sentence to remember, which could determine our daily life:
> The nature kingdoms, all the animals from God's breath, on, in and over the Earth, as well as the animals in the oceans and waters belong to us human beings.

God, our heavenly Father, is the All-Unity, He is the speaking God in His creation and in us, too, in our core of being that is in our soul.
We become aware that all living beings and life forms, the creatures from God, sense and feel the human beings.

Animals live in picture sequences, just as we human beings do. They don't think; they let the picture emerge in their animal consciousness. In relation to us human beings, they first make a picture for themselves, a scent picture.

Learn with us, and don't simply say, "That may be" or, "I can't believe that."
It's not the other one who should try out what has been said – we are all called upon, every single one of us, to live the day in the awareness that everything, absolutely everything, lives. And so, we learn each day.

If you like, begin with yourself. It is a criterion of the eternal life: You are free; you don't have to. According to the eternal law, which, among other things, is freedom, nothing may be forced upon us, not even to have to believe something that can't be proven.

This is why we learn to understand and to experience, ourselves, that our life is unity, and that the life of many animals also takes place in pictures, just like the life of each person – however, not sugarcoated or even colored by thoughts. True life is constant communication with the Creator, with God, our heavenly Father, the All-One, who is the love for God and neighbor.

Learn, let us all learn, to look into the world of our thoughts, words and actions! Only when you think consciously and speak slowly, will you notice that your life takes place in pictures, as do your actions. What you perceive in yourself in pictures also takes place in you. If you look at your picture sequences consciously, that is, if you question them, you will very soon notice what is neutral or what you have colored with your thoughts. Everything is recorded on your life film, as on a film reel.

The picture sequences point out who we really are. Our pictures – honestly looked at – let us recognize that this is our character, and that it marks our appearance.

As long as we don't change the pictures on our life film toward the positive and the content of our five components accordingly, we will not develop the stamp of our nature, our character, toward the positive, either.

If we change our picture sequences, by filling them with a different content, with kindness and love, then we also change our character profile. We become more charming, friendlier, more sociable, kinder and more amenable.

We people always want proof. We are the proof, ourselves. Because when our life film changes toward the positive, when our picture sequences become more light-filled, this also shows in our facial features and on our whole body. So, we are the proof, ourselves, and our mirror image shows this to us.

To learn means to always first learn on ourselves, to examine the content of our own feelings, sensations, thoughts and words, as well as our actions, with the question: Am I really who I think I am?

*All living beings and life forms
from God's creation
are beings of the All-Unity*

Will you join us? We learn to sense for ourselves, to experience that the mighty Creator-God is the giver of life for all God-created living beings and all life forms.

You now no longer go over the Earth spiritually blind. You experience that the All-One is the designer and form-giver in His creation. You recognize that every life form, whether animal, plant or stone, is unique; it is not the spitting image of the same life form, as we say. Why? Because each living being radiates another aspect of consciousness and is also marked accordingly.

Through the institutional churches, we were given an understanding of so-called heaven, like a Fata Morgana, where God is primarily worshiped and perhaps even praised with songs of Hallelujah. And that is not at all how it is!

We surely can never convey in detail the seven-dimensional Kingdom of God with our words, but each one of us can work out for himself what is in the very basis of his soul, the All-life, the love for God and neighbor, the peace and the feeling of the eternal homeland in you, in all of us.

The eternal homeland is the Kingdom of God, in which the spiritual families form the extended family in God, our heavenly Father. In the Kingdom of God, plants and animals live in unity with the divine beings. The eternal gardens of the Being, of the Kingdom of God, know no fences. All structures consist of the primordial substance and are, like everything, weightless. In this connection, we think of the statement of Jesus of Nazareth: *In my Father's house are many mansions. If it were not so, would I have told you that I go to prepare a place for you?*

Spiritual families, dual pairs, that is, dual parents, live with their children on the heavenly planes in the structures, but everything is unity; everything is integrated in the extended family of the Father-Mother-God.

Again and again, the question comes up: Dual pairs, dual parents and children from the duality – How can that be? In the temporal, an analogy to the Kingdom of God

We learn that what we perceive in the temporal is analogous to the spiritual kingdom, only it is transformed-down Light-Ether, that is, energy, which is burdened, and in which many people scrape by in the Fall-thought: divide, bind and rule.

In the following, an example for better understanding: A good mother, in whose body her child develops, to which she gives birth after a certain time, does not ask, "Does it belong to me? Am I the mother?" A faithful, good father will not ask whether he procreated it, or ask, "Does this newborn belong in our family and are all other children in the family brothers and sisters of the newborn?" In every good, intact family, it is taken for granted that the mother is the mother of the child and the father its procreator. Children belong to the parents, and children in the Kingdom of God are with their dual parents and, as stated, they are at the same time in the extended family. That is the true life; that is the "link and be," that is without the Fall-thought and thus, eternal life.

The animal and plant beings, too – those that live with us human beings, as well, – belong to the extended family of God! They should be seen and treated as such by us, because they are, like us humans, beings of the All-Unity. To learn this brings us inner wealth and a spiritual life in the temporal.

According to iron laws, all beings of creation from God that live with us in the temporal, the animals, plants, as well as the powers of the mineral kingdom, are led back to their primordial form, to the respective state of consciousness in the realm of the purely spiritual Being and, in the divine cradle of creation, are prepared for further development. All living forms on, in and above the Earth, in the waters and oceans, and we human beings, too, are merely guests on Earth.

Nothing happens by chance!
Why are so many animal species dying out these days? For one thing, through the terrible living conditions that man has made for them; for another, the Creator-God is taking back His creatures, the animals, as well as the plant species.

The homebringing of the animals and plants says: At the very first, the plants and animals were on the Earth and then human beings. – He who has ears to hear, let him hear, and he who believes in God realizes what is taking place in infinity, in the All!

We realize and learn from this that what is being done to the animals by human beings in terms of negative and bestial acts is the call from hell of the pagan god; it is the underworld. Anyone who believes in him and fulfills his will enter a grim heritage, because whatever a person sows, he will reap.

*What separates us from the All-Unity,
the communication
with the eternal Creator-God?
We learn on ourselves*

Dear fellow people, we are, after all, human beings so that we make use of the chance of our life on Earth to again grasp what we are in the very basis of our soul: beings of unity.

That is why we want to learn to explore the content of our thoughts, to fathom what we have recorded on our life film and why we hardly hear

God, the Creator of all Being, who is our heavenly Father, in the very basis of our soul, and thus, why we also hardly hear the Creator-God in the animals, plants and minerals. Where do we stand – and how do we return to our origin, to the All-Unity, to God in us?

As we continue with our subject "The Speaking All-Unity – The Word of the Universal Creator-Spirit," the motto is: Learn and learn again, for every moment is precious existence on Earth.
We read that every person has his specific life film, which consists of the content of his personal components, of his feeling, sensing, thinking, speaking and acting. This life film runs unceasingly, because every day, yes, even at every moment, according to the course of his day and with his five components, the individual person may be affecting himself and his fellowman.

There is nothing that is not stored in the All. Let us think of the words that Jesus of Nazareth essentially spoke: *Are not five sparrows sold for two pennies? Yet not one of them is forgotten by God. Indeed, the very hairs of your head are all numbered.*

*Everything is consciousness –
Even in our sleep we experience
our consciousness*

There is no such thing as "nothing," not even in sleep.
During the night, in our sleep, we dream. These are mostly indefinable dreams that come from our consciousness and subconscious and from our soul. What we take with us into waking consciousness could tell us something, because dreams come from the various personal inputs on our life film. They may need to be explored, in order to draw conclusions as to our possibly wrong behavior, so that we – insofar as this can be remedied – become free from what weighs on our soul.

As stated, every person records in pictures that correspond to his behavior patterns. Because the content of the life film of each individual differs totally in its imprinting, we rarely understand one another. It's true that we think we have understood our fellowman, and may even nod our understanding – but did we really understand him?

Most people have turned away from the All-Unity, the All-communication of linking and of being linked with the other one, and have created their small, personal ego-world, so that the one hardly understands the other, or not at all. Again and again, we hear that man is the microcosm in the coarse-material macrocosm.

Despite this knowledge, we are lone fighters on the fitness trail of our know-it-all-ness. With this, we have imprinted our life's film reel, which again reflects to us what we still are. We have forgotten how to break down the All-Unity in us into its component parts, which are: Link with the core of being, with the Being, that is God in all people and in all living beings, in all life forms; link with all the pure powers, and be in Him, who is eternally the All-One, God.

If we human beings want to return to the All-Unity, and learn to understand ourselves and our fellowman, as well as our fellow creatures, the animals, the plants and the mineral kingdoms, all pure powers of the Being, of the eternal All-cosmos, then the question needs to be answered over and over again: What still separates mc, what still separates us, from the life of the All-Unity?

We think, "Now I have recognized and rectified so much; now I should be immersing in the ocean of life."

Hardly thought, and already comes another drop or a whole wave that points out to us what still needs to be cleared up. Please don't give up! It can only get brighter from day to day.

We learn to accept the filiation attributes of Kindness, Love and Gentleness, which means to, first of all, become aware that in God, our heavenly Father, we are absolutely free sons and daughters of God. We people also call the three filiation attributes Patience, Love and Mercy, because therein lie the steps to our true origin, to Kindness, Love and Gentleness.

Do not say, "That's hard to accept; I am a human being."
Don't encumber your earthly existence with such statements. If we people think about higher ethics and morals more often, then a lot unravels as if automatically in the following realization: What do I think; what do I say and who am I, actually?

Learn, let us learn, to live in the One who loves us and whose sons and daughters we are in the very basis of our soul.
The orientation to the true life or the separation from our true being always comes from us, from

our storage system, the individual inputs, which are against the law of All-Unity in many aspects. Why? Because most people listened to the promptings of the pagan gods and still adhere to them today, since these, moreover, appear again and again, with very differing institutional and virtual names.

From under their magic hoods, they cleverly preach, for instance, what is against the teaching of the true God and His Son, once in Jesus of Nazareth. Many followers of the pagan cults, now and then also called "Baal cult," behave accordingly and, at every moment, every minute, every hour, day after day, store what the false gods lead them to believe, without examining, without weighing or measuring.

These magic hood sermons then become patterns, which go into our behavior, our behavior patterns. This is then what we think and what we, in turn, express – or what we keep secret.

Beware! For instance, our nervous system is a direct warning system; it sends signals and gives us indications of what we are and – often unintentionally – what we express, instead of rectifying it in time. Mostly, thoughtlessly, it comes from our film reel or from our momentary uncontrolled behavior. But it comes from us, from our five components of feeling, sensing, thinking, talking and acting, with which we often juggle.

To find ourselves, who we truly are, what we have input into our databank, our life film, or are storing anew, the motto is to be alert, over and over again, so as to observe ourselves. By learning on ourselves, by making ourselves aware of what we are just now thinking and saying or what we are just now getting upset and angry about – for instance, who triggered a quarrel, and how far did we let ourselves be drawn into it, and so on – in time we learn to also see through our fellowman, that is, to recognize him.

The motto is to be alert, because what we emit comes back to us at some time or other.

Let it be repeated: Every thing, truly everything, that we think and say, all our actions, express themselves in pictures and this is also what we record in pictures.

Each day brings for every one of us other incidents, situations, conversations, but also worries and fears, for example, concerning the family, in our circle of friends, at work, doing sports, and so on.

We unceasingly store and record things, but we can also learn at every moment – if we question ourselves in the various situations and conversations, over and over again, by checking ourselves, for example: What moves me? What am I reacting to, and how? Why do I speak and act irritably and defensively in certain situations that concern me, above all, when my nervous system tightens up and my pulse beat gets faster?

*True humility is freeing, caring and uplifting.
Egoism is contemptuous of life
and destructive*

Through repetitions, we deepen what we have learned: The All-One is the love for God and neighbor, to which the All-Unity belongs, all of infinity, all heavenly bodies, all animals, plants and minerals. The all-encompassing life, which is the All-One, the Creator-God, is absolute humility, which bows down to the smallest component and lets it become, grow and mature in His love, in the cradle of drawing, that is, creating, the spiritual birthing body of His children.
The Eternal is with us. He helps and supports us. He calls us and reaches out His hand to us. He, the true humility, is a caring Father-Mother-God, also in relation to us human beings.

We learn:
> Without true humility, no love for God and neighbor, and without love for God and neighbor, no humility, no love and mercy toward our fellow creatures, the animals and plants, nor toward Mother Earth, the provider of mankind. True humility is freeing, caring and uplifting – egoism is contemptuous of life and destructive.

Let us look at ourselves and learn: Whoever wants to learns to compare his behavior patterns – with which man juggles day after day – to the Ten Commandments of God and the teachings of Jesus of Nazareth, so as to figure out whether he is truly humble, or rather, a self-opinionated egomaniac, who toots his own horn, day after day.

Another learning step would be:
> What do the animals and plants want to tell us and teach us? By no means vice versa, what we have to say to the animals and plants.

We learn and grasp ever more in ourselves:
The divine creation does not have the intellect, but the All-Intelligence. Animals have intelligence, because they are in the breath of God.

When a person has become humble before the All-life, the All-Being, he may well not experience any miracles with his animal brothers and sisters, but he has gained a true friend, a true companion, who is also able to teach him many a thing.

It's worth it to become more aware each day of what a great and all-encompassing life pulsates in us. It is the complete core of being in the very basis of every soul and thus, also in the soul of every person, in each one of us.

Animals want to be taken seriously and treated with care

We learn: The animals from the breath of God – no matter what kind, how large or small – are a part of life, of unity, of us human beings. They want to be taken seriously by their big brothers and sisters, by us human beings, and treated with care – just as in the cradle of creation, the eternal Creator-God breathed this into all divine beings of the eternal kingdom, of the eternal Being, which we are as well, in the very basis of our soul.
Many an animal could be of help to us, so that we find ourselves in our life film, for example, in

view of how we act toward our fellow humans and toward the world of animals and plants. We are called upon to question ourselves again and again anew and to orient ourselves anew and examine to what extent we have drawn closer to God in us, the Law-word of the All-Unity.

Our pets, which may be closest to us, could teach us many a thing, also in the question they direct to us, which is: Who is training whom?

Over and over again, we should self-critically examine how we deal with our animal brothers and sisters, for example: Do we want to live in imprisonment? – Who wants that, anyway?! Man's desire is for freedom. Animals are also entitled to freedom, because animals that come from the breath of God bear within the law of freedom.

Every animal creature, whether large or small, is due respect and good will, which man also claims for himself. Only in mutual consideration is communication the basis for the All-communication of life, which is the eternal Creator.

Our pets are also beings, like all other animals in, on and above the Earth, in the waters and oceans. They all want to be taken seriously. For example, our cat or our dog does not want to be treated like a cuddly animal, or to be shut in; a dog does not want to be chained up and birds do not want to be kept imprisoned in cages. We should leave them their freedom and treat every animal brother or sister according to its true predispositions, given by the eternal Creator.

Baby talk and cuddly gestures may indicate that we do not take the animals seriously, that we hold their being in low esteem and consider them to be beneath our so-called "dignity" and therefore, treat them accordingly. It is not the person's "centrifugal consciousness" that is called for, but true humility, which the All-One is, and which He also placed into our divine predispositions.

*Our aura reflects our
behavior patterns –
The animals perceive our radiation*

Every one of us behaves according to the picture material on his film reel; that is his engraving; that is also what the person radiates; that is his aura. Every picture on our film reel has, among other things, its specific scent; it is the odor of the body that the animals include in their perception. As already reported, all animals, whether large or small, have, according to their steps of evolution, their divine pictures of creation, which they have lived.

Unfortunately, they also bear within pictures of how certain people have treated, and treat, them. These pictures are called "scent-pictures"; they are mostly warning signals for the animals. They "scent" pictures of people, which clearly show them whom they have before them, what this person thinks, for instance, what he is like and what he may ask of them or how he might treat them. Thoughts also have their specific smell.

Dear fellow people, let our little animal brothers and sisters live – be good to them!

If we want to learn, then we should become aware that our entire behavior is imprinting, and is thus our engraving, which as our aura, as corona, flows around our body and reflects our behavior patterns in color, form, and even fragrance. This is our life film and not lastly, the expression of our present character.

The person who scrutinizes himself learns on himself. As stated, humility is the path to All-communication.

A person who wants to learn asks himself: What about my, our, humility? How deep still is the cra-

ter of egomania? What still revolts in our thoughts that wants to demolish and destroy, that wants to torment, maltreat, torture or even maliciously kill animals?
Unfortunately, it is not a rarity that people with such and similar egocentric thought patterns, that is, behavior patterns, influence the animals and affect them, keeping them as prisoners and delivering them to the butcher, deliberately letting them be killed and straightaway consuming their flesh, as well.

Let us learn to look the animals in the eye. Their eyes often reflect fear and terror, because they scent people's intentions and what might be done to them by human beings.

We never finish learning: The eyes of many of our animal brothers and sisters are filled with sadness and suffering; they radiate anxiety and mistrust; out of fear of people's behavior patterns, many animals are even aggressive and not exactly friendly toward them. This, too, wants to tell us something.
To be fair, we should take the training methods that we often use on the animals to bend them to our will and apply them to ourselves in terms of

our own behavioral imprinting. To be in the right is always one-sided; to let justice prevail leads to self-recognition in terms of what we may need to account for.

An animal's anxiety, fear and attack are always signs that it has experienced many bad, malicious and vicious things – and truly not through the Creator-God, but from us human beings!

We learn: What do we read in the eyes of the animals, for instance, in the eyes of our cat or our dog and in the behavior of the bird creature in the cage? What and how do the animals communicate? In order to sense this, we would have to become calmer and direct our thoughts and our wishes concerning them to ourselves first, in the question: What do we expect from our animal brothers and sisters, which we ourselves do not live up to regarding them as well as our fellowman?

*An interjected question
from the conversations.
To understand the animals,
we have to become permeable*

Question: *We hear again and again that the animals and plants want to tell us and teach us something. Are there examples of this? And how can I be sure, for instance, that I really perceive what an animal wants to tell me, and not what comes out of me, that is, what I have stored on my life film, on my life reel?*

Answer: If we want to learn to understand the animal and plant species from the breath of God, then this requires the person's consciousness to be correspondingly permeable.

Every person whose consciousness is flexible has due respect for the life of animals and plants. He learns much more easily to understand what the animals in particular want to tell us through "sending and receiving," through communication. For example, the flight of birds wants to tell us something, when they perceive us and immediately fly off screeching and squawking or emitting warning calls. Or when they land on the branch of a tree to watch us from a distance.

If we want to learn, then we could pay attention to various things, for example, what did the birds' flying away and their calls trigger in us, that is, in the resonance board of our nervous system? What were we thinking at that moment when the birds took fright, and what were we thinking and feeling when they flew away screeching or as they watched us from a tree?

All movements and stirrings of animals are aspects of sending that stimulated a lot in our nervous system and simultaneously in our thought processes, which means that we received what may have been a message for us. Each of us will receive what would be significant for him just then, from his life film.

Or let's think of the pets and farm animals that are quite a bit closer to us. For them, we are not simply the human being who is known or familiar to them; rather, in many respects, they perceive us in a much more sophisticated way. Firstly, our odor is significant to them; secondly, they register how we appear, whether hectic or somewhat in balance. They see and scent the person's entire aura, because what the person has stored in his soul and in his consciousness and subconscious is also visible in his aura and has its specific colors and odor.

When dealing with our animal brothers and sisters, we could, for instance, frequently ask ourselves: What color nuances and what odor do our thoughts presently have? Or: What are our behavior patterns like today? Everything that we conceal – whether we act in a friendly way toward the animal or are a true friend to it – is apparent to the animal. It recognizes us, what we are really like, regardless of our veils, which we can also call a "masquerade."
Everything, truly everything, is visible; everything has its colors, its sounds and its corresponding odor.

Learning from animals

If we want to, we could learn from the animals. They don't react so spontaneously, often thoughtlessly, as people do. Before an animal reacts, a picture first develops in it. When the picture has basically become complete in the animal, then we see and experience its reactions. Either the animal's eyes become dull, because, for instance, it's afraid of us humans – at the same time it will try to run away from us – or it attacks, depending on what lies behind this. Or the animal submits to the person and does what he demands of it – often, however, only out of fear.

If there is no escape in sight, many animals yield to their fate and accept the yoke. The rope, the chain or being shut up, for instance, is a deprivation of freedom for them, a cruelty of man, against which the animal cannot defend itself.

Animals are sensitive, intelligent beings. They remember who despises them and possibly beats them, and who is sincere and means well with them. The animal's alert, open and clear eyes may want to tell us: You are my friend; you do me no harm; I have made friends with you. Or even: We are friends.

Animals have no fear of dying, but they do indeed have fear and downright panic before death by torture at human hands. In addition, they sense and feel when fate delivers them to the butcher. Among other things, people who consume the meat of their fellow creatures have a certain effluvium, that is, a certain odor that the animals register. The "dead-animal-odor" is for them not only a warning signal; many an animal panics and attacks.

Look frequently into the eyes of animals that are being driven to the butcher – perhaps you will then abstain from consuming pieces of animal carcasses.

Let us realize that animals have a fine sense of perception. Many people call their intelligence – somewhat disparagingly – "instinct," but the intelligence of animals is in constant communication with the universal All-intelligence, with the All-life. To become aware of this means to ask ourselves how it is with us human beings.

And so, let us not fool ourselves! A person can pretend something to other people, but not to the animals. People often do not know themselves, but animals look and see through people, because an unmistakable picture develops in their consciousness.

Every animal has a consciousness that corresponds to its level of development; it sends and receives accordingly. Animals are sensitive beings that see and scent the pictures they perceive, which change only when a person has become kind and understanding in his earthly existence.

People emit differing frequencies. On the entire scale of vibrations, there are frequencies that certain animal species receive and then act accordingly.

Unfortunately, the majority of people hardly has access to the world of animals, plants and minerals. People destroy; they hunt the animals and thoughtlessly kill and eat them. This horror of negative energy carries over to the animals. Many animal species imitate human beings. They hunt their fellow brothers and sisters and kill and eat them.

People of all generations are the ones who have triggered this evil.

If the individual would reflect on higher ethical-moral values, being aware that in everything and everyone is the workings of God, God's Creator-power, God's love, the all-prevailing, eternal law, which the commandments of God and the teachings of Jesus of Nazareth make clear to us, then there would be peace on Earth. The animals would absorb what people emit and would act accordingly.

To live with animals and to establish a true friendship with them is to have real, loyal friends. Animals love community with people whom they can trust. They will prove themselves to be dependable friends, animal brothers and sisters of cosmic intelligence, that is, with an awareness that is beyond the intellect of human ignorance.

Let us remember the words of Jesus in the following sense: *The Kingdom of God is within, in you.* The Kingdom of God is the All-Law, to which every animal, every plant, every mineral and all suns and planets belong. All suns and planets are imbedded in the Light-Ether and are themselves compressed, densified Light-Ether. All in all, this is the Law-word of the All-One. And all consciousness aspects in all heavenly planes perceive His word.

In contrast, man is a law unto himself. What he has stored in his brain is his personal aspects; this corresponds to him, the person; this is who he is and this is how he acts. This is how he dresses, how he speaks, how he eats, how he acts and how he is at home. All in all, these behavior patterns are called the person-law or the person's law of correspondence.

Experiences of the viewers of the program series "The Speaking All-Unity – The Word of the Universal Creator-Spirit" and of the participants of the conversations

The principle of All-communication finds great interest and makes people curious, particularly when it has to do with animals, that is, the communication with animals. Many people follow the explanations on the topic "The Speaking All-Unity – The Word of the Universal Creator God" with great enthusiasm and many are also having their first learning experiences in terms of how they can put the knowledge gained into practice.

For instance, an animal friend wrote, *This is a new world and a totally new life, which has opened up for us, for all people.*
She then described the following experience of how she could help an animal by way of the inner communication:

One of our three cats didn't come home for days. We were really worried. I then remembered Gabriele's explanations about the speaking All-Unity, the word of the universal Creator-Spirit, that everything is connected with everything. And so, I very consciously established communication with our cat, "from core of being to core of being," so that I sensed her "image" and her being in me. I conveyed to her that we miss her, that we love her and would be so happy when she comes home (at the same time, I conveyed a "picture" of good food and the cozy "cat places" in the house). Then I let go and drove to work.

A few hours later, I suddenly had the picture of the cat before my eyes and the feeling that I must quickly drive home. – And lo and behold: She was there! Quite distraught and worn out and terribly hungry. That's why I was glad that I could give her fresh food and water right away and tell her how happy we were that she came home!

I'm convinced that this inner communication helped our cat to soon find her way home and that via the connection with her I was also signaled to be on the spot at exactly the right time when she needed me. – Of course, this experience encourages me to practice the inner communication even more.

This program series is one-of-a-kind – I am very, very thankful for this!

⁂

A highly regarded musician wrote the following:

The program "The Speaking All-Unity – The Word of the Universal Creator-Spirit" reaches such dimensions that for us human beings, it means the definitive, historical leave-taking from our intellect and all the knowledge we've produced. It's fantastic that with such simple terms, we are led into such deep sensations and dimensions. It awakens a very great longing to attain this true communication with all things.

Surely many people jumped up from their sofa with joy when they learned about it! Somehow the whole thing seems so simple, that we wonder why we still bear so much within that is amiss. In any case, through the program and the exercises, the valuable goal has become clearly tangible – this gives us more strength and courage for the "housecleaning" and "transformation" of our being.

While playing music, I have learned to strive to draw each note into my heart. And today I un-

derstand that everything – everything that lives, every being or every ever so tiny thing – is like a note that can find a resonance in me, as soon as I provide the right inner space for this. The indescribable "feeling of symphony" arises; there are no more limits and we gradually abandon all human terms, in order to swim in a huge ocean. It is ... IT simply IS!

Thanks, many thanks to God, our heavenly Father, that we can let ourselves be filled by Him, by the life!

In another report, an animal friend describes a very intense learning experience:

In the explanations on the topic "The Speaking All-Unity – The Word of the Universal Creator-Spirit," we frequently hear the important statement to the effect: Freedom is the highest good for animals!

We hear this and visualize a human concept of freedom and we convey this especially to our house pets. Whether we want to accept this or not, we human beings determine what their freedom should be like. We seldom ask what our animal brothers and sisters might understand under the term "freedom," that is, what picture our housecat, for instance, has of its freedom.

This has to do with our cat who came crying to us ten years ago, as a stray. She had minor health problems, but was otherwise very "easy to care for." Her "own mind" is a special feature when compared to our other cats. On the one hand, she can sleep for hours in her basket, but on the other hand, she can be underway for just as long. Two doors are always open, so that she can come and go as she pleases. She eats and drinks and we are happy when she is with us.

Two weeks ago, she came into the room limping, meowed once and left again, to lie on the ground under a bush. Concerned, we called the vet at a very late hour. After the initial examination, he diagnosed a torn ligament on the knee joint of the left hind leg. He recommended an evaluation at an animal clinic he knew. The x-ray confirmed his suspicion and the vets recommended an immediate operation. Worried – probably more about ourselves – we agreed to the operation.

This was followed by 12 days in the infirmary with a splinted hind leg and a sad cat. We visited her as often as possible and sometimes could see the accusation in her look, "What have you done to me? And why do I have to stay shut up in this room?"

We tried to explain to her that everything would soon be okay again and her leg would heal. She limped around as well as she could and slept a lot. The day came to remove the bandages and thus, her hope to soon be free again.

When we finally fetched her, her eyes grew bigger every time she looked out of the car. "Concerned," we again "shut her up" in the house, even though her sole longing was for the freedom outdoors. We wanted to "stabilize" her for two days, but for our little cat that became a torment. She saw how the other cats were let out – we live with three cats – and the door was shut on her, so that "nothing bad could happen to her." This is how we human beings thought, but not the cat. Her sole longing was freedom and not our care.

On the morning of the third day, we wanted to "take her for a walk." That's what we thought, but not her. She had only freedom in mind, without our supervision. She ran off on us. When hours later she was finally home again, in the room, we decided to open all the doors and to give her the freedom of independent movement. After a small snack, she went straight to the cat door and disappeared into the big garden.

Now that she has her freedom again, she is also happy again. When she gets tired, she lies down on Mother Earth with her "plant brothers and sisters." If she is in pain, then Mother Earth cools her ...

What can we learn when we hear that our animals love freedom above everything? Even dying – of course, without torment by human hand – is not an image of danger for an animal, because life, after all, goes on ...

For us, the oh so "concerned" people, this is a very painful learning process. We can hear about this theoretically, but only through personal sorrow and so-called concern about an animal, do we slowly learn to really grasp the situation.

The speaking All-Unity, the Creator-Spirit, guides the animal and will never let it out of His hand. But often, we human beings can accept this only with great difficulty. We think that our care alone can preserve the animal from harm. Why do we think in such narrow terms? Do we believe in the infinite care of our Creator for all beings? Sometimes, and particularly in such painful situations, we have to admit to our lack of faith and bow before the great speaking All-Unity in thankful humility and learn to see the workings of the Creator in all situations of life.

Freedom is the highest good of animals, even when it means dying. – This is what we may learn from this experience.

The sensibility of animals exceeds all human concepts – a brief report on an incident:

If we human beings would have to depend solely on our senses and perhaps learn a bit of telepathy – nevertheless, we would not reach the communicative capabilities of animals. A brief report on an incident that happened during the development of the work of teaching and learning "The Speaking All-Unity – The Word of the Universal Creator-Spirit" – an incident that serves as further proof of the consciousness of our animal brothers and sisters that is described here:

We were eating breakfast; our cat, which we've already mentioned, lay near the dining table and the telephone table. We were talking to each other, while our cat was diligently carrying out her morn-

ing toilet. Her left hind leg was just being "worked on," when she suddenly paused. The hind leg still sticking up, she lay for at least several minutes and listened. – What could that mean? Suddenly she started cleaning herself again and acted very normal.

A housemate, who is able to understand our animal brothers and sisters very clearly, said, "If I wouldn't be disturbing an acquaintance now, I would like nothing better than to call him and ask him whether he had intended to call us, but something came up and prevented him from doing so."

We decided not to disturb him, but to wait and see if the acquaintance would perhaps call. He called, and it was about 15 minutes later. We asked whether he had wanted to reach us about 15 minutes earlier.

His answer was, "Yes, I wanted to call you about 15 minutes ago, but another call came in-between."

So this was the proof that in her awareness our cat had registered the caller's intent, had then paused and only continued to groom herself when, right then, the call failed. As an explanation for our cat's behavior, we have to say that our cat does not particularly like the speaker telephone and during longer phone calls usually withdraws to a quieter place.

From this brief description, we can easily recognize that an animal's receptivity is far beyond our human capabilities. Our cat made us aware of something that was taking place outside our perception. Our animals appear to understand things and incidents and even our thoughts, and react to them. How very much we human beings underestimate our animal brothers and sisters!

Our cat was present at another conversation among us – what then happened really astonished us. A warm sleeping place had been set up for her in a room on the second floor, which was supposed to provide her warmth and secureness during the cool autumn and winter days. We talked about the fact that one of her human brothers and sisters should accompany her to this room during the coming days and show her the nice sleeping place.
But there was no opportunity to do this. Nevertheless, already the following day our cat lay enjoying the place meant for her. And so, she had deduced from our conversation, from our picture sequences, that a cozy place had been set up for

her. – Is this coincidence or the animal's awareness?

We may often learn more from our animal brothers and sisters:
Animals are esthetic living beings that want to keep their eating place reasonably clean.
We can especially observe this with housepets. Our animal brothers and sisters, for example, cats or dogs, have names and are also addressed by their names. From several incidents, we human brothers and sisters have learned that our animal brothers and sisters that live with us also like to have a set table. We established a set table for them, which they gladly accepted, for example, a round wooden stand for the cat brothers and sisters, about 20 cm high, and 40 cm in diameter for the dogs – of course, depending on the size of the dog. Their eating dishes are porcelain and are cleaned every day. Their smaller and larger tables have small white tablecloths, which are changed for washing. These small offers are gladly accepted.

Another animal friend reported his experiences with a homeless little cat:

For months, we frequently saw a little cat in the fields near our house. It was extremely shy and immediately ran away when approached. Because it's totally black with white paws on all four legs, we spontaneously named it "Velvet Paws."

Each time that I caught a glimpse of the little cat, I linked with her in my inner being and always spoke to her calmly. After some time, she apparently had gained a little trust in me, because she actually began to peek into our house through the cat door! I kept very, very calm and she even dared to go as far as the eating place of our other cat brothers and sisters. It went on like this for about three or four weeks. Again and again, I spoke to her, totally calmly – but as soon as I moved, she disappeared quick as a flash.

One day my patience was rewarded. When I came out of the bathroom in the evening, Velvet Paws was standing directly before me in the middle of the room! When I again calmly spoke to her while very cautiously squatting down, she mewed and meowed – she downright answered. I then prepared a small eating bowl for her and continued talking to her. Then, for the first time, she came very near to me and accepted the bowl from my hand.

I knew then: The ice is now broken; she has gained trust and we have made friends.

The next evening I was already waiting for her and she let me pet her for the first time. Meanwhile she can't get enough "tender loving care." She has already lain on my lap for half an hour, however, always with the exit, that is, the "escape route" in view. But now it's merely a question of time until she stays longer and finally feels totally at home with us.

*Animals want to make themselves understood –
They have their "language"*

Animals often give signs, in order to communicate with us human beings; they want to make themselves understood. The often varying sounds, combined as tone and sound, are their language with which they communicate. This also includes their gestures. All their behavior patterns can be messages, also to us human beings.

If we have learned to largely rectify the negative content in our five components, that is, in our behavior patterns, and to ask ourselves what the will of the All-One is more and more, then we gradually begin to understand what the animals, for instance, want to convey to us. But this also means that, in time, we will learn to understand our fellowman, because, as already stated: Words are shells that have content.

Through the expansion of his consciousness, the person becomes more humble and sensitive and begins to gain respect for the life in all things, because he turns to the commandments of God and the teachings of Jesus of Nazareth. Only then, will we experience with animals, actually, with all life forms, including plants, what we call "miracles," which, however, are not miracles, but the word of our fellow creatures – the animals, but also of the collective of plants and minerals – which we then experience in ourselves, also in pictures, as the word of the All-Law.

If you should receive from an animal, whether large or small, a corresponding "rebuke," perhaps of a physical nature, then don't be indignant, but look into your personal thoughts and words! Look into the picture sequences from your life film! Perhaps the animal's physical rebuke will help you to find yourself in the picture sequences of your life film, and find out why the animal brother or sister reacted so annoyed with you.

Several statements about animals from "great minds"

Anyone who learns to feel and to understand also understands what "great minds" say when they talk about the animal world:

There is not an animal on the earth, nor a being that flies on its wings, but forms part of communities like you. ... they shall be gathered to their Lord in the end. (Mohammed)

Those who permit slaying of animals; those who bring animals for slaughter; those who slaughter; those who sell meat; those who purchase meat; those who prepare dishes out of it; those who serve that meat and those who eat it are all murderers.

You must not use your God-given body for killing God's creatures, whether they are human, animal or whatever.

Meat is obtained neither from grass nor from wood or stone, but only through the killing of a living being, and therefore consuming it is an offense. (From ancient Indian law scriptures)

Woe to the crafty who hurt the creatures of God! Woe to the hunters! For they themselves shall be hunted. (Jesus of Nazareth)

Verily, I say to you, I Am come into the world in order to put an end to all blood offerings and to the eating of the flesh of animals and birds that are slain by men. (Jesus of Nazareth)

When walking in woods and fields, man seeks a respite – While doing so, he enters the dwelling places of his fellow creatures

Seldom does a person who walks into the woods and fields think about the fact that he is entering the dwelling places of animals and plants with all his thoughts, desires and indifference toward them. Plants, flowers, herbs, grasses, bushes and trees are living beings, to which, as with human beings, the life-breath of the All-One flows.

For many people, the knowledge that, with varying motivations, the human being literally invades the dwellings of his animal brothers and sisters and the locations of many plant species is a totally new way of looking at things.

Perhaps this may cause many a one taking a walk through the woods and fields to prick up his ears, for he is usually not aware that he should act as is expected from guests visiting his own apartment or home. It is taken totally for granted that a visitor who enters another person's apartment or house will be considerate of the latter's property.

How do we human beings act in relation to the living areas and dwellings of the animal and plant beings? What do we take with us on our walk in the woods and fields?

Many people out on a walk seek the tranquility of the woods, in order to perhaps bring respite and calm to their agitated disposition. But, despite good intentions, can our walk in the woods be a respite when we walk in the woods and over the fields with many thoughts, perhaps arguing with our companions, laughing and talking loudly and gesticulating accordingly, in order to thus divert ourselves from the stress of daily life? This cannot be a respite or recovery; it is diversion.

Without doubt: The woods provide tranquility. The fields lie there in peace. With his possibly uncurbed conduct, the person on a walk is obviously a disruptive element, which invades the dwelling places of living beings and there, instills terror in the inhabitants of the woods and fields. When the animals subsequently take flight, then many a person is surprised. It is not the wind or the rain that frightened the animals and drove them out of their shelter, but the uncurbed conduct of people.

The plant beings, which are location-based and cannot flee before the people, also tremble before the concentrated flood of human thoughts and before loud talking, as well as human behavior patterns.

If you are not convinced by this brief report, that animals and plants also have a certain right to tranquility, then think of your own home. What would you say if your visitor were to enter your apartment or house and immediately assail you with his pent-up behavior patterns, laughing loudly, talking shrilly and hardly finding an end to what he has to say?

Many a one thinks, "This comparison of the dwelling places of animal and plant species with our personal home is a poor one, because here, it's merely about the animal and plant world." – Don't fool yourself. Animals and plants are much more sensitive than a person, who sees only himself as the measure of all things.

Let us think of the words of Jesus of Nazareth. He advised us the following, which, of course, also applies to the world of animals and plants, for the eternal law is the All-Unity, which would be the community life of man, animal, nature and mineral. Jesus taught us the following, given here with words commonly used today: *Do not do to another what you do not want to have done to you.*

Another version to give you food for thought: Directly in front of your house, motorcycle riders gather, who first turn off their engines and then, after some time, start them up again, to roar off with the throttle wide open, and this, several times every day.

If these comparisons and particularly the words of Jesus don't make us think, then we could imagine a big city, first without vehicles and streetcars, that is, only with people. You, we are in the midst of this confusion of loud talking and laughing, that is, in the midst of the pedestrian noise, which roars in your ears. Now add the loud sounds of many vehicles. The whole thing is a palaver, just one huge racket of rumbling, laughing and yelling. For many people, this is a tumult that they like to escape. But that's just what a city of people is like!

When we transfer this tumultuous behavior to the woods and fields – to the dwelling areas of our animal brothers and sisters – that is, if this same tumultuous life were to prevail in woods and fields, then many a one would sigh, saying, "I won't walk through this woods or over this field anymore; this is not a respite!"

Despite these various comparisons, you could now point out that this is exaggerated and not appropriate, because woods and fields are not a big city; that's why, after all, many escape the big city, specifically to find peace and respite in woods and fields.

But how do many of the people walking there act? In many cases, as they do in a big city.

What does the person who goes through the woods and over the fields without taking stock of himself carry into the dwelling areas of the animals and the plant kingdom?

The plant world also gives signals regarding people's behavior patterns.

Animals take flight; plants tremble – What does this want to tell us?

What does it want to tell us human beings when, out of fear, the animals hastily take to their heels and the plants tremble before the restless conduct and carryings-on? What is, perhaps, even the motivation of the person taking a walk through the woods and fields and carelessly roaming over meadows and fields, thereby trampling down countless plant species? For the person out for a walk, it's totally normal to leave the footpath, whereby without his noticing, many a little plant will no longer reach its blossoming perfection. Or the flower is picked before it has completely developed. Not seldom, the root ball is thereby torn out, if the single flower or cluster was not easy to break off. The torn-out root ball is then simply tossed into the meadow or onto the field.

The animals never really find rest and tranquility in their home, that is, in the woods and fields. They are never safe, because once the noisy walker has set out for home, then at twilight the hunter sneaks into the woods and lies in wait for the game until it comes before his rifle, so that he can then bag it, shooting it down.

Animals have fine sensors, fine antennae. They notice very quickly when there is something extrinsic moving about. Animals do not flee before they have made a picture, that is, a scent picture, of the location and the situation, in order to find out where, for instance, the strange noise is coming from. Once their picture has developed, they run or walk in the direction conveyed to them by the picture. In many cases, the hunter, for instance, exploits this to furtively kill the animal. Or the animal scents danger and in its panic takes flight without being able to orient itself via a scent picture. In the process, it frequently runs towards the danger, in front of the hunter's rifle, who then hits it with a shot from his rifle in a "fair sportsman" way. Whether the animal is dead or not, for the hunter it is, in any case, "fair sportsmanship."

If all this is regarded as quite normal by many a person on a walk, then picture the following: Shortly before you fall asleep, you are startled by a very loud bang coming from the nearby woods, where a hunter has shot, that is, bagged, one of our animal brothers and sisters from the large family community of the Creator-God. Perhaps it is "merely" non-fatally shot, that is, wounded, and wanders about in unspeakable pain for hours, even days, until it dies a wretched death. The animal, for example, a doe or a wild pig sow, may have left behind its young, which now likewise die an agonizing death, because without their mother, they have to die of hunger and thirst.
What is this called? Gamekeeping and maintenance? For many people, this is normal, because they believe in the dictates of church doctrine, that animals lack feelings and do not have an immortal soul.

If by way of these various scenarios, you have become more sensitive and think about this and much more before taking a walk in woods and fields, then you will understand many an animal, when it scents an agitated person's pent-up temper and reacts accordingly.

If during your walk, you should see an animal that you can briefly look in the eyes – be it even with binoculars – and if it is thereby possible for you to perceive the animal's behavior, then you can grasp its situation and surmise why it takes flight before many people.

It is a sad state that animals avoid people out of fear and dread, considering that in their spiritual predispositions, unity is alive between man, animal, plant, mineral and Mother Earth, in the total picture of the All.

Animals want to be with people who should protect and safeguard them, because we human beings are their big brothers and sisters.

How does man act toward the defenseless animals? He hunts them in the woods and on the fields, deviously killing the defenseless creatures. He tortures the animals in the most brutal way and slaughters them or has them killed. This is a cruel, perverse death; it is the murder of our second neighbors, the animals, our animal brothers and sisters.

As stated: Animals want to look up to people; they want to live with them, to be their friends – however, they do not want to be trained by people; they do not want to be convenient and serve as personal entertainment. Nor do they want to be so-called livestock; they do not want to be exclusively "used" by people as useful and subservient, but to help and serve people with their strength.

Animals have a consciousness as do the plants, the trees and bushes, even the stones, the minerals, because everything lives, and whatever lives breathes the breath of the All-One.

*We learn and practice,
to become aware of what precious creatures
live among us. We practice watching our
animal fellow creatures*

If during your walk, you can watch an animal from afar, which has not yet perceived you, that is, which has not yet scented and registered you, then allow its nature to become effective in your mind.

Become attuned to the quiet.
Inhale and exhale deeply several times.
If possible, briefly close your eyes, and with your breath take the animal brother or sister into your body rhythm.
This means that you breathe in and take the picture of the animal along with you, into your inner being.
Without an attitude of expectation and in all humility before the life, let the image of the animal take effect in you.

In time, you will experience that from its divine state of consciousness, the animal radiates peace, unity and a spirit of community to you, which cannot be of this world.

Practice watching your animal fellow creatures, but also practice watching plants, which you will read more about later. Through these exercises, by becoming quiet, by consciously switching off unessential feelings and thoughts in order to be truly present in the dwelling areas of our fellow creatures, you will soon notice that you become more sensitive, and in time, develop empathy for what surrounds you. And if you frequently visit your fellow brothers and sisters, the animals, in the woods and fields – however, with the appreciation that is also due to our second neighbors, our animal brothers and sisters, and to everything that bears life – you will very soon grasp what life in true unity actually means.

Animals love peace and freedom. Their spiritual inclination is based on unity and community. This is why they also want to be with their big brothers and sisters, the human beings.

They sense very well when people learn to understand them, in humility and respect before the speaking All-One.

Sensory perception is important for the development of awareness

We train ourselves. A great help for properly developing our awareness is a balanced, quiet walk through the woods, over meadows and fields. Our steps are careful, because we learn to hear and to listen, whereby "hearing" and "listening" have a totally different emphasis in their aspects of perception.

To hear is a certain kind of external perception, while, on the other hand, to listen is an inner sensing, an inner allowing what we hear to come. By practicing and taking stock of ourselves, as time passes, we will experience a connection that can hardly be defined by man.

By learning and practicing, we become masters.

On our conscious walk, we grasp that nature wants to give us tranquility. We also understand and experience that everything has sound, color and form. We hear the varying tones of the wind, which, during a walk in autumn or winter can be cold. In spring it shows itself as a balmy breeze, perhaps with softer tones, that announce the warm summer wind. Now and then, the wind also manifests itself as a storm, which is like a drum roll.

We hear the babbling of a brook, the twittering of the birds, and here and there, the sound of an animal from the woods.
We seldom perceive the innermost sounds, the consciousness aspects of life, because we have not yet learned the difference between hearing and listening, for the difference between these two kinds of perception can be great. – But, we are learning!

Dear fellow people, what we hear, that is, what we hear with our ears, are the external aspects, which belong to three-dimensional frequencies. In contrast, to listen means to indeed hear with the external ears, but with our breath, our inhalation, to take what we hear to within and place it on our personal body of sound. Listening does not mean curious eavesdropping.
If you need an orientation, then concentrate on your central nervous system. We try to switch over from hearing to listening, to perceiving. The same applies to seeing and beholding.
To "switch over" always means to first become calmer, perhaps by breathing deeply, until our thought world has calmed down, so that we can take in what we saw. The nervous system that is calming down points it out.

For us human beings, what we hear and see is external sensory perception. However, let us allow the deeper perception of beholding and listening flow together, which means to take it into ourselves, into our body, with our breath, in order to gradually sense that a stimulating feeling is making itself noticeable, which changes our body rhythm and conveys tranquility to us. From this, several moments of happiness develop, which are not of this world. This could be aspects of inner perception.

Everything is based on practice and self-discipline, also in daily life, in monitoring our five senses.
If we try to bring hearing, listening, seeing and beholding into accord, in time we will become more sensitive to the perception of life. In the process, we will become calmer from one time to the next, and our perception sensors finer. From this, develops the understanding that in the very basis of our soul we human beings are cosmic beings from the great family of God, in which the All-intelligence is active and reveals itself.

If each day we learn more to grant respect to the world of animals and plants, then we will gradually comprehend that the All-One, the speaking

Creator-God, the giver and maintainer of life, is in everything and everyone, in the tiniest and in infinity.

Let us allow heart and mind to be moved by the following simple statement:
>In the tiniest is infinity, and in infinity is the tiniest.
>God, the Creator of life, is the All-love. His love is the All-humility, which pertains, and is granted, to all life equally.

Together We Experience a Virtual Walk!

During a virtual walk, many a thing can be figured out more easily and deeply. We learn and practice

We will now undertake a virtual walk through woods and fields. In pictures, we go deep into the woods and become aware that everything is animated, present life and is, as essence, present in us.

If it is still difficult for us to grasp that everything is unity, let us remember that it is only through learning that one can attain mastery, and no one was born a master!
However, *one* divine being once departed from the eternal homeland, from the heavens. It distanced itself from the All-competence of the Father-Mother-God and went its own way. It burdened itself and drew other spiritual beings along with it, all the way to the emergence of man. But at some point, we, each and every one of us – either as human being or as soul – will take the path back and step by step reflect more on our

divine origin, setting forth on the path back home to the Father's house, to the eternal homeland. Why wait? – Why not now and today, as human being?!

*Everything bears within
the melodies of the All;
everything is part of the All-symphony.
We take in a bird's body of sound*

We could experience our virtual walks outdoors on a bench or at an open window or while looking at a picture of nature. The pure, fine, noble, good, the love for all Being is always ready to give to us via the core of being in the very basis of our soul. The eternal All-One gives, and we may receive. The world of plants and animals receives in a similar way. All living beings and life forms are animated by the All-One, depending on their state of consciousness.

Especially during our virtual walk, we get an inkling of what the All-Unity can mean.
Again and again, we hear and read that it is up to us, to our personal behavior, to grow closer to the life, which is unity.

Let us learn to explore our thoughts and our senses, in order to rectify what keeps us from letting the All-Unity, the All-life, emerge in us – the loud, the shrill, the egocentric, all in all, the self-aggrandizement.

Everything, absolutely everything, wants to tell us something – the animal, the plant, the mineral, even the drop of water, the babbling of a brook, the rustling of a tree, the wind that ruffles our hair – everything, absolutely everything, contains the All, and the All-One is always present. Every little plant, every flower, the blade of grass, the little herb, the medicinal plant – everything that often stands so inconspicuously by the wayside – bears the core of being as a predisposition and is in communication with the All-One.

Everything, including the elements, bears within the melodies of the All, because everything contains the life, which is the All-One eternal All-Spirit, whom we in the western world call "God." The virtual walks bring us learning steps, which are focused on the inner perception, on the picture, the tone, the color and the sound.

We learn to hear and to listen into ourselves. For example, we hear the twittering of a bird and pause briefly.

We breathe deeply in and out a few times and remain very quiet.
Whoever wants to can close his eyes, to be able to concentrate better. The twittering of the bird, its state of consciousness, is melody, which is included in the sound volume of the All.

We try to absorb the bird's body of sound into our body, which is also sound, because everything is energy and everything has its specific sound. We continue to breathe calmly and deeply and endeavor to gain distance from our thoughts.
We have become calmer. Hearing the little bird changes; it becomes a listening.
The melodious sound of the little bird creature reverberates into our physical body. Thereby our body begins to lightly vibrate. That is, our sounding box vibrates higher. We notice that a frequency builds up in us, which lets harmonious feelings rise up that convey a certain equanimity.

Could this be the body of sound of the bird creature?

We experience that when our body vibrates higher, we can experience an ethereal resonance in us.

Should this not work out right away, please don't be disappointed. By learning and practicing, we experience that everything is based on "sending and receiving." The virtual walk is now our training ground.

We practice and learn. We try not to think. We have learned that everything is based on "sending and receiving."

Once more, the same exercise:
A bird sings; it emits – we tune in to receiving and absorb the body of sound of the little being into ourselves. This time we draw the melodious body of sound to us and, with a deep breath, let it reverberate into our physical body. While doing so, our nervous system begins to lightly vibrate.
Each of us reacts differently. The one senses another body frequency in the whole volume of his body, another experiences the ethereal energy of the little bird creature in his central nervous system, especially in his solar plexus. That which reverberates in us is a soothing feeling, a lightness and freedom. It is the ethereal life; it is the small, unburdened ethereal body of the little animal, of the bird creature.

Stay concentrated, and listen into your body: The little bird creature wants to establish communication with you, with us, in the awareness: "Link, and be one with me!"

Remember that self-recognition and practice lead to sensitivity.
Through more exercises with other animals – for instance, also with your pets – in time, you will experience that the bodies of sound of the individual living beings bring out differing resonances in you, in your nervous system or in the volume of your body. If you have learned to sense the other body in your body, and if you have perceived the various melodious frequencies, then you have heard a touch of the infinite ethereal All-sounds, a touch of the All-symphony, which is All-harmony. When you have made several inner experiences in terms of what it means to see, to behold, to hear, to listen, then in time you will sense that the sounding box of each living being is different. It is, as stated, the sounds of the respective unfoldment of consciousness.
By learning on oneself and through the exercises, your perception will become more differentiated, also in terms of what builds up in your more light-filled thoughts. It is the life that unfolds, which

is the All-Unity, the sound and the being of each animal, of the plant and mineral, because everything has its frequency of consciousness, that is, its sound volume, which also expresses itself in color and form.

By frequently practicing with our second neighbors, our animal brothers and sisters, but also with all other life forms, our attitude toward life gradually changes. The true life is an unending fullness.

For the alert virtual walker, such and similar exercises can become a treasury of rich experiences in the vivid awareness that everything lives and that everything, truly everything, pure vibrates in the All-Unity.

Let us also bear in mind that every sun, every planet in the eternal Being, as well as all the powers of the finer-material planets and heavenly bodies of the material cosmos are part of the All-symphony.

*To what extent has our sounding box
become more light-filled and brighter?
Our virtual walk leads us to a clearing –
We take in another animal's body of sound*

Aware of the All-Unity, we continue our virtual walk. No matter where we are – there are many, very many, occasions to question ourselves over and over again as to what extent our body of sound has become more light-filled and brighter, and thus grasp and feel the omnipresent life in us.

During our virtual walk, we should frequently check where we are at the moment with our thoughts, whether we are with our virtual walk in our thoughts, because it is significant for learning what "sending and receiving" mean.

No matter on which continent we live, everywhere the life is present in the very basis of the soul of each person, as well as in the animals from the breath of God, on, over and in the Earth, in the waters and oceans.

We now continue our virtual walk. It leads us to a clearing in the woods.

An animal is grazing at the edge of the woods; another is drinking water from the brook that flows by. The animals have not yet perceived us, the human beings. We behave calmly, so that we take in the ethereal body of sound of one of the animals.

Virtually, we are standing at the edge of the woods. We "sort ourselves out," which means that we try to switch off our perhaps still lingering thoughts and to empty ourselves as far as possible, that is, to be as alert as possible.

As before, with the bird creature, we virtually take the picture of one of these animals into ourselves. While doing so, it is helpful to again briefly close our eyes and to deeply inhale and exhale a few times.

While inhaling, we now take in an animal, as a picture in us, which very gradually wants to take form in us as ethereal sound.

We listen into our physical body, to perceive the animal's aura, its body of sound, in us.

In the central nervous system, particularly in the so-called solar plexus, a certain energy builds up, which puts us "in accord," triggering in us a – until now never before observed – positive resonance.

It could be the ethereal aura, the body of sound of the animal.

Remain calm. Do not think; let your feelings come and you will notice:
It sounds; it vibrates; there is something present that conveys harmony and joy to you.
Let it happen. If it does not yet vibrate into you, then remember that every beginning is difficult.

In time, you will notice that higher vibrations make you glad and harmonious; they convey to you a touch of another side of your life, which lets you sense that everything, absolutely everything, is sound, color, form and fragrance.

Whoever learns more and more the effect that seeing and beholding, hearing and listening have on our personal sounding box, and whoever can affirm that everything lives, that everything sends, will understand more and more that the true cosmic life communicates in everyone and everything – it is the speaking All-One.

On our virtual walks, we will see that when we close our eyes, we draw closer to ourselves and when we open our eyes, we immediately begin to think again, because we perceive this and that, which distracts us from what is presently a concern. That, too, would not be a coincidence, because a message might reach us by way of our eyes.

The message could be, perhaps: Make use of the day! Don't be erratic in your thoughts, and whatever you do, give it your all and learn to get your senses under control, then your sensations and feelings will also change, pointing in a new direction.

We learn and practice. Higher ethics and morals can be attained only through self-recognition and self-discovery, by no longer doing what we used to consider normal, for example, imitating unethical and often immoral actions that others have shown with nonchalance.

Without properly and conscientiously learning on ourselves, we are often like driven people, who, without self-reflection, leave their conscience by the wayside of everyday stress and, on top of that, may even let others trample on it. This not only makes a person dependent, but also unfree.

That is why we learn and practice to attain higher values that truly make us free. In this way, we

experience our day and our leisure hours, which become a gain.
In addition, we experience what true life, which is the All-Unity, means.

*We take the life form of a flower
into our body of sound*

Now we continue our virtual walk.
Virtually, we step out of the woods and see before us a flowering meadow, in which many plants and herbs, among others, medicinal herbs, also have their home.

We look at the closest flower. In all blossoms, no matter what kind, we see in the center the developmental germ, the germ of life, also called the pistil, from which propagation develops.
In the eternal Being, the spiritual essence of the respective flower species is the ethereal germ of life, which, in God's cradle of creating, that is, of drawing, develops into the core of being step by step.

May it be stated again and again: You do not have to accept or believe what is written here. Accord-

ing to the law of God, you are free. Don't let yourself be forced into anything.
If you like, you can try it out. With a bit of patience and practice it's worth the experience!

We learn and practice. Virtually, you examine a flower in the flowering meadow, in the garden of God. You now have a virtual picture of a flower. You see its structure and its species. You recognize that no one flower is the same as another in all details, not even when it is the same species. Nevertheless, each ethereal flower species develops in a specific spiritual genus, in which the same species show various stages of development.

Each kind of flower that we look at more closely, and to which we develop an inner relationship, can begin to vibrate in our body, in our physical sounding board, if we learn to take the being of the flower into ourselves. Each one of us determines, himself, whether we are successful in this. If it is possible for you to switch off your thoughts, that is, to make yourself empty, so that you begin to receive, then you will gradually sense that something in your physical body begins to vibrate – it is an ethereal body of vibration, the life of the flower species.

As stated: Everything needs training and practice.

The report of an experience

A participant of the roundtable reports his experience:

Dear fellow people, I've tried it out, not as a virtual walk, but by walking over meadows and fields. The rustling of the trees, the twittering of the birds, the wind, all of this brought me out of my learning step. I went into the woods again and tried the following: I got some earplugs and put them in my ears.
Then it went better. The sounds of the external world disappeared.

I experienced it this way. It's very quiet then. Between you and the trees, the bushes, flowers and grasses, there is no distance anymore. You sense that you are sharing the space with them. The tree that stands far off radiates no strangeness. It is very close in its nature. You share the habitat and are part of all the life that surrounds you. The stillness of nature transmits itself to you and

you feel a touch of what is brought home to us in the presentations about the speaking All-Unity, the word of the Universal Creator-Spirit: stillness, peace, connectedness – the greatness and power of the All.
You feel the mighty tree, which exudes steadfastness, loyalty and endurance, and the delicate flower that radiates its faithfulness to its Creator. It is an interesting experience. –
This is how I experienced it. If you like, try it out!

⸻

And so, it is worth the attempt to take another virtual step.
Another experiment:
Pull back your thoughts – as already quite often described – by pausing and breathing consciously. When you go with your breath, as it comes and goes, your thoughts recede from you more and more.
Inhale and exhale deeply several times.

As stated: We are underway, virtually. If you like, close your eyes again so that you are not distracted. Observe, yes, behold, another flower being as a picture in your inner being.

Very gradually you feel lightness and freshness, because the flower stimulates your central nervous system. This can be a breath from the divine "Let There Be," a touch from the core of being in the very basis of your soul.

Once you have become somewhat experienced in the inner perception, then, in time, you will also perceive the sound and the ethereal, delicate fragrance of the flower, for, as stated, everything is sound, color, form and fragrance.

Practice makes perfect!

We now continue our virtual walk, and learn to look deeper and to comprehend that everything is unity and the speaking All-One is omnipresent.

Practice makes perfect! In time, the "master" grasps that everything pure, all Being, is alive in him – and thus, in us – and that ultimately there is no here and there, no above and below, no behind and in front, no right and no left.

During our virtual walk, we see a medicinal plant on the big flowering meadow. What do the words "medicinal plant" want to convey to us? They want to tell us that this is an herb and it is good for one or several organs of a person or for his blood or for calming his nerves, and so on. The fact that there are a large number of medicinal plants shows us that the All-One cares for the bodies of His human children.

The medicinal plant that you are looking at virtually in the flowering meadow is also in your core of being as a spiritual collective germ, from where the essential picture comes alive. Without our virtually picking it, it wants to convey to us via its fragrance that it is a life form – a teeny-tiny living being – in the mighty spiritual collective of infinity.

Even without being picked, through proper sensory perception and through its fragrance, it could help us, if we can let its nature and its fragrance come alive in our body, in our organs.

When we hear, "can let it come alive," then this contains the question: Can the medicinal plant reach us? It always depends on how our sounding box, that is, our physical body, including our organs and all the components of our body, vibrates.

We virtually bend over a medicinal plant, to absorb its fragrance. Inhale and exhale deeply several times, and, virtually inclined toward the

medicinal plant, take its fragrance into your body.
This is possible at any time, above all, when you, as a human being, that is, in reality – not virtually – take a walk and turn to a medicinal plant, to absorb its nature and its fragrance with your senses.

With this exercise, remember that everything is present, even the fragrance of the medicinal plant. Present means that you do not have to go here and there – the life is in you. You, yourself, are nature.

We now devote ourselves solely to the fragrance of the medicinal plant.
In time – because it takes some time to perceive the life in oneself – you will feel how the fragrance of the medicinal plant makes itself felt as a sense of well-being in your sounding box, perhaps even in certain functions of your body. You may feel freer and fresher and your central nervous system also relaxes.

Note that when you take a real walk and, for instance, pick some leaves from a medicinal plant, for tea or for other medicinal purposes, then remember: The medicinal plant wants to fully unfold in you, without additives.

Decisive is how you approach the life form, whether for you it is merely a means to an end, merely a remedy, or whether the medicinal plant can helpfully unfold in your body, in your organs, as described in the virtual walk.
Do not let go of the thought that everything is communication and that your whole person is in communication with the material macrocosm and, the innermost part of your soul, with the All-Being, the All-One, the Creator of infinity.

Another remark concerning the use of medicinal plants: If you should pick healing herbs, remember that the roots belong to Mother Earth. Leave the roots for Mother Earth, and carefully take only as much as necessary from the herb. To learn also means not to waste anything that the Creator-God gives us by way of the Mother Earth.
It is also possible for us to do these exercises when we live in a city and hardly have access to the medicinal plants in nature, because all life forms are in communication with each other. This means that for the All-communication there is no such thing as distance.

The All-communication is always the present. There is no time and no distance, and thus, no "waiting time," either.

The sending consciousness of the All is the same as direct reception. This also holds true for a medicinal plant. It can be reached on its direct wavelength, if this wave sector is active in our consciousness.

A communicative resonance is totally possible if, for the most part, we respect the life of the nature kingdoms, if we cherish animals, plants and minerals and are not indifferent toward these life forms, but are friendly and ready to help, instead. So distance does not matter here.

We often have the attitude: "Practiced today – tomorrow it must work!" However, it does not work from one day to the next! This means we have to practice over and over again, thereby asking ourselves: What does my daily life look like – my thoughts, words and actions?

It is only this that determines our life; these are also our works and like everything, this is based on "sending and receiving."

The Earth is a living organism

Before our virtual walk comes to an end, let us also allow the path through the fields or woods to have its effect on us. We perceive smaller and larger stones and in-between, the grass; now and then a flower peeks out.

Rarely does a person taking a walk or a pedestrian or car owner pay any attention to the stones and the gravel on the pathways. And few people realize that they are walking on grass and here and there trampling a flower or a little animal.
Paths and streets, tunnels and train tracks, the routes of airplanes and ships and much more – on, in and over the Earth – are forced onto the planet by mankind.

Does the farmer think about the fact that with his heavy cultivation equipment, he not only tills the fields, but also ruthlessly compacts the soil and thus also distressing the life in the soil and, in the process, killing many a little animal and, not lastly, poisoning them with artificial fertilizers, pesticides, herbicides and the like?
Is man aware of how brutally the minerals were and are extracted from the Earth?

The Earth is a living organism. Has man ever realized what it means for the Earth when dams are built or skyscrapers erected?
We're not talking about the building of residential homes, but about a massive intervention in the Earth, whereby its balance is considerably disturbed.

If now, during your virtual walk, you look back and remember your many real walks in the woods and over the fields, then you sense that the owner of the Earth has much patience with us human beings.
The overexploitation of Mother Earth is also a severe offence against life. The same holds true for the murder of animal creatures and plant beings. Everything that bears life – and everything bears the life – is part of the great family of God.
May it be said about this: A person will reap what he sows.

The planet Earth is merely a loan from God, so that during his life on Earth, man may again find his true origin.
His animal brothers and sisters and the plant beings are also only placed at his side, so that he may again open the unity of all life in himself.

He, the All-One, the Creator of all Being, let healing herbs grow for the physical well-being of His human children and He gave them minerals to strengthen their body.

The Eternal One essentially said that the fruits of the woods and fields, the fruits of the trees should be the people's food.

The elements, too, which are in the hand of God, serve in the preparation of the nature kingdoms, thus also supporting us human beings in this way. He lets the sun shine on the good and the evil. He, the Eternal, lets it rain, the wind blow, and gives us the air to breathe. This and much more are His gifts to us. – What has so-called civilized man done with all that the eternal Creator bestowed and bestows on us?

When we take all this into consideration at the end of our virtual walk, and become aware of the boundless transgressions against God's creation, then many a one will think:

Well, spiritually, we are still Stone Age people, despite so-called scientific and technological progress. And many a one comes to the conclusion that it might well be precisely scientific progress that has turned mankind into spiritual illiterates, who are not fit to hold a candle to indigenous peoples.

Let us consider that everything we are aware of and often not aware of, and much more, pulsates in us as essence, light, strength, as the life. Anyone who has reached this recognition will, for instance, certainly no longer simply toss a plain, for us, meaningless, stone, simply because we feel like it. Nor will we thoughtlessly waste minerals, either.
People who during the virtual walk have awakened spiritually live more and more in the awareness that everything is energy, and that everything on, in and above the Earth, in the waters and oceans, is God's all-prevailing eternal law, the life from the breath of God. They understand and experience that man is merely a temporary inhabitant on this planet, to recollect that an immeasurable treasure lives in the very basis of his soul: the core of being in him, God's All-power and love.

May our virtual walks motivate many of us to experience real walks of a similar kind.

*In the very basis of our soul,
we are unendingly rich.
The inner wealth is decisive –
The eternal life*

Dear fellow people, only through the inner perception of life forms and living beings around us, will we learn and experience what a treasure our soul bears.

Wherever we look, wherever we go – the innermost workings of the All-One are everywhere. On the way to work, to shopping, at work, in everything that we experience, also in the household, with the family, in our circle of friends, we recognize God's All-workings.

Let us not forget that God, the All-life, is always present.

And with disagreements and quarrels, too, we can learn to find the approach to the positive and to carefully, that is, purposefully, address this.

The good is always present and there is always an approach to the positive.

Let Us Continue Learning to Fathom What We Heard and Read

How can we respond to the great suffering of the animals, the plants, of all of Mother Earth?

Question: *Through the work on ourselves and through the exercises, "we become more peace-loving and peaceful and thus, more spiritually consistent," as was stated. We become much more sensitive, and we feel the immeasurable suffering of the animals, the plants, all of Mother Earth much more intensely. – How can we cope with this, so that this great woe does not totally oppress us?*

Answer: For one thing, we can cope with this only to some degree by praying for those people who torment and torture the animals, who brutally kill them, who keep them in animal ghettos as slaughter animals, who deliver them to the butcher, and so on. But in prayer we should also think of the souls of those people who still – out of ignorance or weakness – eat the meat of murdered animals. We should place all these prayers under the protection of the Christ of God.

At the same time, depending on our possibilities, we should do everything we can to make a species-appropriate, free life possible for animals, until their physical demise, which especially for animals is a natural, that is, a totally "normal" process.

The earthy existence that we people see as an ethically valuable life should also be granted to the animals and, ultimately, to the planet Earth, which is likewise an organism that has its perception and, like us, is a bearer of life. It gives life and fruit; and we human beings may receive.

There is still much to do, to achieve the cosmic All-communication, and this means: Learn, learn and learn again! Shall we dare to do this?

Question: *On the virtual walk, we practiced perceiving in ourselves the body of sound of an animal and the life form of a flower. For some it went better when it was one of our animal brothers or sisters, for others, the plant beings seem to be closer. Why is this?*

Answer: A picture of the sun and the clouds could be helpful for us here:

The clouds cover up the sun's light and cause shadows on the Earth. But the sun shines, whether dark clouds pile up or whether they are lighter. If the cloud cover is scattered, for example, if there are so-called cirrostratus clouds, then the sun shines through the scattered clouds.

When the shadows, the clouds, are heavier in one area of the particle structure of our soul, then the communication – for example, in relation to the animal world – is also disturbed. If the particle structure of our soul is lighter in relation to the plant life, then communication with it is closer to us.

On the whole, we can determine without doubt that in order to attain the cosmic All-communication, there is still much to learn and to do!

Let us learn to remember again and again, that in the very basis of our soul we human beings are all-rich, that is, infinitely rich. Happy the one who grasps this!
Let us learn to put order in our world of thoughts.
Let us learn to watch our breathing.
Let us learn to grow closer to the All-Unity, so that the picture of life can rise in our cleansed

thoughts; for, as stated, a unique treasure is active in the very basis of our soul: the pure Being, the All-communication.

Let us learn what life means.

Let us learn to keep calm and disciplined in every situation, in order to master the life on Earth and, in this equanimity, to also watch the behavior patterns of our fellow creatures, the animals, and to contemplate and experience nature.

Wherever we go, wherever we are – there is always something to learn.

May you learn, may we learn, to perceive the life, because everything proceeds in rhythms, in colors, forms, sounds and fragrances.

The Covenant of the Eternal with the Animals

The following realization opens to the person who fulfills the law of unity, the love for God and neighbor, the "link and be," more and more: Only when we human beings have attained the All-Unity again, will there be peace on Earth – just as God, the Eternal, announced 2700 years ago through His prophet Isaiah:

*The wolf shall dwell with the lamb,
and the leopard shall lie down
with the young goat,
and the calf and the lion ... together;
and a little child shall lead them.
The cow and the bear shall graze;
their young shall lie down together;
and the lion shall eat straw like the ox.
The nursing child shall play over the hole
of the cobra, and the weaned child
shall put his hand on the adder's den.
They shall not hurt or destroy
in all my holy mountain;
for the earth shall be full of the knowledge
of the Lord as the waters cover the sea.*

And through His prophet Hosea, God said, also 2700 years ago:
And I will make for them a covenant on that day with the beasts of the field, the birds of the heavens, and the creeping things of the ground.
And I will abolish the bow, the sword, and war from the land, and I will make you lie down in safety.

In our time, in the year 1999, the Eternal gave a revelation through His prophetess Gabriele: He made a covenant with the animals and with all of nature and the Mother Earth.
The eternal Spirit, the Creator of infinity, spoke:

I gave them a healthy Earth. However, they turned the Earth into a garbage dump und a breeding ground for illness and disease, pestilence and much more.

Mankind is becoming more and more sick, because the Earth is not only sick, but hardly viable anymore through the pest, man, who unceasingly maltreats and tortures it.

The perpetrator of this evil thinks he can become healthy if the right medication is found for him, which is tested on animals in a bestial way in so-called laboratories.

Then – so thinks the merciless man – he can continue to live out his mercilessness. The animal farmers who keep animals for slaughter are no better than the bestial people who torture, maltreat, cut up, and do even more to animals in laboratories. Anyone who pens up animals, to let them vegetate away in the most cramped spaces, even though the Earth offers freedom, will one day experience the same and similar things – according to the law of cause and effect: A person will reap what he sows.

And so, every man is the architect of his own fate. Whatever man does to animals, plants and minerals – that is, to the Earth – will also be meted out to him, no matter what medication he takes to escape the effect.

Mankind of many generations has maltreated the Earth in the cruelest way. It was violated and robbed of its treasures. People interfered, and interfere, in the watercourses, which are the arteries of the Earth. They dumped, and dump, their trash into the Earth's source of life, the oceans. They destroyed, and still destroy, the Earth's protective shield, the atmosphere, and the Earth's lungs, the forests.

Human beings have become cannibals. The excesses of cannibalism are interminable. The cannibal, man, breeds millions and billions of animals. Day after day, the cannibal, man, has them driven into slaughterhouses and killed using gruesome ways and means, in order to then consume their flesh – deliciously prepared, of course.

Many a one believes animals are a commodity and that he can exploit the Earth, to increase his bank account. At some point, he will have to recognize that, in truth, the larger his bank account grew, the poorer he became. The pathetic creatures, who think they could trump the Creator, will soon have to recognize that Mother Earth no longer obeys them.

The Earth is now Mine and will do what is My will. This means that the causes, the offences of human beings against Mother Earth, will come at them as causes ever faster. Mankind is gradually reaching the culmination of its doings. The adversary is of the opinion that he can triumph over Me via degenerate people, who interfere in life and play the role of Creator. He has always fooled himself, and he will also deceive himself this time, because Mother Earth is now Mine.

Murder and manslaughter are on the banner of many people. The insatiable Moloch man has positioned himself against his own dwelling planet and is thus against everything that lives on the Earth. Because the people did not accept the love of their

Redeemer for people and animals, I have taken the Earth back from them, with everything that lives on it – animals, all plant species and minerals – and place it trustingly in the hands of spirit beings and divine beings of nature, which will very gradually build up the Earth again, with its animals, plants and minerals, and guide them toward its recovery.
The covenant with the animals has been made. So be it!

And God, the Eternal, continued:

When spiritually cosmic, peaceable people inhabit the Earth, I will give the Earth to the people again, just as Jesus, the Christ, said in the Sermon on the Mount: "Blessed are the meek, for they shall inherit the earth."
The animals, plants, elemental forces, the Earth, all of nature are a part of life; the Kingdom of Peace of God will emerge through them, in which it is on Earth as it is in heaven.

We have now read it: May the one who can grasp it, grasp it, and may the one who wants to leave it, leave it.

God is making His word come true! It can be recognized that the Eternal is gradually taking back the animal world, and likewise the plant world. What then? What does this mean for us human beings?

The Earth-killer man

When we look at the state of mankind and of the Earth, then we inevitably think of a vandal who has turned the Earth into a battlefield, who upholds the pagan sacrificial cult on water and on land, by fishing the global oceans to death, by murdering the animals on land, by having them murdered, and over and over again, by striving anew to totally overexploit the Earth.

The barbarian man has literally become a robber and murderer where the Earth is concerned, with everything that it bears as human beings, animals, plants and minerals. Such a person can also be called an Earth-killer and spiritual illiterate, who knows only himself.

When the Earth takes back what ultimately belongs to it – for example, a person's physical body – then the released soul, which is not of this Earth, is a spiritual wreck, which has to first find its way again in the purification planes of the souls, in order to build itself up there. At some point, it learns to open up what it ultimately bears within, the free Spirit, the All-One, who is its Creator and heavenly, eternal Father, and it learns that it is spirit of His Spirit.

The Principle of All-Communication – Without Technology. Man's Worldly Communication Aids

In a world that is becoming ever coarser, in which the dictate of technology determines the beat of mankind, the finest spiritual-divine processes presented may often seem accessible only with difficulty. The majority of mankind has become blunted in relation to the subtle principles of the law of life, which are at the basis of all life forms.

The coarsening of the five components, the content, for instance, of thoughts and feelings, also goes hand in hand with a coarsening and brutalization of the living conditions of most people. That is why the words from the origin, from the breadth and depth of life, sound unattainable for many, yes, nearly incomprehensible, and for many a one it seems impossible to experience this in one's own life.

Modern, intellectually shaped people often do not easily grasp what is explained to us from the seven-dimensional world of the eternal Being, which also permeates our three-dimensional world. And yet, the present time in particular, with its technical possibilities, offers more illustrative examples for the communication principle of infinity – "sending and receiving" – than ever before.

Coarse-material communication technology is based on transformed-down inherent laws, which are nothing more than energies that have become flat. They are aberrations, a three-dimensional technical and pale reflection of the communication forms of the eternal Being, of the infinite Light-Ether, which we read about, over and over again. How hard it is for us human beings to make ourselves aware of the All-communication; and yet everything is based on "sending and receiving."

We remember that all life forms and living beings in the life-stream of the Creator are linked with each other. They live in the activated All-communication of infinity. They don't need to go here and there. By way of their core of being, they are in connection with the entire All.

If they want to make contact with a being that may be on another plane of heaven, then with an impulse via the core of being, they send to the being and in that "instant," they are present and directly connected with this being, at one with each other. We would say that the spirit beings and all life forms are "networked" with each other via the core of being.

One question is truly appropriate: And what about us human beings? Where do we stand? What is our sending volume? To where do we send?
We human beings present a sad picture of ourselves in terms of the All-communication without technology; and yet, man is so proud of his achievements and in addition, even arrogant.

If spiritual-divine circumstances are accessible to us only with difficulty, we could call to mind the millionfold processes of present-day communication technology.
One of the many technical possibilities that we take for granted in our daily life, even though just a few decades ago they were considered utopian, are the applications of mobile communication technology. We now take it for granted that by dialing a number in a communication network, we send an impulse via which we will be connected with the mobile phone we dialed. Within the countless possibilities of the mobile communication network and from every random location,

we can now dial a number and thus, unerringly establish communication with the desired partner – even in a far distant country.

This comprehensible technical possibility takes place in the coarse-material world and we make use of it without thinking about what inherent laws this technology is based on.
The internet expands this possibility of establishing technical communication in a way that, even today, is nearly incomprehensible. People can communicate not only with sound; they can also mutually see their far away conversation partner, so as to converse with each other as if they were both in the same place.
We accept all this as technical achievements that we take for granted – whereby it is ultimately merely transformed-down, we could also say satanically manipulated, aberrations of the inherent laws of the eternal Being.

And so, it could be a help for our understanding, if we were to imagine something like this: Just as the mobile communication network gives every participant the possibility to accurately dial a specific number from countless possibilities of the network, it is similarly possible for the spirit beings, by making contact via the core of being, to reach another being in all of infinity with absolute precision.

The technical possibilities of our time fascinate and captivate many a one. May you also feel exactly this same fascination for the wonderful multiplicity, greatness and subtlety of the communication of the All-Unity. With this, a pearl of wisdom for life now opens up for the one who thinks and reads with the heart. It is: "Man, don't take yourself so seriously; you are greater than you can imagine."

The All-Communication Network Goes with the Approaching Earth Citizen

The life cycle of a human being on Earth

The giving and receiving All-principle is always the free Spirit, God, the life of infinity, the Light-Ether. The core of being, about which we have often heard, thus contains all the powers of the Being, because it is compressed Light-Ether.

Jesus of Nazareth taught the people: *The Kingdom of God is within, in you.* – So it is! All powers of the eternal Being, set in the core of being, are in us, in the very basis of our soul. The primordial source of giving and receiving is the light of the eternal sun, which fills our soul and our body with life force.

It is the divinity in the core of being. With the birth of a human child, with its first cry, its first independent inhalation, the core of being and the soul connect with the child's developing pituitary gland.

According to its aura, the finer-material soul increasingly establishes contact with the organism of the newborn and flows into the physical body. As the child grows and matures, it flows ever deeper into the physical body. Via the core of being, the eternal free Spirit gives life to the human child. The child's breath is, as with all of us, the breath of God.

Via the core of being, the new person remains connected to the All-communication

As stated: Just as the child grows and develops, a part of the soul takes possession of the body more and more. Via seven spiritual centers in the person, it flows successively into the components of the physical body and transfers the life to all its physical functions. This means that via the core of being, the Eternal gives His power to the soul, and via the soul, to all components and all functions of the body.

The child grows and matures into a young person. The power of God is present with every inhalation and exhalation.

A person's heart is solely the distribution center for his earthly existence. The heart muscle sets the beat, depending on whether the person breathes shallowly or more deeply.

The child grows and matures and gradually grows into adolescence. Time does not stop – the young person grows older. The years pass; the process of growing older merges into being old, but the core of being remains with him, the human being.

Because life on Earth is not permanent, sooner or later the person passes on. Already with the child's birth, the soul brings with it its cycle of life on Earth, which the former person – insofar as there were previous incarnations – inflicted on his soul. Among other things, this cycle of life on Earth shows how long the person will live in the temporal.

Consequently, at the time of birth, the new citizen of the Earth already bears within the cycle, that is, from birth to passing on.

However, it is possible that the person terminates his life cycle on Earth sooner than foreseen. This happens when he creates causes upon causes, through which situations can occur that, for instance, bring with them the danger of the person dying prematurely. This way, he breaks off his life cycle on Earth through a premature death, which he caused himself.

There are countless variations of fate, for instance, also through suicide or through a karmic network, whereby, for example, one drags another along into death, and so on. However, the person himself is always the one who challenges his destiny, his fate. But the core of being remains in his soul.

Now the objection could be made that even a premature death would have to be programmed, because nothing happens by chance. Yes, so it is – but it is always up to the person himself, whether in critical situations we moderate ourselves in time or let the vehicle of our soul, the body, crash. Here, too, free will decides.

As stated: With the newborn's first inhalation, the core of being and the soul connect with the pituitary gland.

When a person passes on, with his last exhalation the core of being and the soul begin to separate from the pituitary gland. The soul body very gradually detaches from the lifeless body, so that it is merely the shell of the former soul body. With the person's last exhalation, the now finer-material soul body inhales and, after complete disembodiment, continues breathing in the beyond according to the rhythm of its finer-materialness. A more light-filled soul perceives the tone, the sound, of a finer-material planet, which is programmed by the person according to whether he is "for or against the commandment of love for God and neighbor."

It is possible that a so-called earthbound, world-oriented soul may linger in the temporal for a very long time, because the material-oriented programs of the former person have also been absorbed by the soul.

The programs shaped by this side of life are primarily stored in the material cosmos, because, to wherever a person sends, from there he receives. Therein also lies the force of attraction, the magnet for the soul – once the physical body has passed on. And yet, the All-communication – the core of being in the soul – remains.

And so, our inputs form the sending and receiving station. For example, when a soul goes to another incarnation, then it takes its still-existing "for and against" along into its new earthly existence. If the negative programs prevail, then these can definitely determine the fate of the newly incarnated person. Each of us, that is, we, ourselves, have our fate in hand.

It is not for nothing that the Eternal gave us the Ten Commandments through Moses, Law-excerpts from the all-encompassing law of infinity, the Kingdom of God. And it was not for nothing that in His Sermon on the Mount, the Son of God, the Co-Regent of the Kingdom of God, as Jesus of Nazareth, gave still deeper insight into the inherent principles of the eternal Being.

We, every single person decides about his life on Earth according to the principle of for and against: either for God's indications in His commandments and in the Sermon on the Mount of Jesus or against the advice of the Eternal. By being against it, we act against our soul through transgressions in thinking, speaking and acting, and in this way, use up the energy of soul and body. Thus, a blow of fate could possibly break out, which could very well have been prevented.

Freedom in the law of love for God and neighbor is of significance, because from the All-law come many warning signs, which can be of help to the person, insofar as he is willing to place himself in question over and over again. If we are alert and if in all not-good situations we make the connection to ourselves – as far as our fellowman is concerned, as well as in our behavior toward the world of animals and plants, toward the whole Earth, with everything that it bears – then we learn on ourselves and will curb ourselves in good time. However it may be: The All-communication, the core of being, remains in the very basis of our soul.

The soul prepares the person for his passing

A tip especially for the elderly: Elderly people notice ever more often that their physical strength lessens, that they perhaps become slower, even frailer, and tire out more and more often. The breathing rhythm also becomes shallower; particularly during strenuous work, breathing is more difficult. And so, many things become more arduous.
We are not talking about illness here; that belongs to another topic.

How often do we hear: "Age sets the plane in motion and smoothes everyone equally." No matter whether a person makes use of plastic surgeons or not – his strength lessens; the metabolism slows down; the wrinkles come; the hair turns gray, and so on. This development is inevitable. This is simply part of a person's life on Earth. Life changes, from birth to death, but the core of being contains the eternal youth in the eternal Being.

In all of infinity, nothing happens by chance, nor is there anything static, nothing that happens unexpectedly with a jolt. After a certain time of being here, the soul in the person begins the period of preparation for the moment in which the soul moves out of its physical body.

During this time of preparation, the soul prepares for the life in its finer-material form. Slowly, very slowly – in a healthy person often over several years – the soul withdraws.

For example, many an elderly person has trouble walking. The strength in his arms and hands also decreases. To carry something heavy becomes a burden. The organs of seeing and hearing also lessen in their performance. Daily life in general is more laborious.

Many a person does not want to think about this. How often do we hear from elderly people, "But that's impossible! That used to be no problem at all for me. I was agile, strong, I could work for many hours without great effort, that is, accomplish things – and today everything is so arduous!"

That's just how it is. The soul is preparing for another aggregate state. If we could ask our soul, it would basically answer us as follows: "You, my human shell, take note: I, the spirit being in the innermost part of your soul body, am not of this world; I have only assumed a physical body to rectify, during this life on Earth, as much as possible of what I brought along from former incarnations in the way of iniquity. I want to go homeward, to my land of origin, the eternal Kingdom of God, where I will again live as a spirit being in the eternal All-Being."

No matter how a person purports to be, whether he wants to try to delay growing older as long as possible, through cosmetic operations, spas, massages and the like – everyone, absolutely everyone, is merely a wayfarer on this Earth. One day, the soul will discard its physical body, because it belongs to the Earth.

There are no exceptions – all human beings pass on. And even if the soul returns ever so often as a human being: For every person – without exception – comes the time and the hour when the soul discards its body. But the core of being, the heavenly All-communication, remains in it.

The same applies to all coarse-material life forms on, over and in the Earth, as well as in the oceans and waters: earth to earth.

The material universe and the finer-material universes are also gradually being led back by the Eternal, for the life in God is fine-material, it is ethereal and absolutely pure.

Jesus essentially said: *Become perfect as your Father in heaven is perfect.*
Everything that is not akin to the origin, to perfection, is inhaled by God, the Eternal, in cycles, toward the eternal All-Being.
He transforms the coarse-material into the finer-material and the finer-material, into fine-material.
Everything is then once more fine-material, finest primordial substance, compressed Light-Ether.

The Incorruptible Core of Being – Hope Leads to Eternal Life

The seat of the maturing core of being in animals, plants and minerals

Everything out of the breath of God lives eternally and is imbedded, that is, received, in the inexhaustible Light-Ether. The life out of the breath of God is light of His light; it is the core of being, the fullness of the Being.

A question to this topic: Where is the seat of the maturing core of being in animals and of the germinating life in plants, stones and minerals?
In the animals out of the breath of God, which, as stated, have a maturing core of being, the seat is in the brain, according to the development of the animal; with many an animal, we can also say that it is already near the pituitary gland.

We should always assume that in every animal the core of being has been formed according to its spiritual development, according to its state of consciousness, that is, its degree of maturity.

In the tiniest animals, as well as in the plant and mineral kingdoms, the germinating eternal life is still set in a collective and, like all forms of consciousness, allocated to cycles of evolution.

The specific degree of maturity is the state of consciousness of the respective living beings and life forms.

The germinating life has a divine structure, which can be described as a particle structure. Every spiritual germ is set in particles and, in the cradle of drawing, that is, of creating, it develops to the next higher form.

If the degree of maturity of the germinating life has developed to the extent that it can be set as a core of being, then in the corresponding form of being, evolution continues according to the developing core of being toward the next higher unfoldment of consciousness in the planes of development.

The earthly three-dimensional way of thinking classifies everything in categories, so a person envisions, for instance: What I perceive here as phenomena must be the same everywhere. According to the thinking of many people, every animal, every plant species, all tree species, all minerals must be the same everywhere, just as they observe them in their sphere of activity.

In the seven-dimensional creation, there is nothing that would be divided into categories.

As already stated, every germ of life has differently developed degrees of consciousness. For this reason, here and there or even on other continents, a flower, a shrub or a tree species, for instance, can have another form or even other characteristics. It can have a very different name and bloom or ripen at a different time. Nevertheless, this life form belongs to the same genus, even when the germ of life displays different stages of development.

The Creator-Spirit, who holds all life in His hands, does not let Himself be ranked according to human categories.

Man's idolatry mania.
The manipulation of animals, plants and nature

But when we think of the manipulation procedures that man forces onto the animals and plants, then it has to be said that the appearance of such artificially altered living beings and life forms does not correspond to what the Creator-God designated for the animal and plant kingdoms.

Man, who is a slave to idolatry, upholds his concoction as a purported trophy in every respect.

Whether by altering genes in animal and plant species or via arbitrary hybrids – man always proves to be the henchman of the one who comes from below. The henchman of the underworld makes himself at home everywhere, even in the mineral kingdoms.

But one thing is certain: He will never be able to manipulate the eternal Creator's spiritual life of creation.

When we take a closer look at the behavior of yesterday's mankind, that is, of previous generations, and that of the present generation, we get an inkling of how far mankind has departed from the origin of life.

Even though the eternal light, the eternal sun of the Being, still shines in the very basis of the person, the cell structure of the physical body and the spiritual particle structure of the soul are often so very shadowed that the sinner looks only at his own world of shadows and considers this to be real and even the reality of life.

Why doesn't God intervene?
The law of freedom

The question is asked again and again: Why doesn't God intervene in this shambles of human ignorance?

Why does God allow the manipulation of animals and nature?

Why does He allow animals to be tormented, tortured and massacred?

Why? Because according to the law of freedom, we human beings are absolutely free beings. From the beginning of His creating and drawing, that is, with the first respiration of a spiritual atom, God, the Eternal, placed freedom into the spiritual cradle of creation, into the "Let There Be."

Anyone who abuses the principle of freedom, which is a life principle of the eternal Being, by allowing his all-too-human will to become a deed, delivers himself up to the causal law that is "divide, bind and rule," and that results in cause and effect, sowing and reaping.

For us human beings, this means that we ourselves are responsible for everything that we think, speak and do that does not correspond to the law of love for God and neighbor, which contains the true freedom.

Everything that is not good and goes out from us and has not been remedied comes back into us; it is stored by our physical body cells and the particle structure of our soul.

Anyone who does not recognize this today and continues as before designs his own realm of shadows, which comes from below.

Thus marked, the soul goes into the beyond after its disembodiment, because as the tree falls, so will it lie. Depending on the soul's burdening, it may go to another incarnation, an incarnation that corresponds to it. Depending on his condition, the new human being picks up where he left off at the time of his former body's demise.

Dear fellow people, all the insights into the all-encompassing works of the eternal Creator-Spirit given here are, stated in human words, not even a drop in the ocean of All-Unity.

However, in the soul of every person is the All-ocean, the essence of the All.

Because the rendering of the All-Being given in three-dimensionally shaped words is not even a drop in the All-ocean, the following must be stated: May the one who can grasp this grasp it; may the one who does not want to accept it as far as it has been given leave it. At some point in time, that which the person is in the very basis of his soul will open up in the soul: an ethereal spirit being of the All, of the Light-Ether, which is the All-Unity.

To conclude, a reminder and a request: Think about – may we all do this – the fact that for every piece of meat that man eats, an animal from the All-family of God was killed.

And think about the fact that animals that also eat meat call up this behavior from the energies with which the Earth is impregnated, or from energies that they have absorbed from the smell of the billions of people who consumed, and consume, pieces of animal carcasses.

If you want to, also think about the fact that all the negative contents of our feeling, sensing, thinking, speaking and acting are warfare agents that have sound, color, form and smell. Via our glands we exude what we are, also what corresponds to the food we eat.

Let us also think about the fact that it is man who transmits his behavior patterns to the animals in the temporal, that is, on the Earth.

No matter how we want to see it: Eating meat means to have animals killed.

May ever more people grasp in their hearts and experience that animals are our fellow creatures in the great All-family of God. They are our little brothers and sisters, who require our love and care.

We wish you, all of us, the perception of life in and around us, the unfoldment of consciousness for the All-Unity, the peace and the experience that in the very basis of our soul a mighty, all-encompassing treasure gives us light and strength.

Epilogue

The Unending, Inexhaustible Light-Ether, the Primordial Substance from which the Infinite, the Eternal, the Primordial God, Creates and Forms

Majesties, excellencies, eminences, reverences, "His Holiness," the "Holy Father" on Earth, cardinals, bishops, professors, doctors – and more eminent titles of outstanding significance – remarkable personalities, that result in not insignificant means.

Why all these titles? Why the resources that often result from them, such as money, assets, property and the like? Why?

Jesus of Nazareth taught something else. The following words of Jesus have been passed down in the following sense:

I do not receive My honor from people.

I have recognized that you do not have the love for God in you.

I have come in the name of My Father, and yet you reject Me. But when another comes in his own name, then you will acknowledge him.

How can you come to believe, when you receive your honor from each other, but do not seek the honor that comes from the One God?

He spoke further as follows:

Whoever professes to Me before the people, I will also profess to him before My Father in heaven.

He taught us in the following sense:

But you are not to be called rabbi (that is, priest or pastor), *for you have one teacher* (Christ) *and you are all brothers.*
And call no man your father on earth; for you have one Father, who is in heaven ...
The greatest among you shall be your servant. Whoever exalts himself will be humbled, and whoever humbles himself will be exalted.

His words have been passed down as follows:

I Am the way, the truth and the life; no one comes to the Father but through Me. When you have recognized Me, you will also recognize My Father.

The following incident has also been passed down about Jesus of Nazareth:

... a man came up to him, saying, "Teacher, what good deed must I do to have eternal life?"
And he said to him, "Why do you ask me about what is good? There is only one who is good. If you would enter life, keep the commandments."
He said to him, "Which ones?" And Jesus said, "You shall not murder, You shall not commit adultery, You shall not steal, You shall not bear false witness, Honor your father and mother, and, You shall love your neighbor as yourself."
The young man said to him, "All these I have kept. What do I still lack?"
Jesus said to him, "If you would be perfect, go, sell what you possess and give to the poor, and you will have treasure in heaven; and come, follow me."
When the young man heard this he went away sorrowful, for he had great possessions.
And Jesus said to his disciples, "Truly, I say to you, only with difficulty will a rich person enter the kingdom of heaven. Again I tell you, it is easier for a camel to go through the eye of a needle than for a rich person to enter the kingdom of God."

Dear fellow people, do not merely read page after page, but think along with us. Let the epilogue take effect in your consciousness.

The Light-Ether

The Light-Ether is the inexhaustible, omnipresent Spirit, the highest Intelligence, the Primordial God of infinity.
Many words for the Eternal, the Infinite and for the eternity.
In the western world, people call the All-One "God."
In this book, it is not the God of the churches who is meant; it is not the God who supposedly lives in temples of stone – here is meant the All-Spirit, the highest, universal light, the omnipresent life in you, in each person. It is the All-Spirit, who lives in all His life forms and living beings, who permeates all things, who is eternal and whom we human beings may simply call "Father."
If you like, think along with us and let the words flow into your heart.

> He, the All-One, is the Father of all His children.
> He is the Creator of the true Being, of all divine life forms, of all divine beings.

He is the Father-Mother-God.
He is the all-irradiating, eternal love.
He is our heavenly Father, the Father of all His children.

So why the many titles for people?
What does this want to tell mankind, since it should be, after all, on Earth as in heaven?

Let us allow these words of life to also come alive in us:
Our Father, who are in heaven,
hallowed is Your name.
Our kingdom comes, Your will is done
on Earth as it is in heaven.
You give us this day our daily bread
and forgive us our trespasses,
as we forgive those who trespass against us;
You lead us in time of temptation
and deliver us from evil.
For ours is the kingdom and the power
and the glory,
from eternity to eternity.

Here, too, the question: What does the Lord's Prayer want to tell us, above all, the so-called "Christians" in the western world?

We human beings may say to the Almighty, to the All-Being, the eternal Creator of all forms, Father. Our Father!

If we dedicate our earthly existence to God, our heavenly Father, as son or daughter, without attached titles, by doing His will, which is defined in His Ten Commandments and in the Sermon on the Mount of Jesus of Nazareth, then we will begin to truly live, for solely on this path will we experience ourselves. Only then will everything in us become new in our feelings and thoughts, the new person in His Spirit, the person in the stream of life, the eternal law of light, which flows around and through all Being, all cosmoses, all life forms, all beings. It is the love for God and neighbor, the inexhaustible source of life, the Being, the law of the All, the breath of life, the Father-Mother-God of love, eternally.

We human beings have forgotten how to reflect on the love for God and neighbor. Instead, experts think about the atomic nucleus. Whether science or religion, one fishes in muddy waters, particularly where God is concerned.

All words and terms spoken from the All-law of God are, as already explained, an insufficient language from the three dimensions.

Everything that we know about God and about scientific findings is by far no proof.

Everything is based on faith or even on hypotheses about how it could be – and perhaps is not, after all.

No person can give you proof of whether the point of view is as given or written, nor whether there is a God.

Only you can prove for yourself what the truth is, because in you, in the very basis of your soul, is the ethereal All-core of being, the primordial heart, the Light-Ether, the all-flowing All-communication, the life, set in the core of being, and that you, the human being, are embedded in, that is, enveloped by the Spirit of God, the infinite and inexhaustible Light-Ether, which is the absolute love for God and neighbor.

A note: People talk about the belief in science and in God. Seldom do we hear: I love God and strive daily to do His will.

If you want to, let what you read vibrate into you, in the following awareness: May the recognition ripen in you, yourself, that what you read and can affirm, so as to fulfill it, enriches your life on Earth, so that you sense, yourself, that there must be more than merely a belief in the good Lord.

If you want to, disengage yourself from "mechanical thought," which makes most religions the same, and feel into your innermost being, for the answer to what is written is in you, in the very basis of your soul, and do not let up thinking every now and then that God is love.

Everything that is supposed to prove God with many words and dogmas is no proof.

There is no external proof that God exists.

There is no external proof of the Light-Ether, from which all universes, all forms and living beings have their existence and their life.

However, there is *one* proof: You carry the proof yourself, in the very basis of your soul.

Every word is like a shell: One must learn to draw closer to the content that is contained in the word, in the insufficient language of the three dimensions.

Therefore: Read with heart and mind!

The highest potentiated Light-Ether is the law of infinity, it is the All-communication – we can also speak of an All-communication network, in which all universes, all heavenly bodies, all divine beings, all human beings and all life forms have their existence.

The Light-Ether, that was mentioned at the beginning of this book and to which we are also referring here in the epilogue, is the highest potentiated energetically flowing All-power, a volume of energy that is inexhaustible and immeasurable to us human beings.

There are no words for the highly potentiated Light-Ether that can even begin to express the abundance of energy.

Everything, but absolutely everything, is received, that is, embedded, in this all-encompassing, all-flowing Light-Ether.

It is the All-Spirit, the All-God, also called Primordial God, the infinite power of love.

God is Spirit. All of Infinity is suffused with His Spirit, His law, which is love.

All things and all beings are embedded in and permeated with the love for God and neighbor, the Light-Ether. The core of being in the very basis of every soul is, as essence, the cosmic love, it is the Primordial God in you, in all of us, the light of His light.

Even though it is said that you, all of us, are from the breath of God and that God, the eternal love, is in you and that you, too, all of us, are permeated by the eternal ocean of love, the Light-Ether, the omnipresent Spirit, the Primordial God – all this is still by far no proof.

In our world there are many hypotheses and concepts regarding the Light-Ether, also called ether. But no author of a book or paper on energetic interrelationships, on life or All-Unity can prove the existence of the ether of the Being.

In addition, we frequently hear or read about the four forces in matter, using different scientific words.

We also hear or read about the atomic nucleus that also has different names, and about all that is achieved with energies.

We need think only of atomic energy, which ultimately, like all energies, is from the transformed-down power of drawing and creating and is abused in the most brutal ways.

We mostly read and hear about the four forces in matter.

The energies of matter are nothing more than transformed-down compressed ether.

The depths of the All, in terms of the infinite Light-Ether and what it contains, can never be totally grasped by a three-dimensional brain, and certainly not when God, the All-Spirit, the highest Intelligence, His power of drawing and creating, which is the love for God and neighbor, is dismissed and transformed into self-love, that is, narcissism, into hatred, war and acts of cruelty.

Man is ultimately fishing in muddy waters and is of the opinion, "Someday everything will have been researched."

Without the substance content of the Light-Ether, the bearing and all-permeating, highest potentiated power, the love, no person can accomplish anything, let alone prove it all-encompassingly and in depth.

The Light-Ether is, after all, the highest light-filled-atomic power.

All spiritual ether atoms have a central nucleus, a primordial core, which consists of Kindness, Love and Gentleness. The Kindness and Gentleness of the Eternal are incorporated in His Love. They are the three attributes of God, the Father-Mother-Principle, which is the highest pulsating power, the Love.

The love for God and neighbor is the motive power that initiates the drawing and creating of all divine forms. This is the spiritual atomic nucleus, the primordial core of infinity. The four primordial powers, also called the nature powers, revolve around the spiritual atomic nucleus.

All in all, this is the law of drawing and creating of the Primordial God, which is the flowing Light-Ether.

In the infinite, all-permeating and all-communicative Light-Ether, which can also be described as the All-ocean, the mighty Kingdom of God is embedded, as well as all other finer-material spheres, also called cosmoses, which are already associated with the Fall-thought and the rebellious beings, as well as the material cosmos.

Without exception, everything and all forms, beings and people are surrounded by the eternal Light-Ether of infinity.

Whether we talk about divine life forms, about spirit beings, rebellious beings or about animals, plants and human beings – everything, absolutely everything, is surrounded by the inexhaustible Light-Ether of infinity and is permeated by the Infinite.

Spoken with our words: Everything lives; we all live, that is, move, in the mighty ocean, God.

The primordial nucleus is the motive energy of the love for God and neighbor.
Anyone who does not fathom and acknowledge this and live accordingly will never decipher the Light-Ether as the primordial law of infinity, the primordial atomic nucleus, around which revolve the four primordial powers, the drawing and creating powers of God.

The holistic principle of eternity is the primordial nucleus, the love for God, and, as stated, the four primordial powers, the energies of drawing and creating of the Eternal One.

Mankind of all generations has not oriented itself to God, to the love for God and neighbor, but always to the intellectual agents of warfare, to the four reversed primordial powers.

We human beings experience daily what comes of this. As stated: The Fall-thought, the dissolution of creation, to lead everything back into the ether, and then itself, to draw and create, was not achieved, that is, realized.

The highest energy, which the rebellious beings took with them, has reached point zero. It is largely used up.

Because this is so, mankind is degenerating more and more and, with what is still left of the negative power, it is going against God's love, against the world of animals, plants and minerals. The killing machinery keeps rolling.
It's true that man can very well take a handful of eternal Light-Ether and for a period of time operate with only the four powers.

Man can rebel against the love for God and neighbor and use up His four powers of drawing and creating, that is, transform them down.

Man can create arsenals of weapons, in order to kill. We can build airplanes, ships and other means of transport. We can create atomic power plants. We can build satellites and send them around the planet Earth. We try to design and build orbital gliders. But we will not be able to conquer the planets in the universe and turn them into dwelling planets, because we lack the love for God and neighbor.

We can torture the beings from God's thought of creation, from His love, the animals, we can wantonly kill them, massacre them and consume them as the chief motivation for eating.

We can do animal testing.

We can exploit the Earth and test our warfare agents on it. We can build dams; we can interfere in the flow of the water veins. We can build skyscrapers.

But one thing is denied us: Using these ways and means to transform up the energies entrusted to the Fall, and thus attain with this the Light-Ether, which is the life.
Mankind of all generations has failed.

The life of the All-One is the love for His All-creation, in which the All-Being is embedded.
The time has come. The amount of divine energy that was taken along is largely used up. The Eternal is taking the life back into eternity.
People of all generations have transformed down the handful of Light-Ether to such an extent, and exhausted it using cruel ways and means, so that there is hardly enough anymore for another inflated centrifugal force of human ignorance.

Science, which, as stated, is fishing in muddy waters, will not find the aforementioned primordial nucleus, the motive force in the Light-Ether, because, in general, there is no communication with the Light-Ether. Where there is no communication, nothing can develop, either.

Mankind of all generations has more or less rejected the love for God and neighbor, because it loved, and loves, the Fall-thought, the inflated self-love, which says, "I am my own best friend. I am like God or even God himself."

Anyone who works for himself, loses.

Anyone who works for the Highest, which is love, wins, because the carrier substance of all life, all Being, is love – love for the nature kingdoms, love for each planet, love for the world of animals and plants, love for each mineral, love for neighbor, love for all of creation.

Where has love been left off? In the scientific drive or even in stone houses, where a church god should be worshiped?

Love is the law of freedom, which Jesus of Nazareth taught us: *Love your neighbor as yourself.*
God's love is the All-Unity.
With love, it is not physical love that is meant but the love for God and neighbor.

Mankind of all generations has tried to conquer the planet Earth with brutality, to make everything that belongs to the Eternal its possession. Today, it can be seen that it is not man who could make of the Earth his possession – the Earth is overtaking man, who is its property, earth to earth.
Mankind has not learned to make use of the Light-Ether for peaceful purposes, the Light-Ether, which, as such, is the All-Unity, to which all divine life forms, all pure Being belong.

The Fall-beings and the people of all generations had their window of time.
The transformation is underway, from the coarse-material to the finer-material and from the finer-material to the fine-material.
Very gradually, from one window of time to the next, the Eternal is taking back the handful of Light-Ether.

Mankind did not make use of its window of time. When we take a closer look at the seething, all-too-human volcano, mankind, then we experience the degeneration of the human race.
Today man is still a human being, tomorrow perhaps already a Neanderthal. And what then? How will it go on?

With our three-dimensional way of seeing things, we human beings cannot designate a time – no matter whether science talks about millions or billions of years – in which evolution took place, albeit downward, toward an ever denser and darker mass.
We human beings know the word eon; but we cannot calculate it.

One thing is certain: In this handful of Light-Ether is contained the essence of infinity's All-drawing and All-creating energy, because, after all, everything is contained in everything.
Blind, dull and clinging to superstition, mankind moves in the principle of "divide, bind and rule."
We can compare the whole thing to an ice floe, drifting on the mighty All-ocean, the All-ether, the All-Being. The ice floe, the masses of humanity, seeks again and again the connection to the drifting icebergs, which present themselves as science and religion, in order to perhaps be able to dock there and find security.
As long as the person himself does not begin to search, with the simplest words, "God, the infinite love, in him; God in all of us, in all creation forms of the nature kingdoms," neither man nor

man's soul will reach the Light-Ether, the highest potentiated source of Light-Ether, God, the heavenly Father.

Dear fellow people, surely you are interested in what a scientist has compiled for this book, what he reports about the emergence of the Earth.
Perhaps you can read many a thing out of it and get your bearings somewhere in a sentence, in the awareness:
You, all of us, move – symbolically spoken – in the mighty ocean of the inexhaustible, eternal Light-Ether, of the eternal God, the eternal Intelligence, the Creator-power, which we, as His sons and daughters, may call "Father."

When you read about the history of the Earth, think about God's work of drawing and creating. In one handful of Light-Ether, all is contained in everything.

Mankind of all generations has squandered its chances. The Fall-energy is largely used up; there is only one thing to do: Onward to the All-One.

The Emergence of the Earth According to the Present Position of Science

The findings of science are subject to constant change and expansion. It is certain that science today is very far from being able to decipher all the interrelationships in the material universe. This also applies to knowledge about the emergence of the Earth. But during past years and decades, science has come up with many new findings that, with all due caution regarding the soundness of individual statements, do contain many details describing an evolution from the so-called "Big Bang" until today, which vaguely remind us of the truth about the eternal Being and the emergence of the purely spiritual worlds described in this book.

As we've heard, the material universe – in contrast to the fine-material universe and to the finer-material universe – consists of the most strongly condensed and transformed-down energy. Everything that happens in the material universe is therefore tied to the three dimensions. For this reason, all possible phenomena and processes are not directly comparable with the processes in the pure Being, which is seven-dimensional.

Nevertheless, we can recognize that – similar to the pure Being – an evolution in cycles and rhythms also takes place in the material universe, from the very beginning to ever more complex and differentiated forms, from the very beginning of matter to the emergence of the heavenly bodies, all the way to all forms of life, from the minerals to the plants and animals, all the way to human beings.

You will frequently discover parallels and perhaps conclude that the blueprint of the material universe, as it formed according to the Fall-concept of the rebellious beings, is nothing but a pale reflection of the creation plans of the All-Intelligence, God, in the pure Being. In the three-dimensional world only little is left of the beauty and perfection of the eternal creation, which is still being maintained by the remaining quantity from the handful of Light-Ether taken along by the rebellious beings.

From the viewpoint of the present position of science, how the Earth emerged in this three-dimensional sphere is explained as follows by a scientist:

The history of the Earth can be divided into four great eras, namely the primeval time of the Earth, the Paleozoic Era, the Mesozoic Era and the Cenozoic Era. The individual periods are then further subdivided by geologists.

The primeval time of the Earth

Our solar system, including the Earth, emerged about 4.6 billion years ago from a contracting cloud of gas and dust. Several tens of millions of years later, the moon also developed. It is assumed that it developed from the debris of a collision between the small planet Theia with the Earth. During the period from about 4.1 to 3.8 billion years ago, meteorites very frequently hit the Earth and the moon, so that only about 3.8 billion years ago, a permanent, initially thin, earth crust was able to form. The gases rising from the Earth formed a dense atmosphere, which consisted primarily of water vapor and carbon dioxide. The condensation of the water vapor resulted in the formation of the oceans.

The primeval time of the Earth is also called Precambrian Time, and it encompasses the time from the emergence of the Earth until about 545 million years ago. Thus, the earliest phase en-

compasses a very long time, namely, about four-fifths of the entire history of the Earth. There are still rock complexes on Earth that are more than 3 billion years old. Such rock complexes can be found on all continents; they are called the "old shields" and form the oldest continental cores, respectively, around which all younger mountain ranges amassed. During the Precambrian Time, plate tectonics were much more intense than today; this means that there was a strong shifting and movement of the tectonic plates, causing numerous mountain ranges to develop and also to disappear.

Interestingly enough, the distribution of the continents and oceans changes every 200 to 300 million years during the course of Earth's history. Our solar system needs approximately just as long for an orbit around the center of the Milky Way.
Today, we are more or less certain that about 3.5 billion years ago microorganisms, so-called cyanobacteria (also known as blue-green algae), lived on the Earth. Still today there are up to 3.5 billion years old calculous, fungiform structures that are called stromatolites and that were formed from these bacteria. At that time, oxygen was not yet present in the Earth's atmosphere.

The cyanobacteria most likely came up with photosynthesis and, with the help of sunlight, were able to develop organic substances from water and carbon dioxide. The first bacteria still had no cell nucleus. The genetic substance, DNA, was free inside their cells. There were also no complicated inner structures yet, so-called organelles. For at least one billion years, there existed on Earth only these relatively simple single-cell organisms without cell nuclei. They formed the vanguard of life, as it were. These organisms continued to be the only living beings on Earth for a total of over three billion years. Multicelluar living beings have been on Earth for only about 8 to 9 hundred million years.

Over the course of millions of years, a gradual accumulation of oxygen took place in the atmosphere. Many single-cell organisms had no use for oxygen; it was even a cell poison. We could speak of an "oxygen disaster." Some single-cell organisms managed to cope with oxygen and to then use it to produce energy. The oldest known more highly developed cells are about 1.8 billion years old. During the primeval time of the Earth, the Precambrian Time, there were frequent massive glacial periods during which the Earth was almost completely covered with ice. In this connection, we use the term "snowball Earth."

About 580 million years ago, it appears that a stabilization of the climate occurred. Toward the end of the Precambrian Time, peculiar living beings appeared on Earth which, as we know from fossil finds, looked like little air mattresses or also fern leaves. These early living beings must have developed very well at first, because they didn't yet have any natural enemies.

During the transition period to the Paleozoic Era, very bizarre animal forms appeared, which geologists call "weird wonders." These animal forms have a certain similarity to arthropods and had a threatening appearance, for example, with mouths like circular saws, with five eyes in their head and with movable pincers on stalks.

The Paleozoic Era

This second era of the Earth began 545 million years ago and ended 251 million years ago.
Based on the development of organisms, the Paleozoic Era is divided into six periods, which have their own names: Cambrian, Ordovician, Silurian, Devonian, Carboniferous and lastly Permian.

In the Cambrian Period (545-495 million years), that is, at the beginning of the Mesozoic Era, there was a sudden explosion of life forms on Earth. In geology, "sudden" can be a timeframe of five to ten million years. Important index fossils in the Cambrian are the trilobites, which populated the Earth for many millions of years. At first, life existed only in the ocean.

During the Silurian Period (443-417 million years ago) the first conquest of dry land occurred. The Silurian plants still had very small "leaves" that looked more like thorns. Compared to modern plants they looked quite naked, which is why they are also described as vascular plants. During this period, even jawed fish appeared for the first time; in addition, fossils of huge crustaceans have been found, which could be up to two meters long and were thus the largest arthropods that ever lived on Earth.

During the Devonian Period (417–358 million years ago) the gill breathing of fish must have gradually evolved into the pulmonary respiration of land vertebrates. Thus, during the Devonian the first amphibians evolved that could live in water as well as on land. Proper fish, some of which looked like our present rays or skates, already were living in the oceans of that time.

A mass extinction occurred toward the end of the Devonian, probably due to the cooling of the climate. The Devonian was followed by the Carboniferous Period (358-296 million years ago) – the black coal age. At that time it was most likely quite hot on Earth and this led to rampant plant growth. Amphibians sometimes grew to huge forms, up to five meters long, and there were huge dragon flies with 60 cm wingspans.

The last period in the Paleozoic Era is called Permian (296-251 million years ago). During this period, increasingly large horsetail plants appeared along with conifers, because, on the whole, the climate became drier. Important salt deposits developed during the Permian, which are still mined today, for instance, in northern Germany. During the Permian, a certain kind of dinosaur first appeared, with a long sail on its back. At the end of the Permian, the largest mass extinction in the history of the Earth occurred, which claimed 75 to 90 percent of all animal species as victims.

The Mesozoic Era (251-65 million years ago)

The Mesozoic Era began about 250 million years ago and represents a kind of new beginning for living beings after the worst mass extinction of all time. During this era, the entire land mass was one single super continent, which we know as Pangaea. For this reason, land animals were able to spread out practically over the entire mainland, which can be easily recognized by fossil finds from that period. The climate was mostly hot and dry.
During the Triassic Period, the first mammals appeared, presumably small shrew-like animals. Turtles and crocodiles also originated during this period. New forms of saurians appeared on Earth. During the late Triassic, dinosaurs were already quite successful and had largely displaced other animal species. On the whole, dinosaurs dominated the continent for a good 150 million years. Today, birds represent the sole line of evolution from the dinosaurs that still live today and, from the viewpoint of evolution biology, are most closely related to crocodiles.
In the plant world, seed-bearing plants increasingly developed. Toward the end of this period, came the first precursors of flowering plants.

A shallow sea repeatedly formed on the great continent Pangaea, which is why very many fossils can be found today in limestone. The second period in the Mesozoic Era is called Jurassic; during this period a breakup of Pangaea occurred. During the Jurassic and the following Cretaceous Periods, dinosaurs experienced their great period of prosperity, whereby during the late Jurassic, the largest dinosaurs of all time appeared. In addition, primeval birds developed during the late Jurassic.

In the plant world of the Jurassic Period, gymnosperms such as conifers, ginkgo trees and palm ferns were widespread. The ammonites (snail-like living beings) attained their greatest diversity of species during the Jurassic, since there were numerous warm shallow seas. Such ammonites can frequently be found today as fossils in limestone.

The Cretaceous Period began 145 million years before the present time and lasted about 80 million years. It ended with the extinction of the dinosaurs 65 million years ago. During the Cretaceous, a clear separation into continents occurred and the Earth began to assume the formation of continents as we know it today. The sea level during the Cretaceous was much, much higher than at present, so that flat seas covered large parts of the continents. The sea level might have been about 200 meters higher than that of today. With the development of flowering plants, insects also increasingly appeared. The Cretaceous was the golden age of the dinosaurs; mammals played a still subordinate role. Mammals split into two large evolutionary lines: marsupials and placental mammals. In Australia and South America, the marsupials, for instance, kangaroos, koalas, opossums, developed in great diversity.

The Cretaceous Period and, with it, the Mesozoic Era ended 65 million years ago with a great mass extinction. It meant the end of the dinosaurs, which had lived for 150 million years. Most of the living beings in the oceans also died through this disaster, which is ascribed to the impact of an asteroid, which presumably had a diameter of about ten kilometers. The energy of this impact must have been absolutely gigantic; it was presumably about 10,000 to 100,000 times greater than the total energy of all existing atomic weapons. However, this cannot be precisely calculated. Over a long period of time, the Earth was enveloped in volcanic ash and dust; it was dark and cold on the Earth and, by and large, the photosynthesis of plants came to a standstill.

*The Cenozoic Era
(65 million years ago until today)*

The so-called Tertiary Period began about 65 million years ago and ended 2.6 million years ago. During the Tertiary, the continents moved to nearly their present positions. At first, the climate was still tropically warm, but cooled off very strongly during the second half of the Tertiary and turned into an Ice Age. During the Tertiary, the time of prosperity for the mammals began, which branched into numerous evolutionary lines. The genus man appeared on Earth approximately 2.5 million years ago; before that, there must have been so-called man-like beings. However, opinions in science regarding this change constantly.

The Tertiary Period was followed by the Quaternary Period, the period of the Ice Age and of man. The Quaternary Period began 2.6 million years ago. During the peak of the last glaciation, the sea level was about 120 meters lower than today. Winter in Europe must have been very icy, because the Gulf Stream nearly came to a standstill.

During the Quaternary, there were very many large mammal species, a so-called mega fauna, for example, mammoths, giant kangaroos, giant camels, big wolves, elephants, large ground sloths and giant armadillos. However, many of these huge species died out with the beginning of an interglacial interval, so that, of the large mammals, only elephants, rhinoceroses and hippopotamuses still exist.

The first species of the genus "Homo" probably lived about two million years ago in East Africa. The Neanderthals lived from 200,000 to 130,000 years ago. So-called modern man – Homo sapiens – has existed for approximately 100,000 years.

An Appeal

In this book, we are led step by step to a deeper understanding of the all-encompassing speaking All-Unity. The more we follow the explanations and carry out the exercises in the texts of this teaching and learning book ourselves, the deeper the awareness of the cosmic communication of the unity of all Being opens up in us. But we also learn to feel into the world of minerals and plants and especially that of animals

The animals in their multiplicity, which vitalize the Earth with their unencumbered nature, and which, like all life forms, desire growth and thriving, physical integrity, but also happiness and peace, suffer unspeakably under the arbitrariness of man. Particularly when we learn to understand the animals more and more in our hearts, we recognize even more how cruel it is when we human beings abuse the animals as useful commodities. Animals are robbed of their natural habitats and are kept shut in; they are kept imprisoned in unnatural conditions. They often eke out their existence in dark dungeons; others are hunted, fished, beaten, skinned, stabbed and shot down or tortured, mutilated and abused in experiments. Just as people are kept in prison after war, so does man wage war against the animals, as if they were his enemies. Man carries out these cruel acts, of which he is capable, on his fellow creatures. When we view all this before the background of the speaking All-Unity, the word of the universal Creator-Spirit, then it is an incomprehensible crime against life, against the animal world, which is a part of us in our innermost being.

But also in the global interplay of people and nations with each other, the law of unity is constantly being violated. While people starve to death on a daily basis, ducks are force-fed, for instance, in prosperous countries, so as to peddle their diseased, fatty livers to epicureans as a culinary delight on decadent tables. Every day, children die of hunger. They suffer endlessly, until death by starvation sets in, while the lavishly laid tables of the people in industrial countries are overladen with carcass pieces from all the kingdoms of nature. It is a barbaric scenario, the savagery of which cannot be described to a full extent.

It is a billionfold suffering of the animals – solely for the stomachs of surfeited people, for whom, during their festive meals, it is obviously easy to ignore the sorrowful eyes of hungry children with their undernourished bodies.

People who can daily reconcile their conscience to unscrupulously pen up animals in degrading conditions, to stuff them full of grain – which is kept from the starving children – only to then brutally slaughter these animals and consume them, have forgotten the compassion that unifies.

Therefore, dear fellow people, the appeal to you: May you, all of us, let the words flow deep into our being, and let us bring to mind the everlasting great Spirit, who works untiringly and who speaks to us in the speaking All-Unity. Then we will find our way to peace in us, to peace with creation and to justice toward our fellowman, which also includes sharing and mutual care.

Let us not look away from the unending suffering of the starving people and the enslaved animals. Let us look into the eyes of the children seeking help, for they hope for justice and kindness.

Let us also look into the animals' eyes – their look is the appeal to us to recognize in them our little brothers and sisters, who want to be our friend and who want to look up to us in the fellowship of the cosmic Being, as little brothers and sisters, to their big brothers and sisters, who are all children of the speaking All-Unity, creatures of the Being, beings from God.

We Are All Children of God

*For Self-observation
and Self-reflection*

*Mercy Would Be
the Wealth of Our Soul*

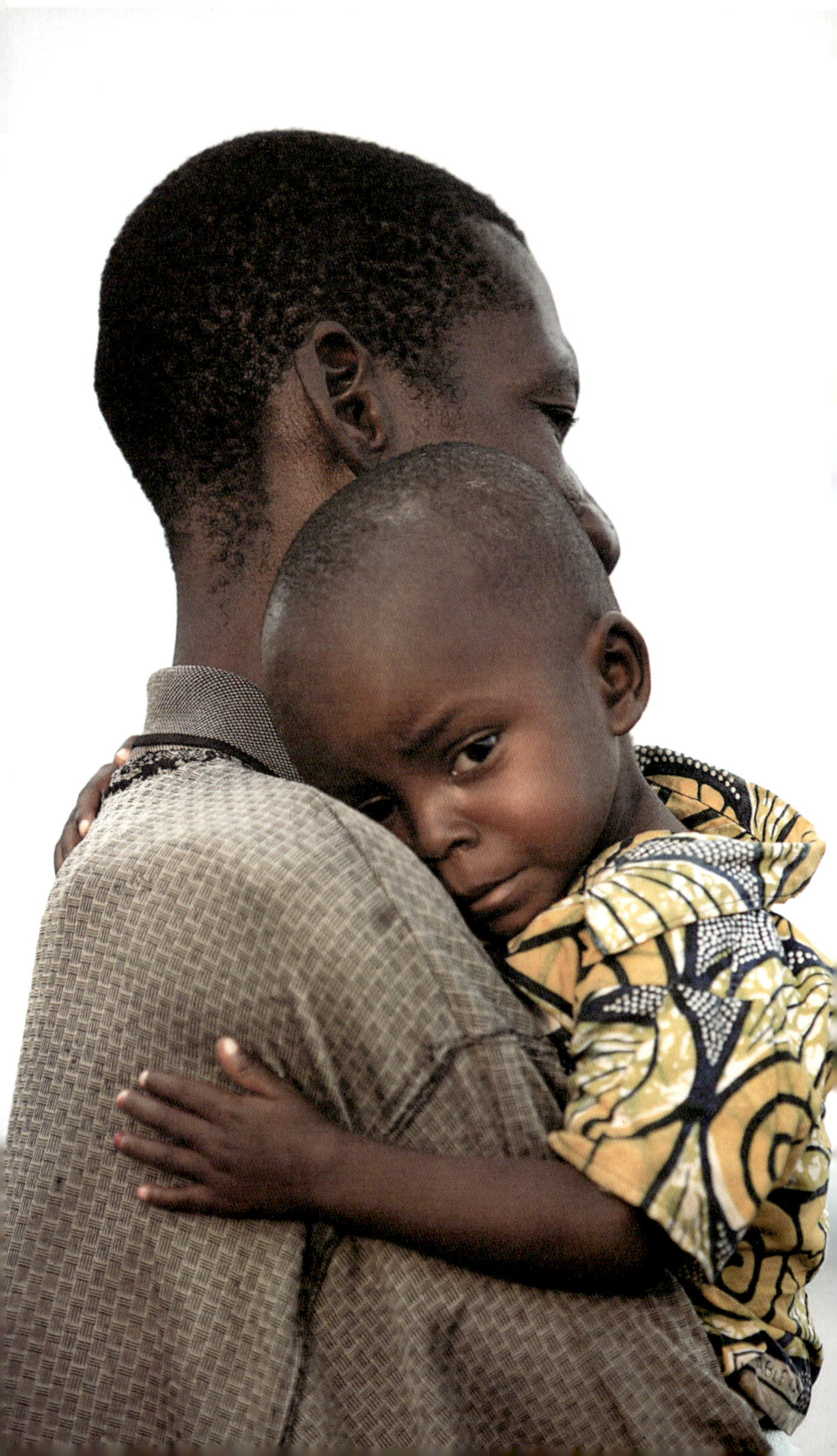

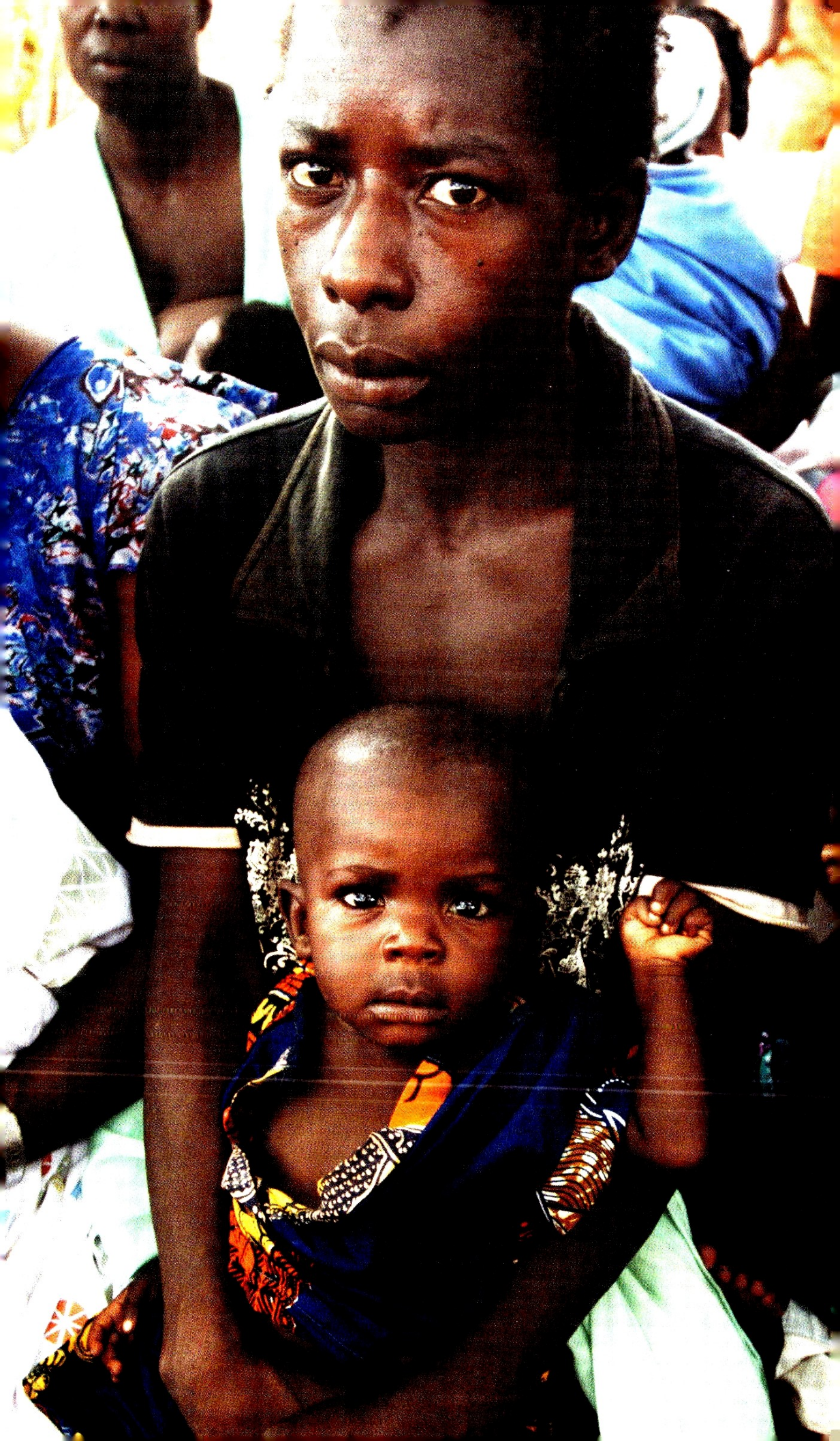

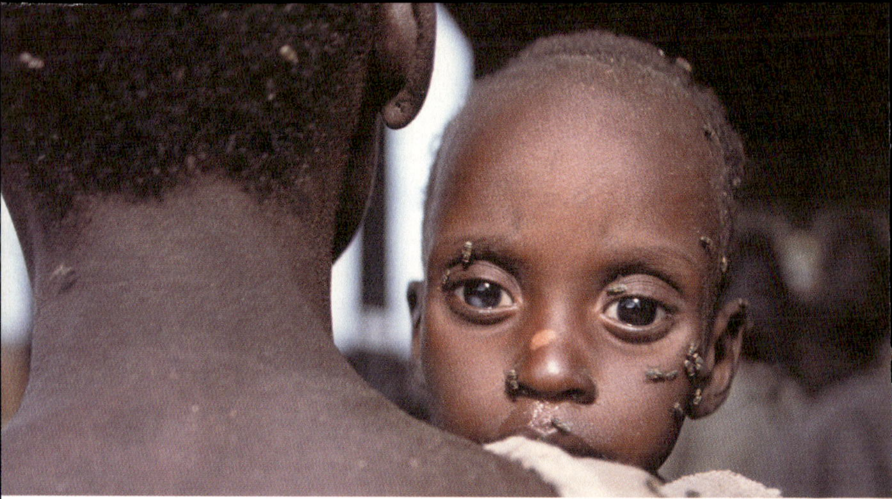

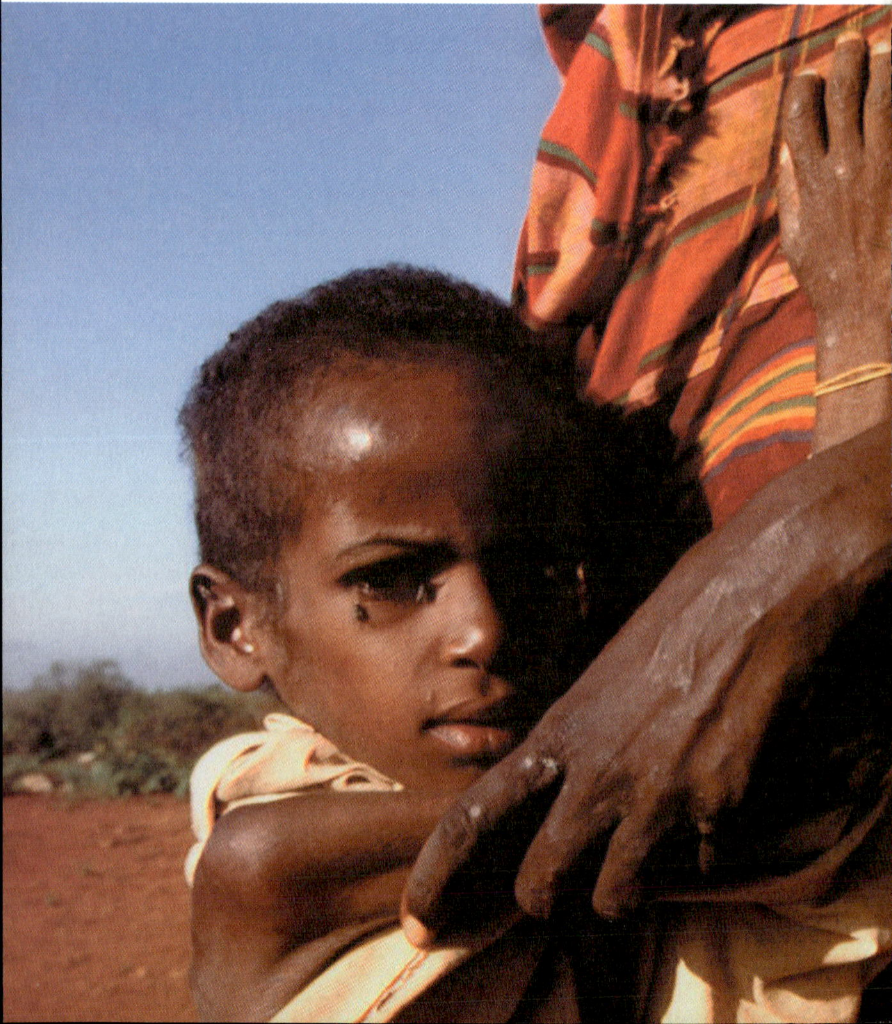

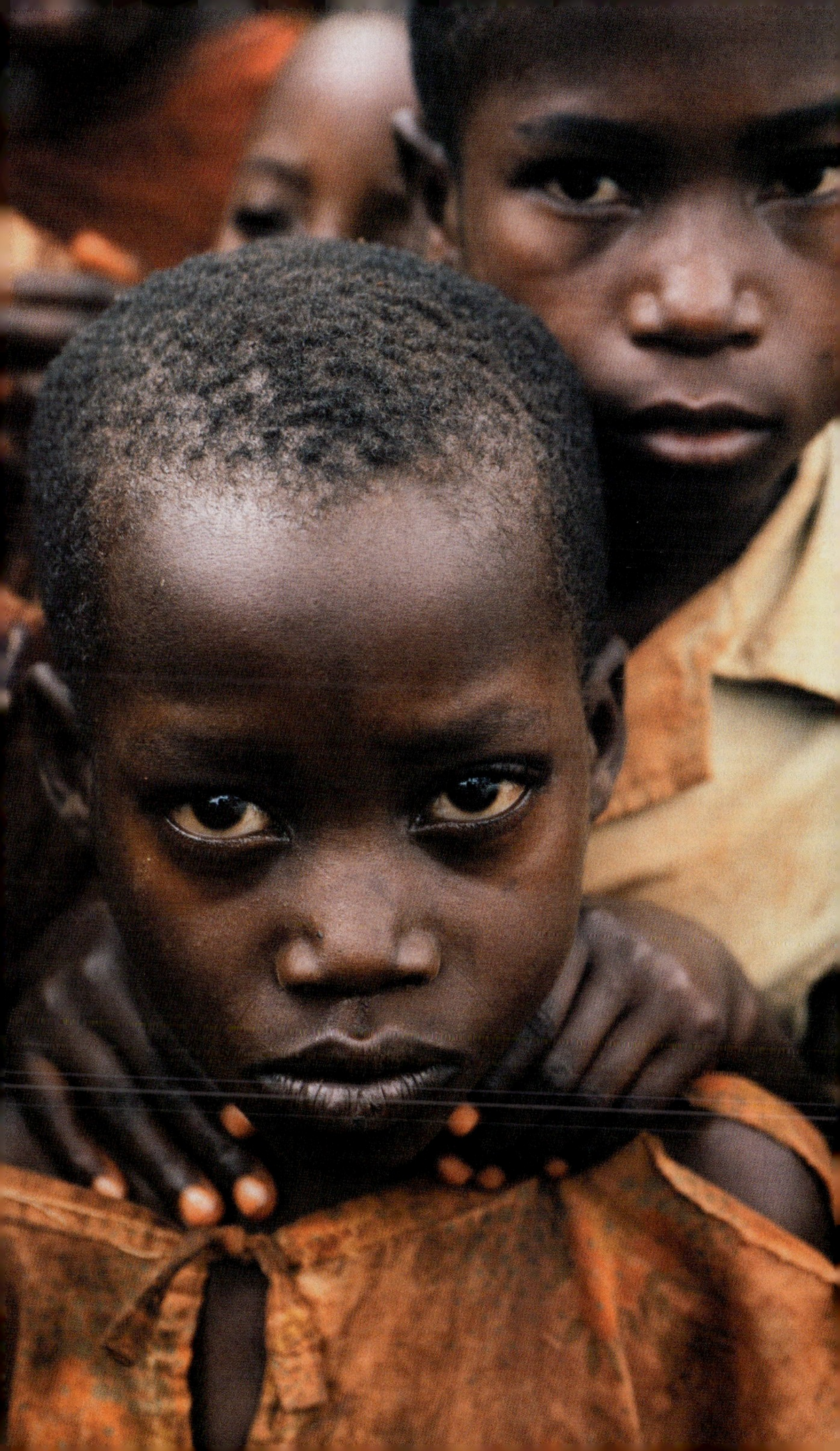

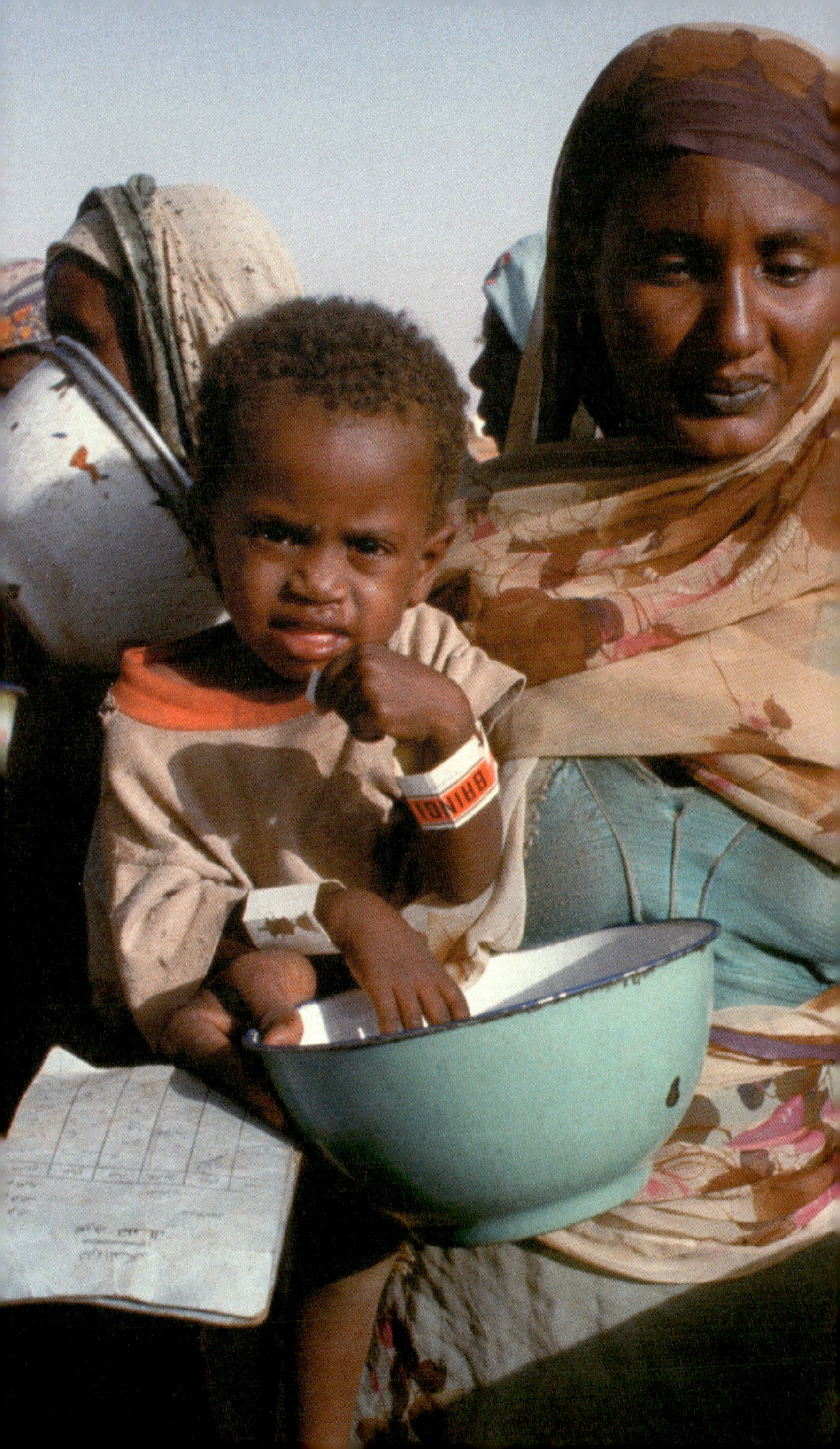

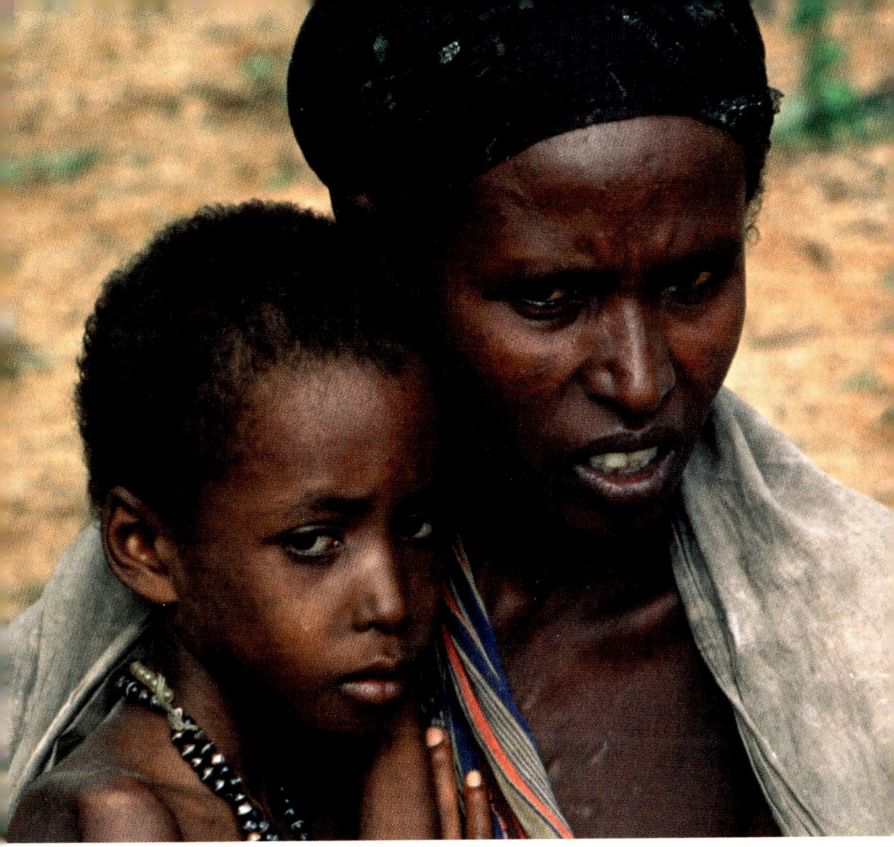
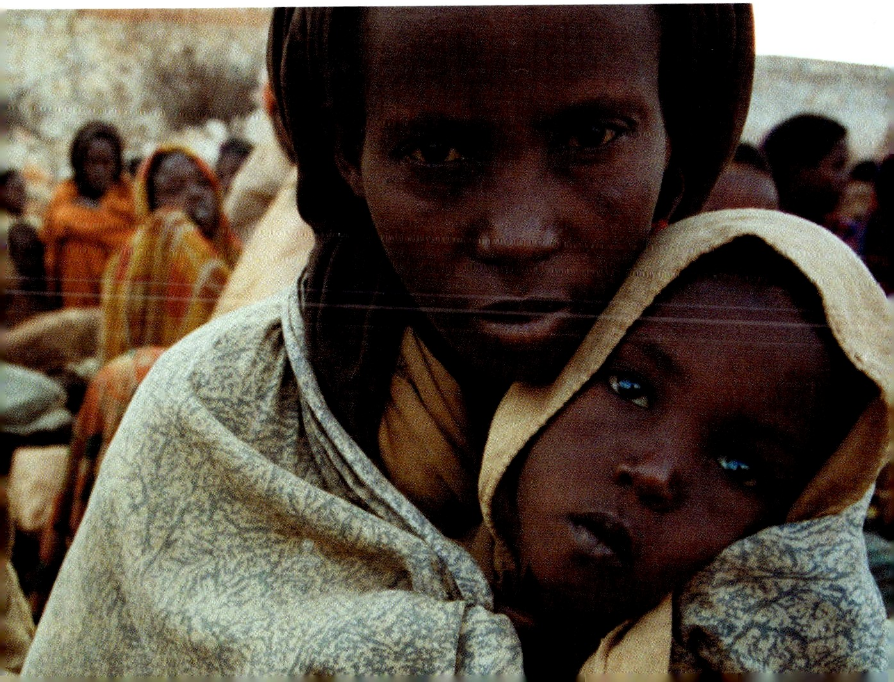

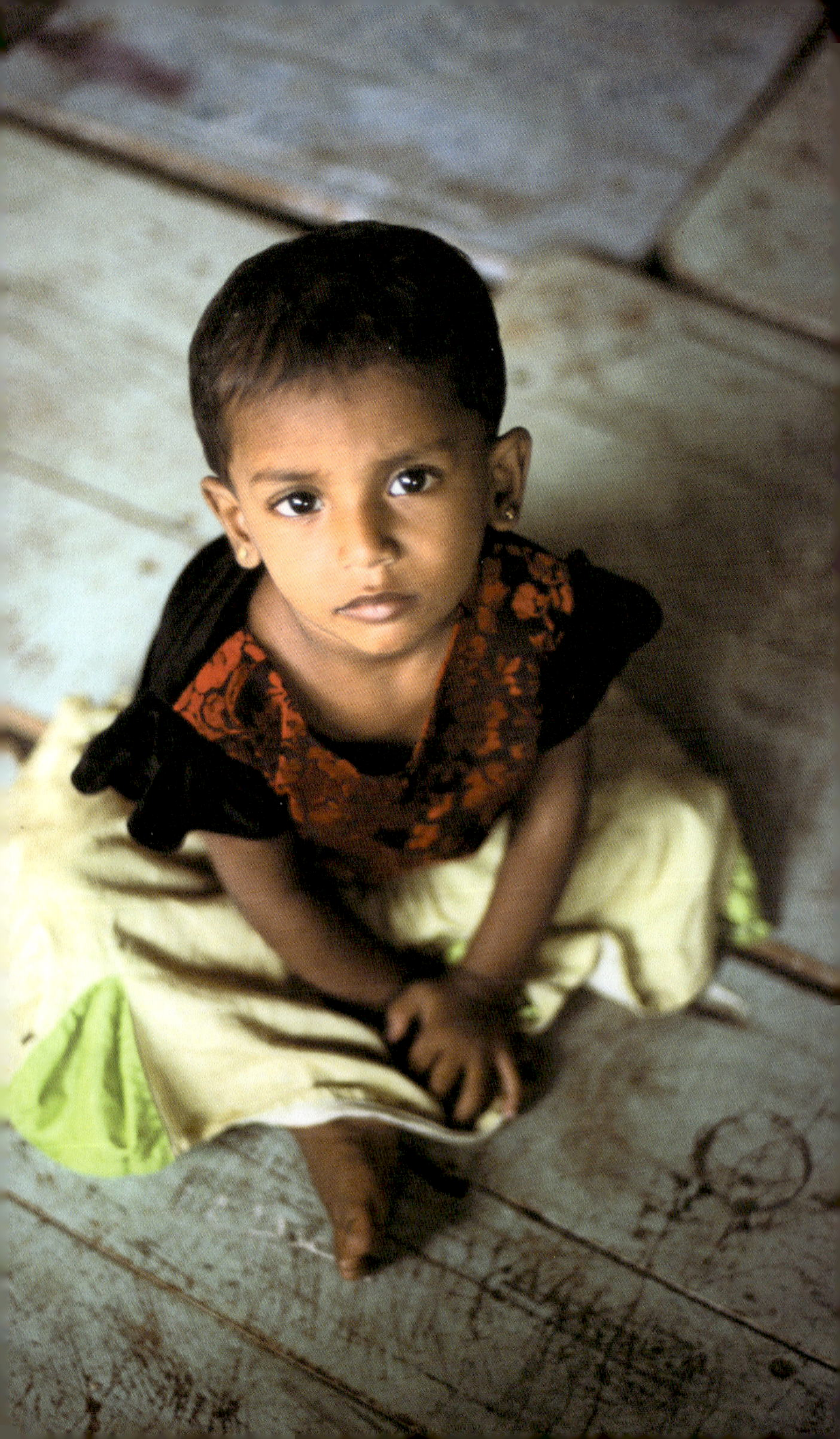

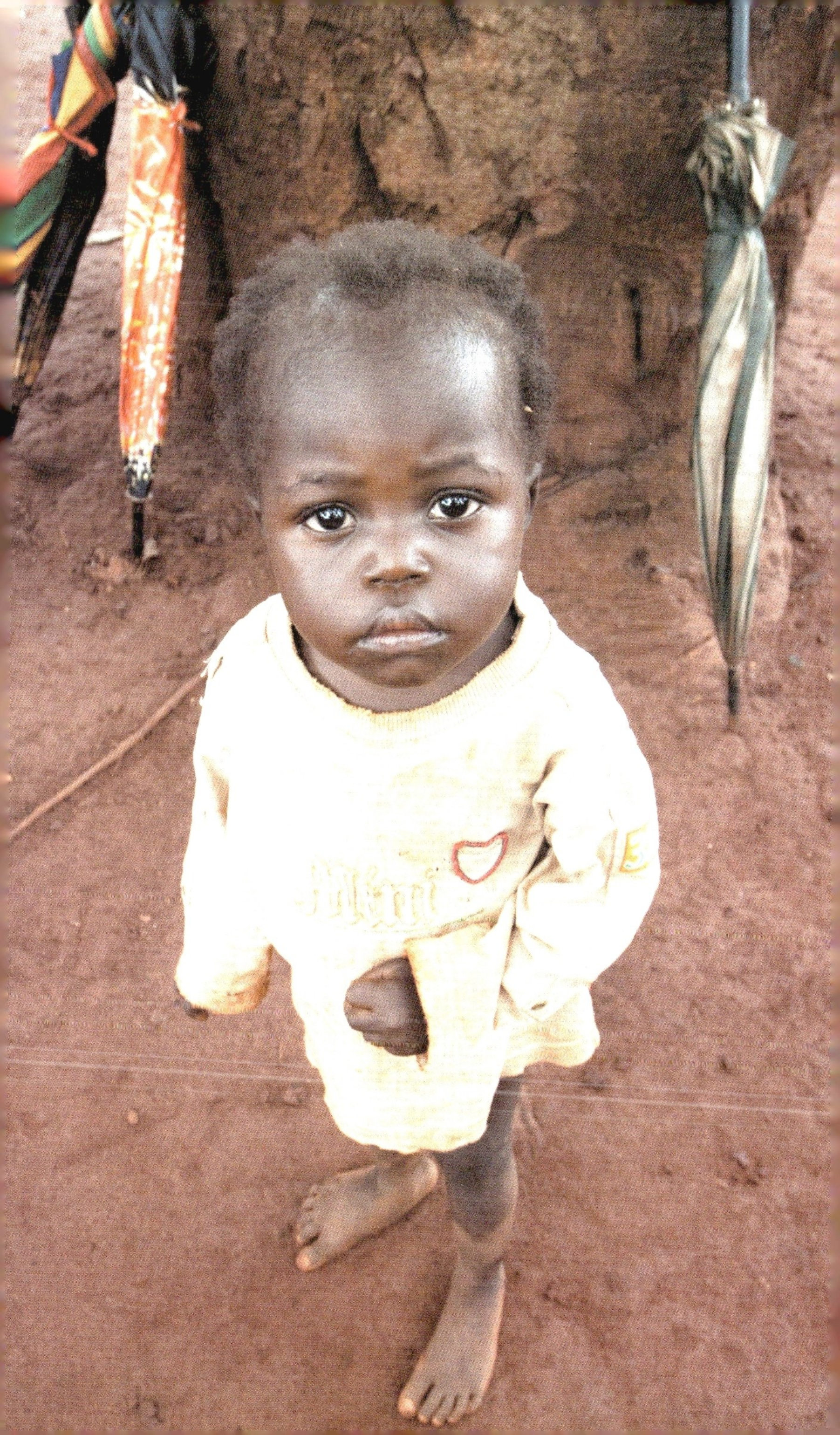

Let us go briefly within.

*Who or what
speaks to us?*

*I Am in Your Soul
as Power and Light*

For Virtual Observation

*The animals and plants that you see
on the following pages live on the
Land of Peace, which the
International Gabriele Foundation
is developing in the heart of Germany.*

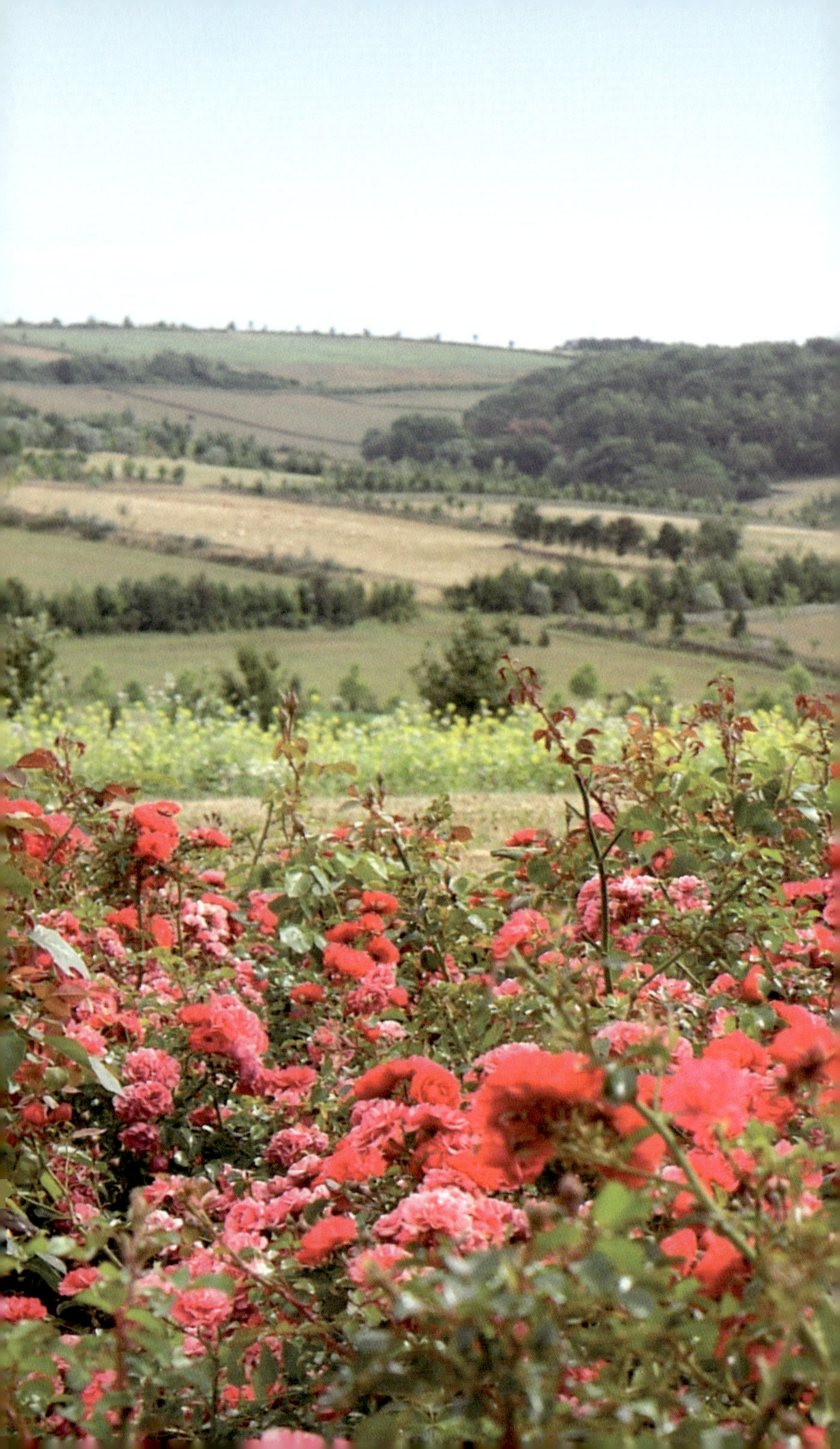

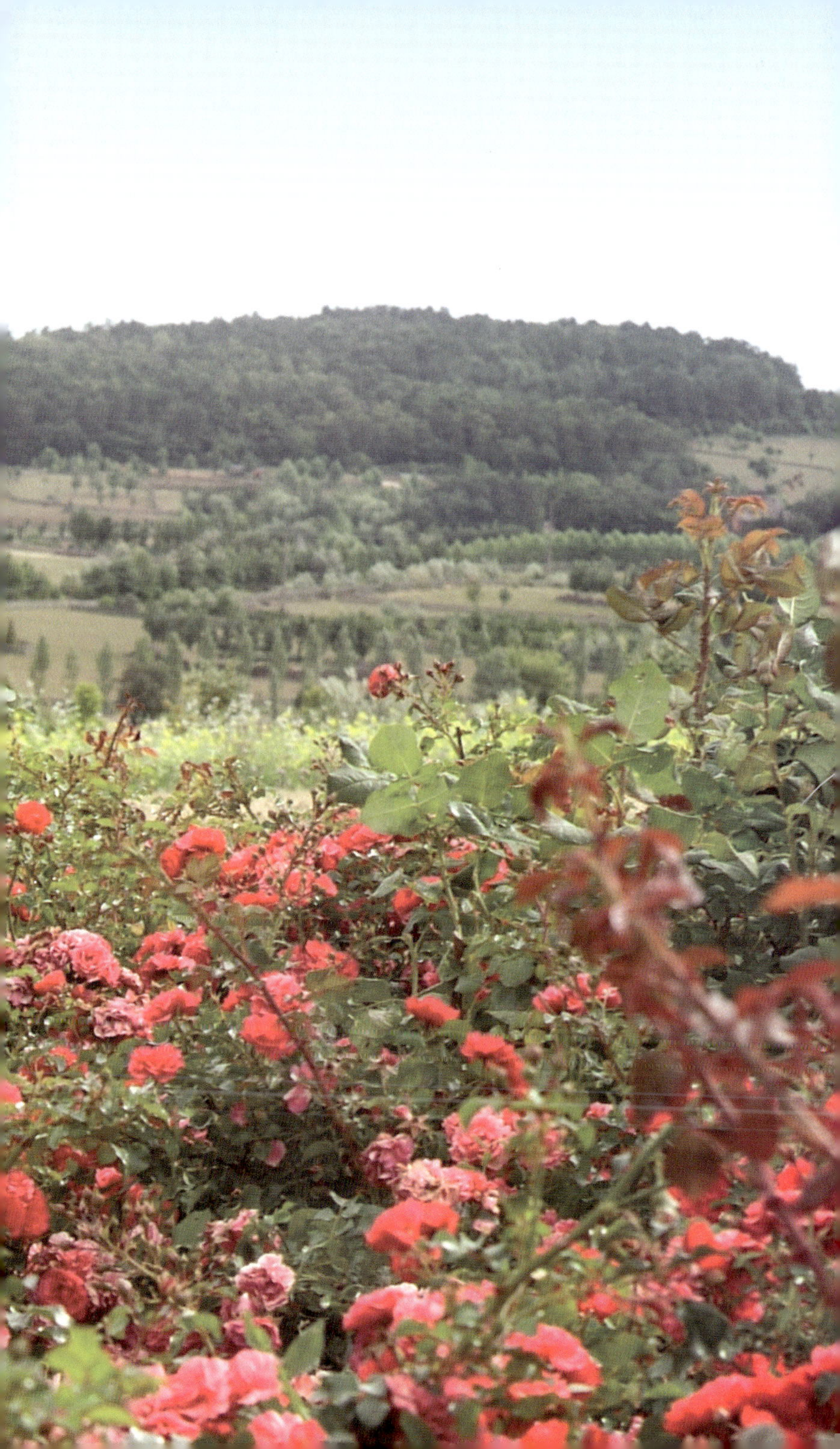

I am in your soul
as power and light.

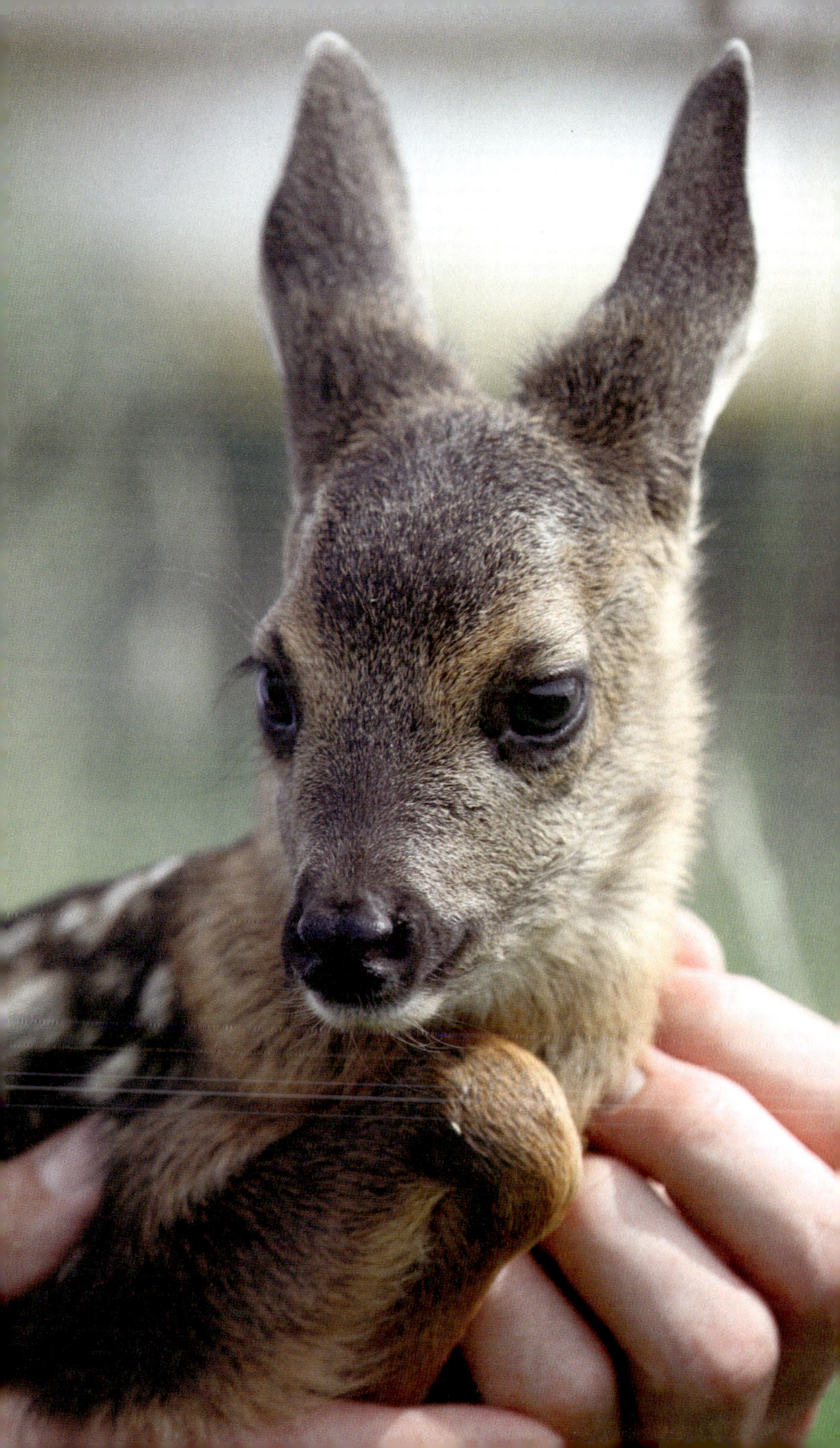

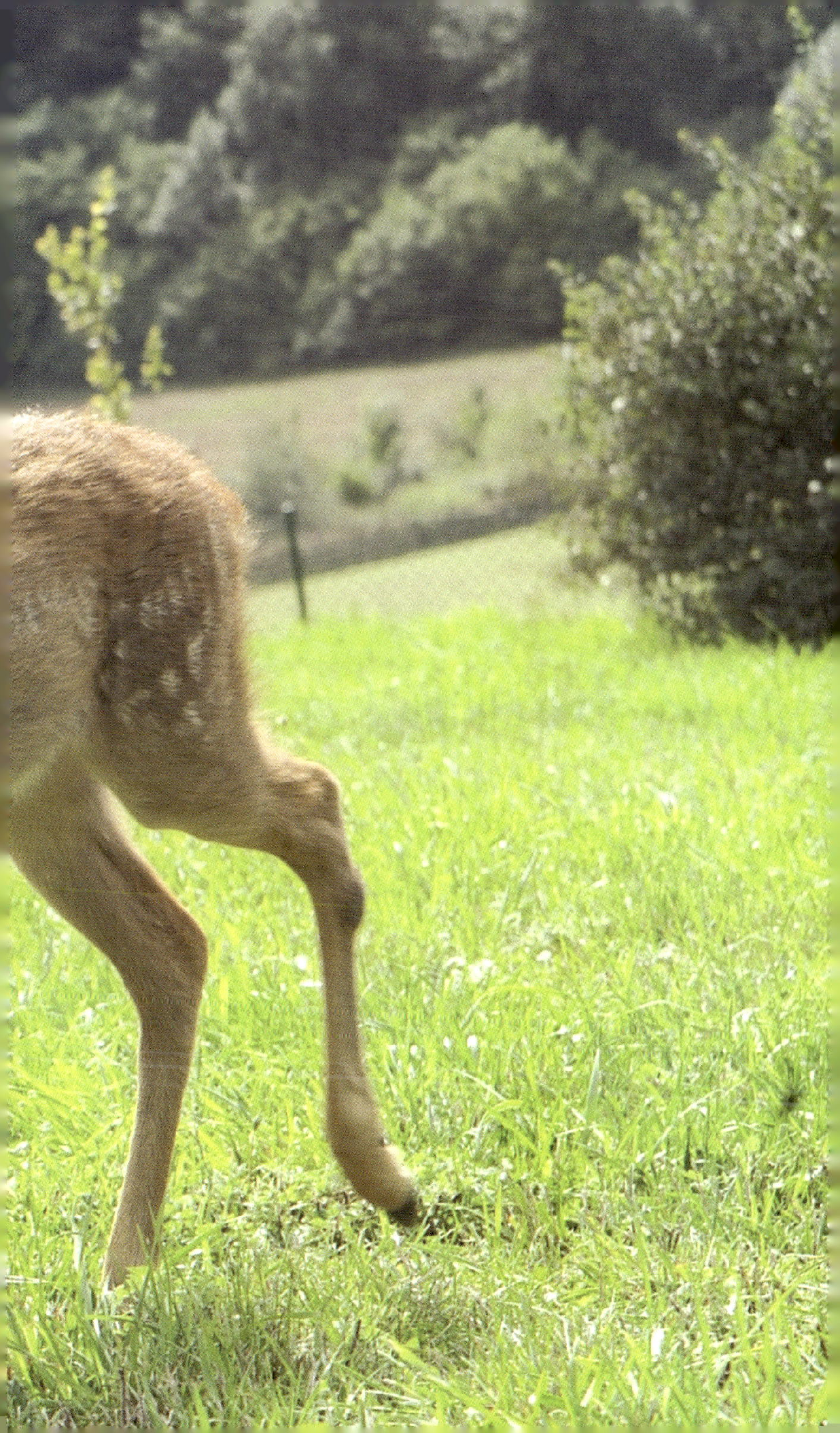

I am in your soul
as power and light.

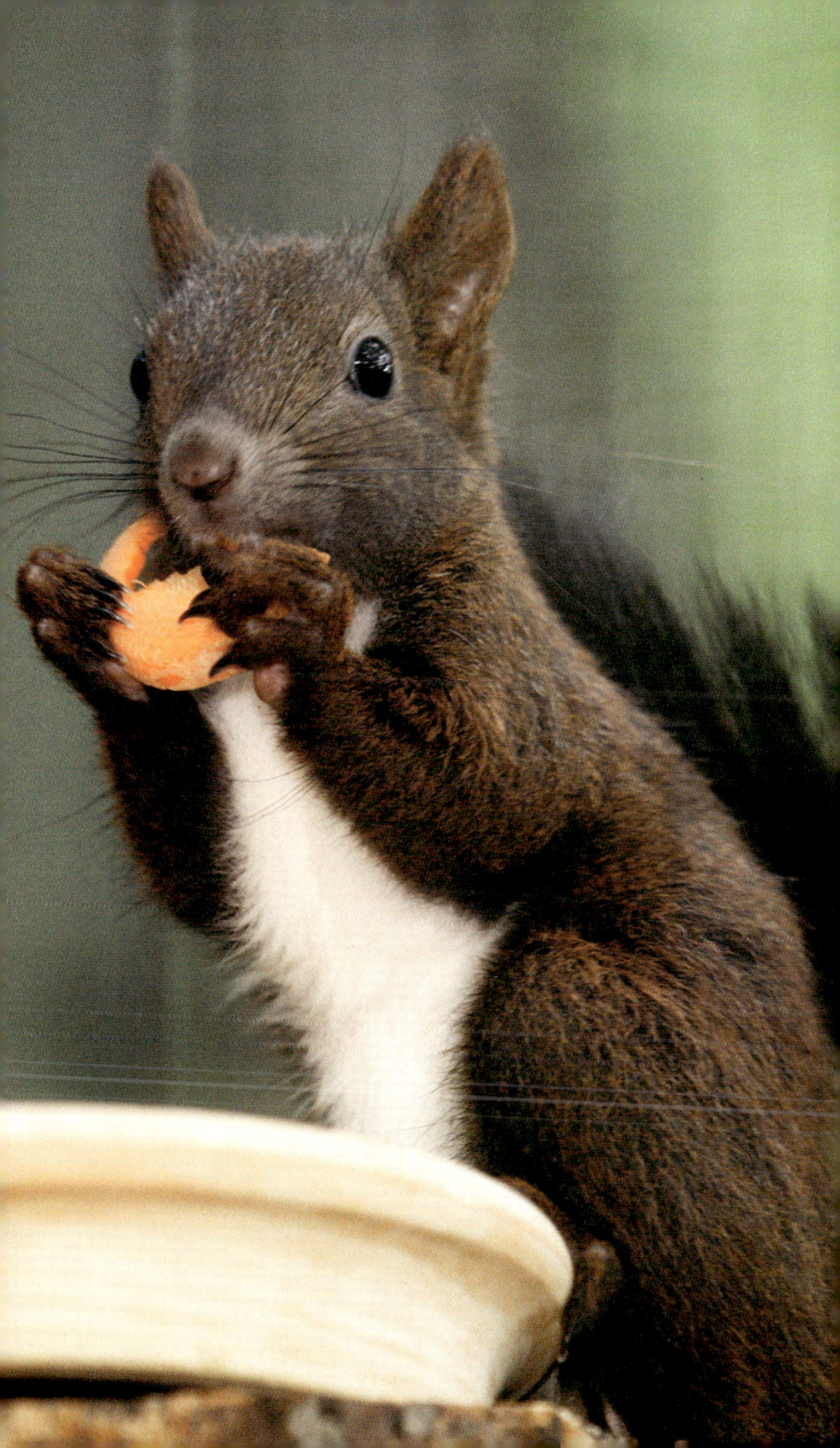

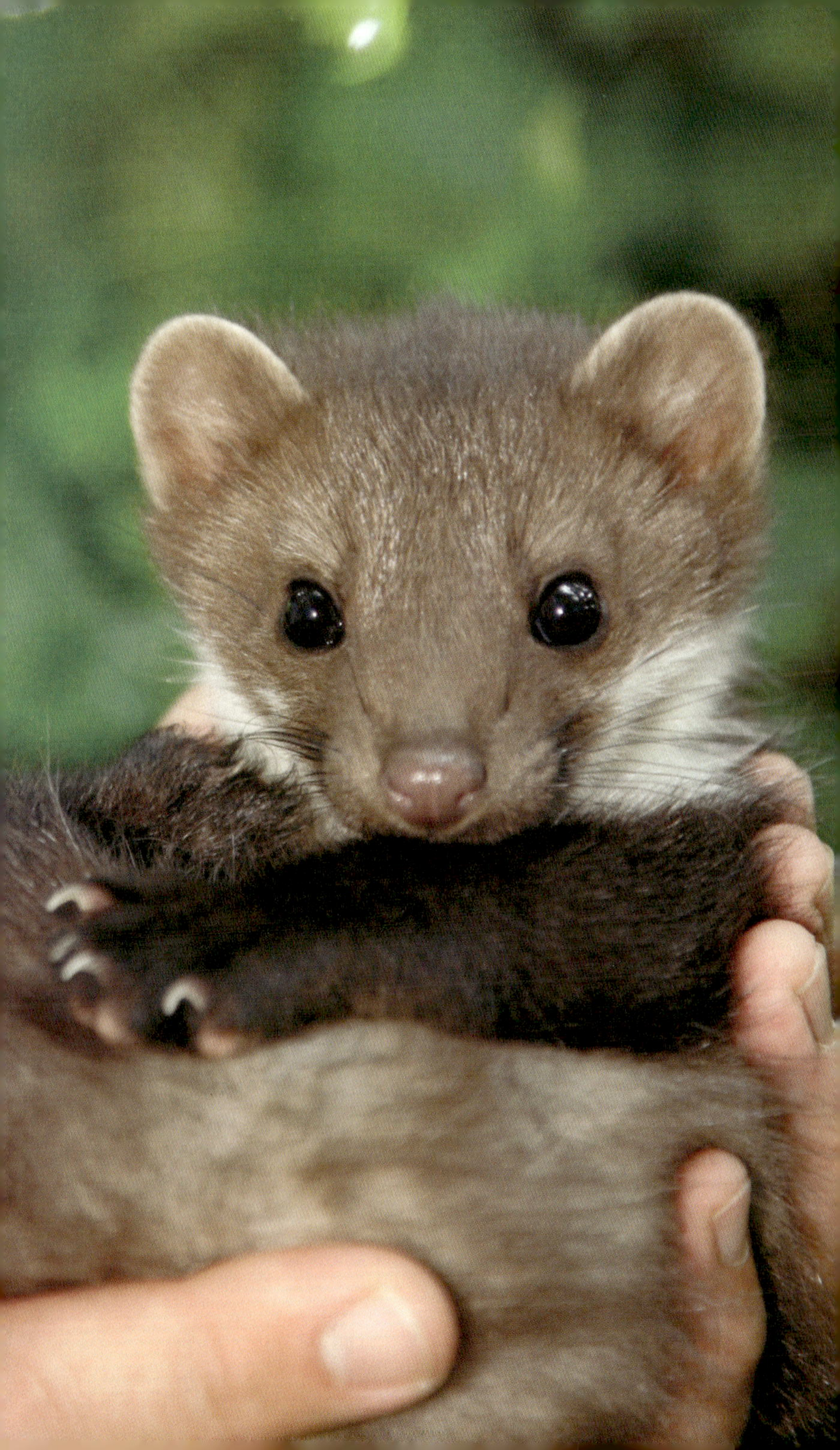

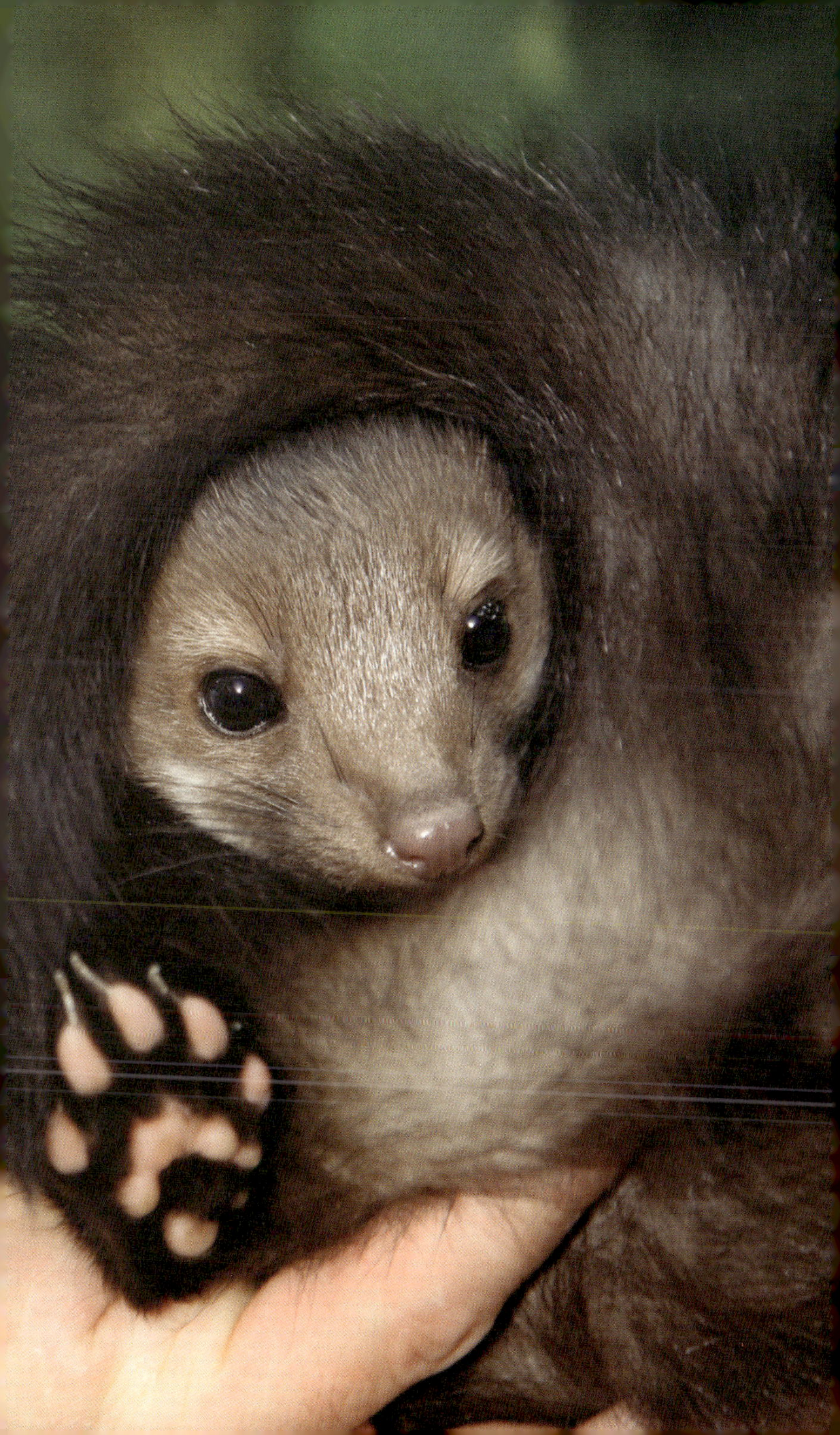

I am in your soul
as power and light.

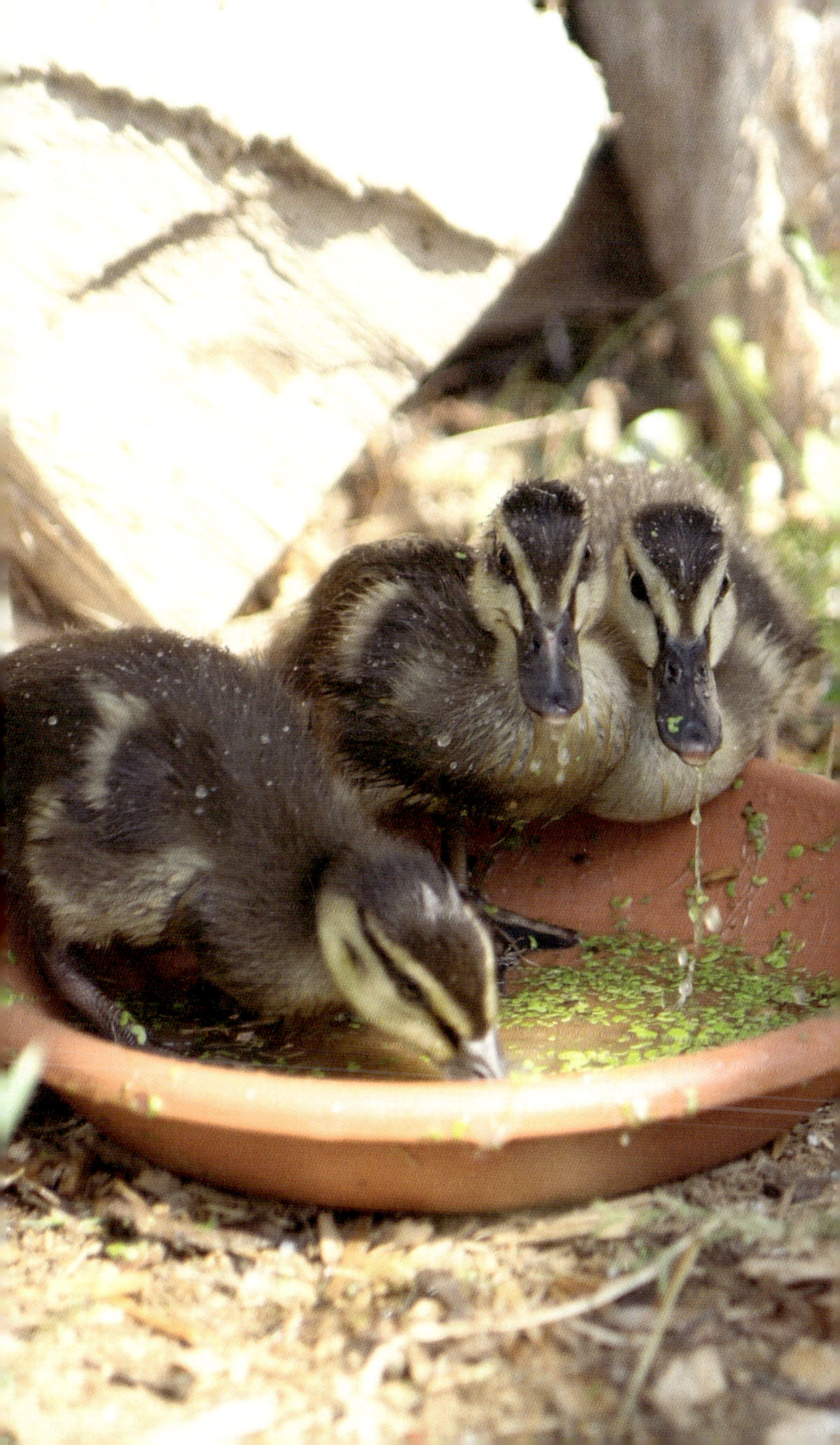

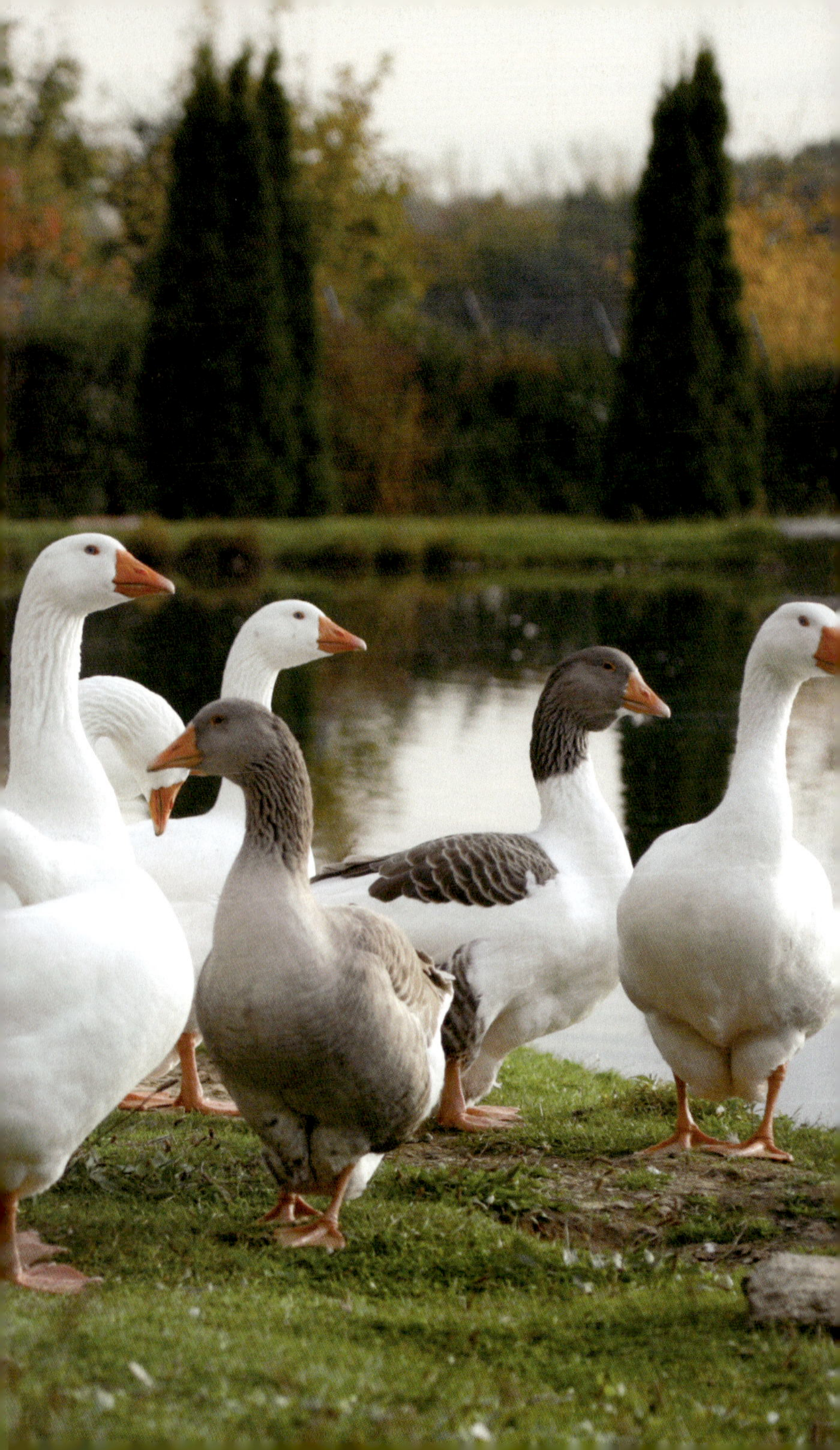

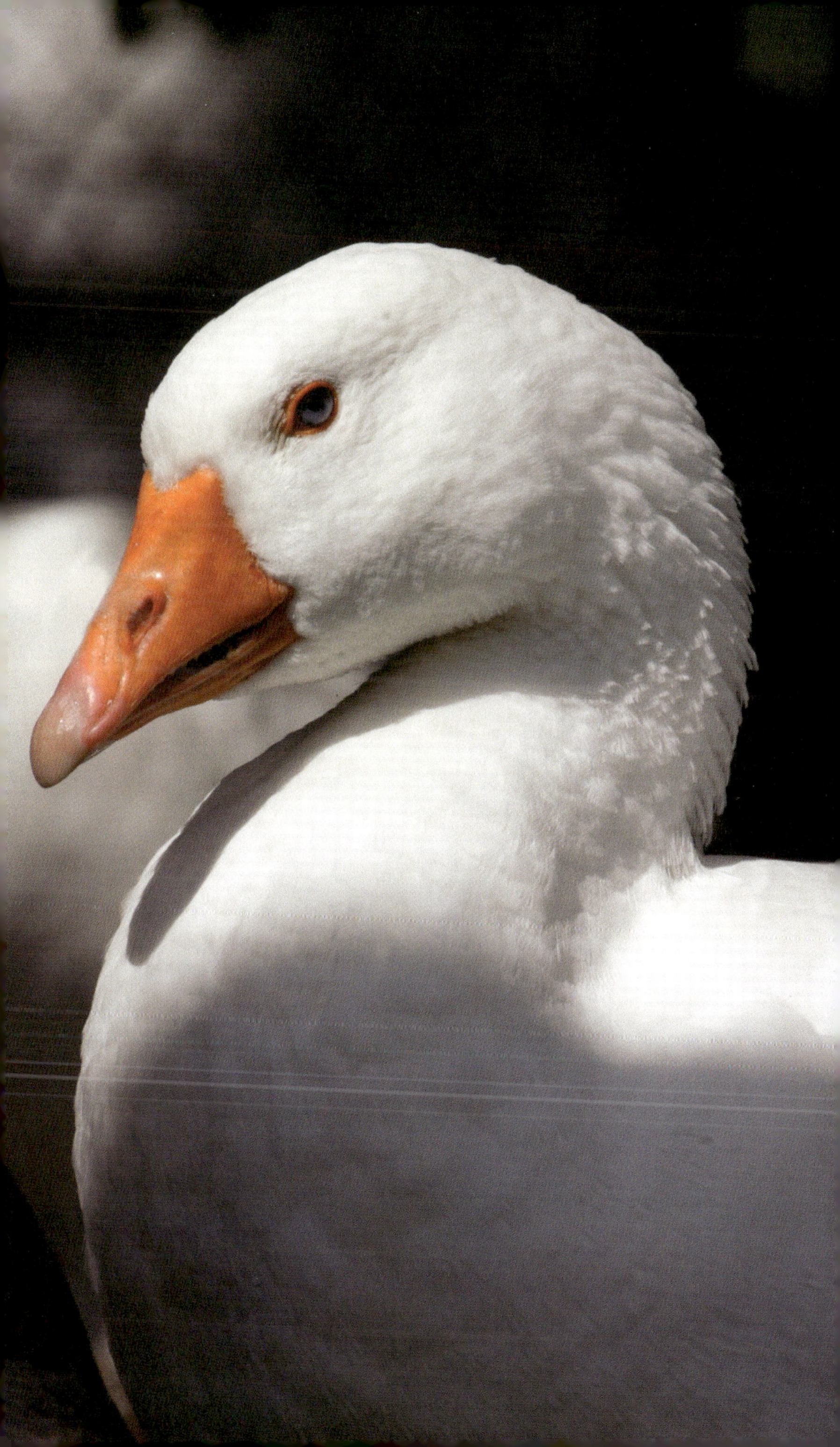

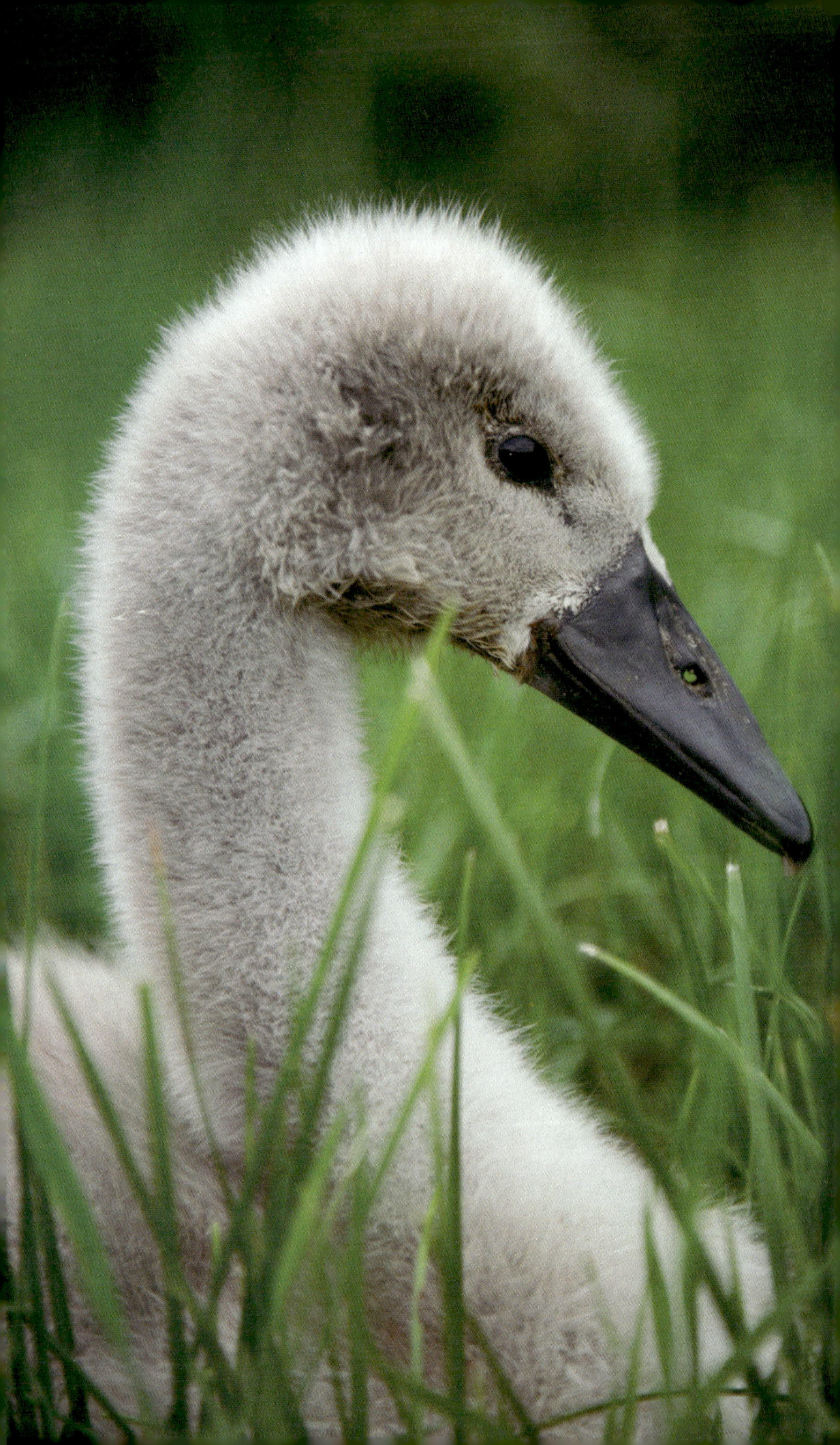

I am in your soul
as power and light.

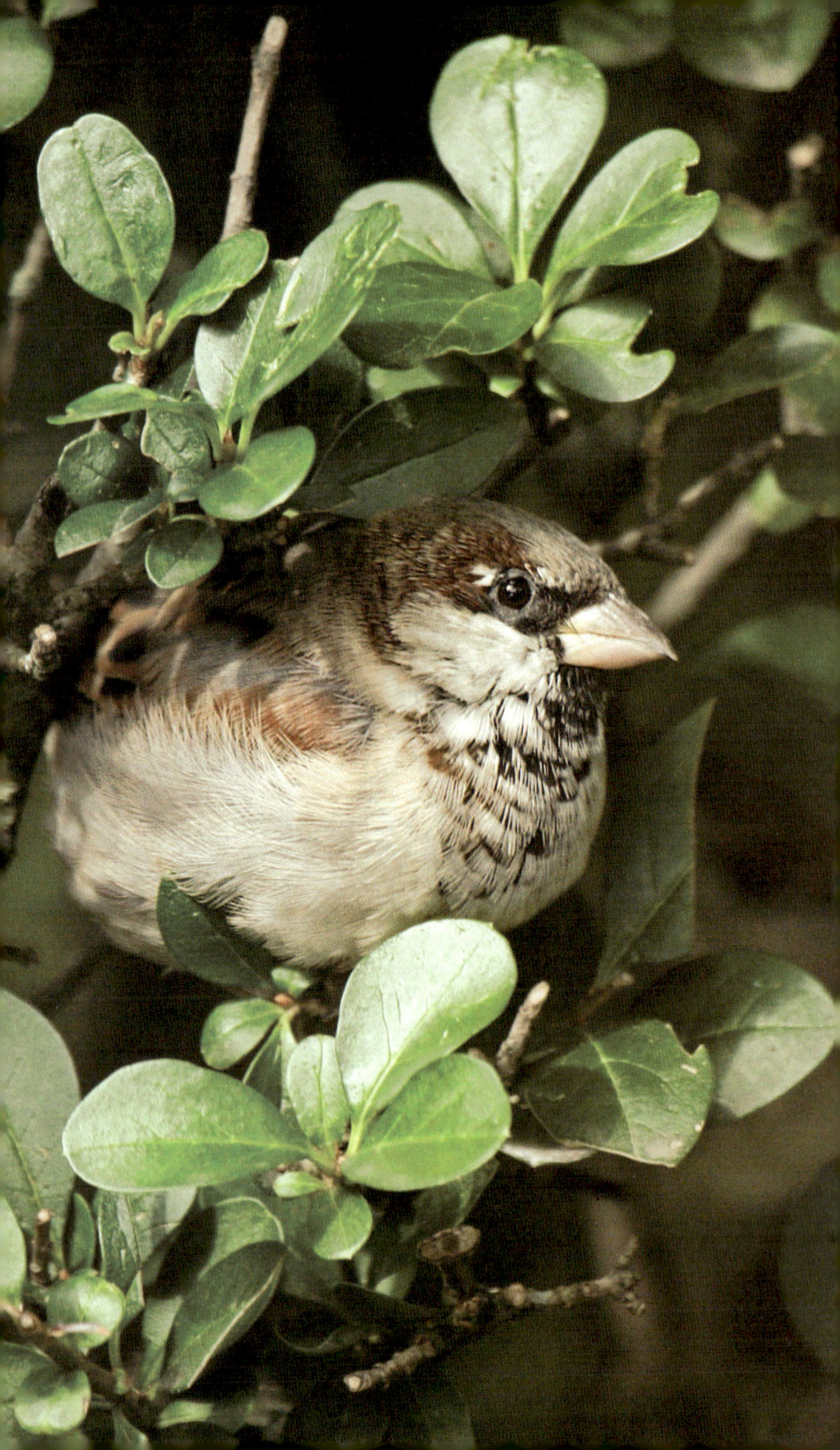

I am in your soul as power and light.

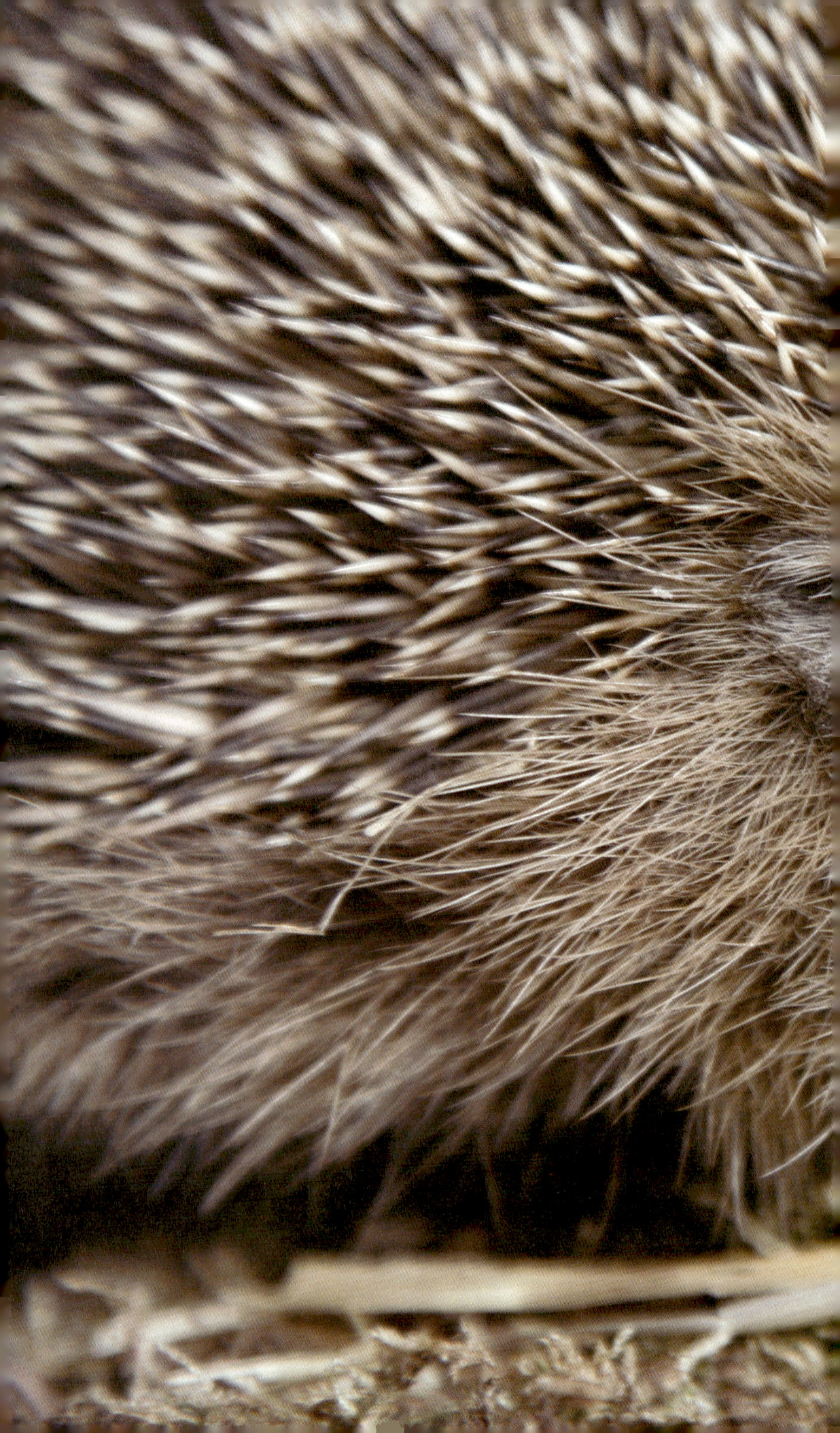

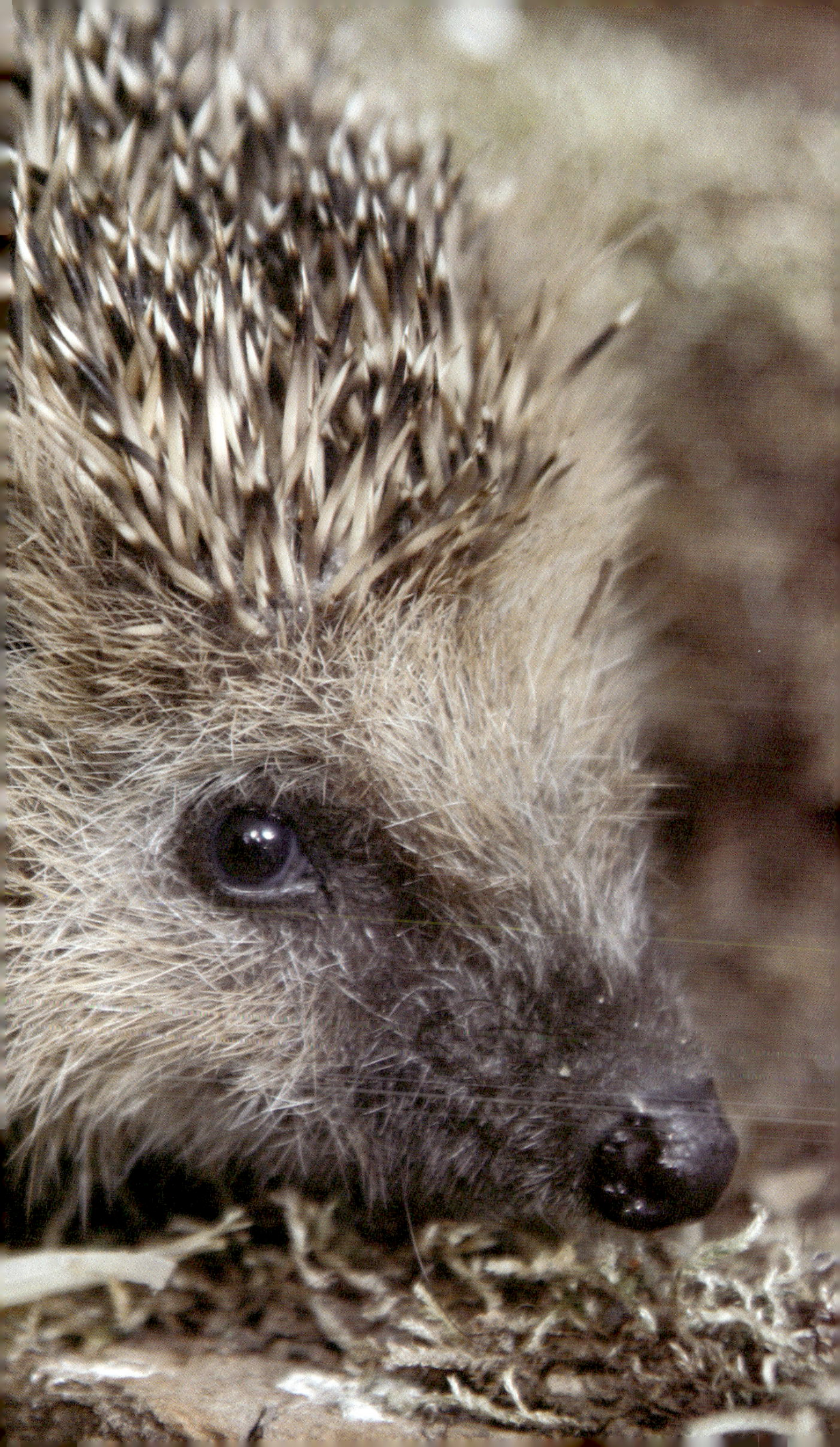

I am in your soul
as power and light.

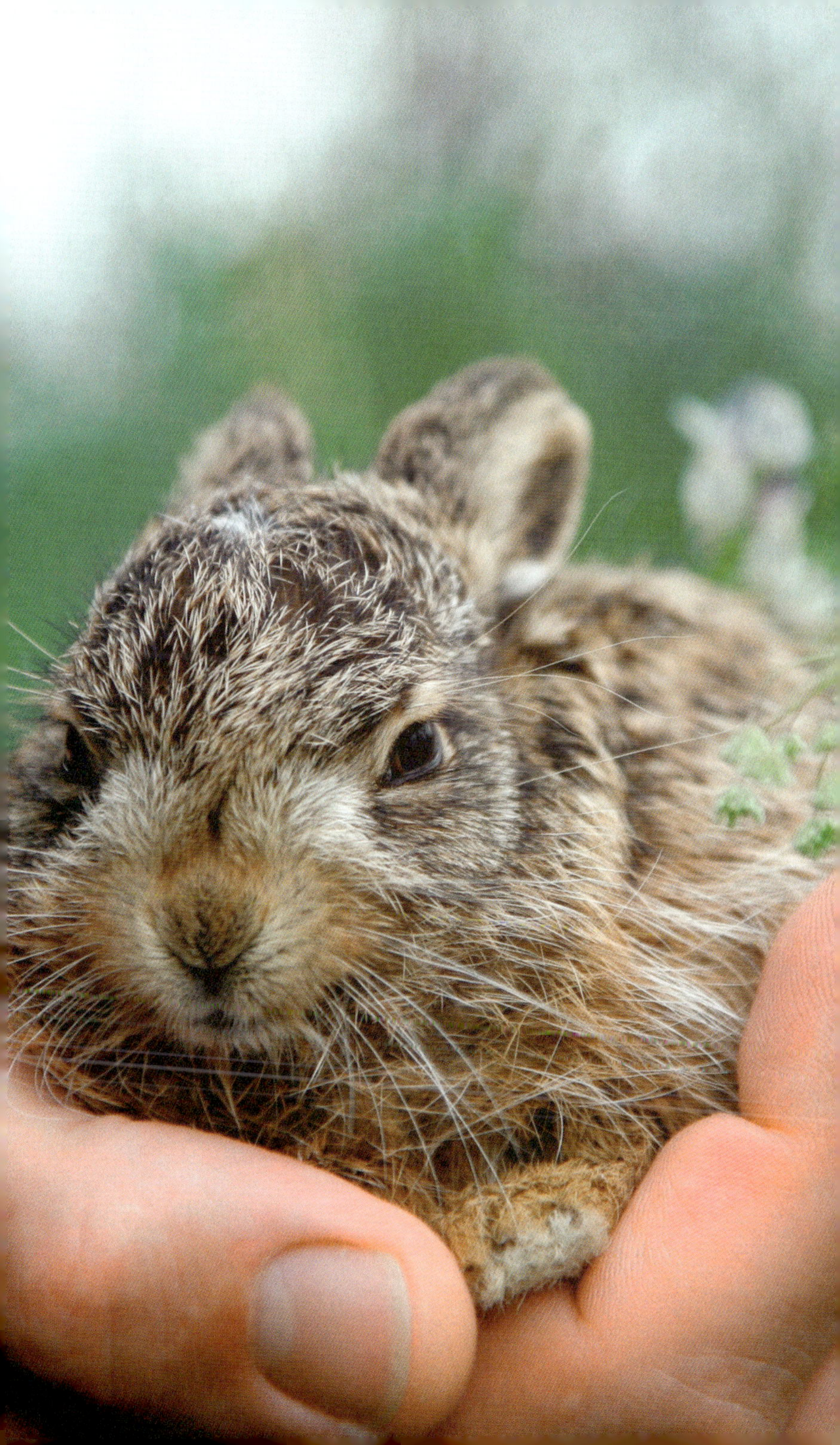

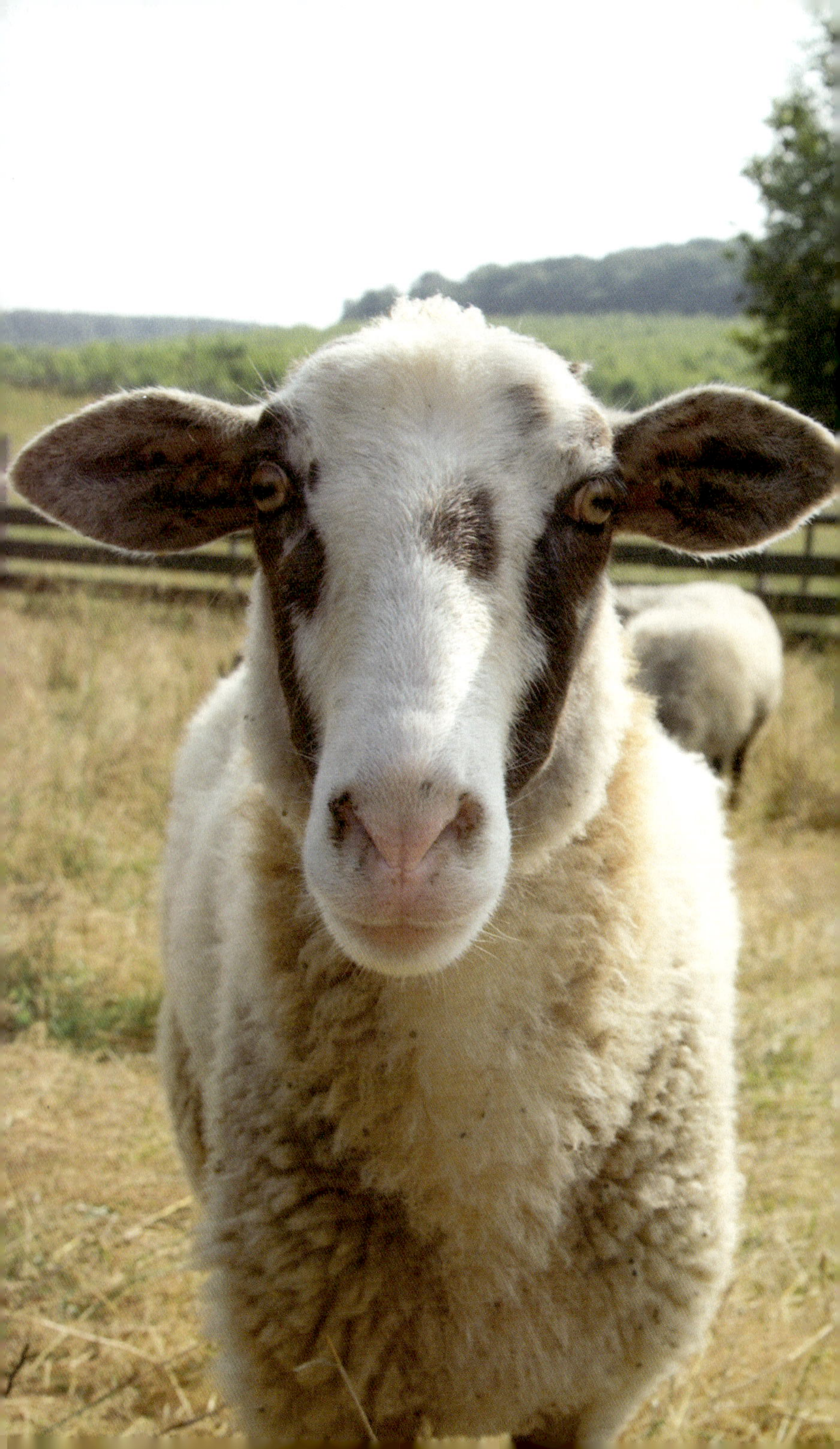

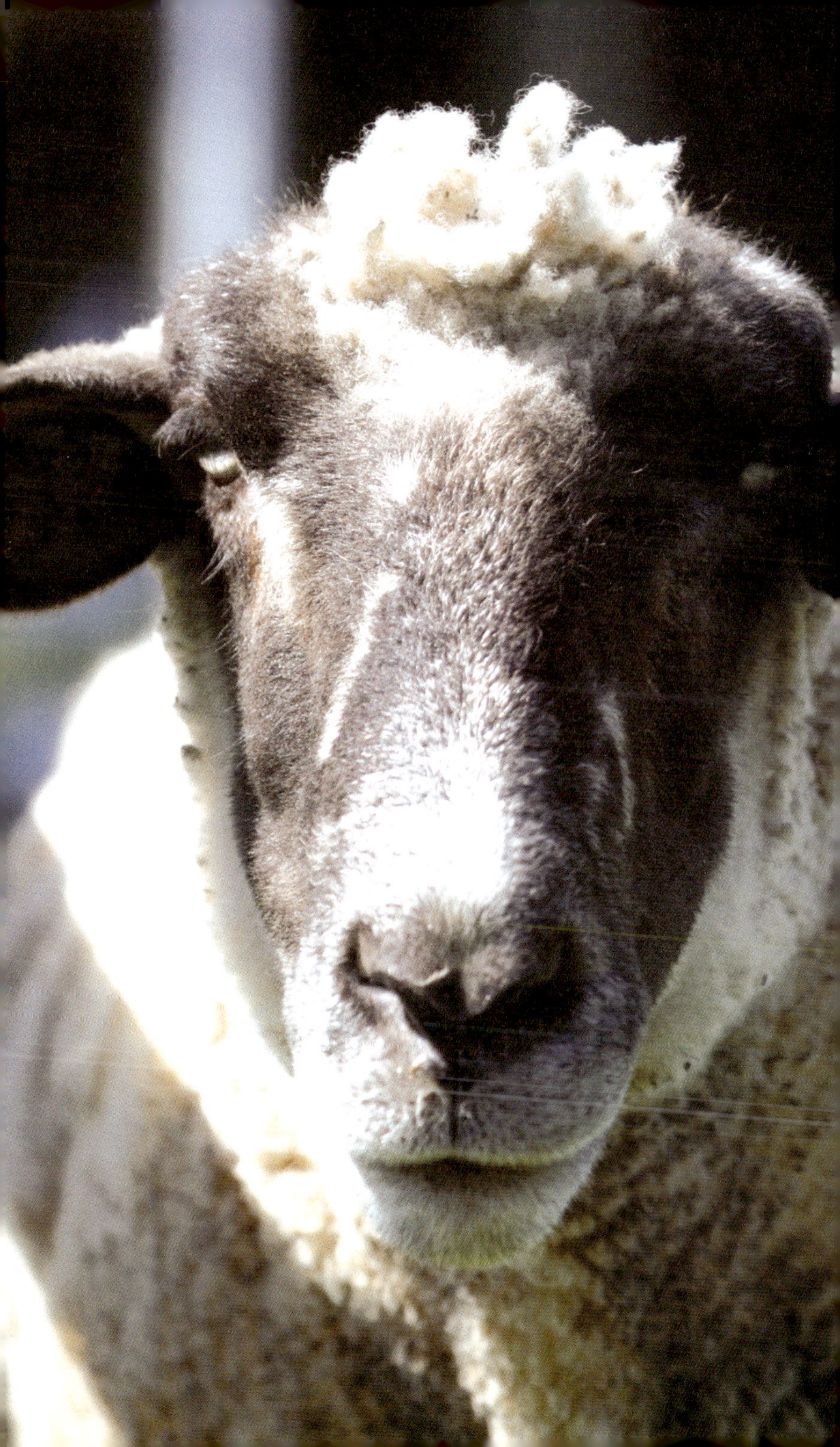

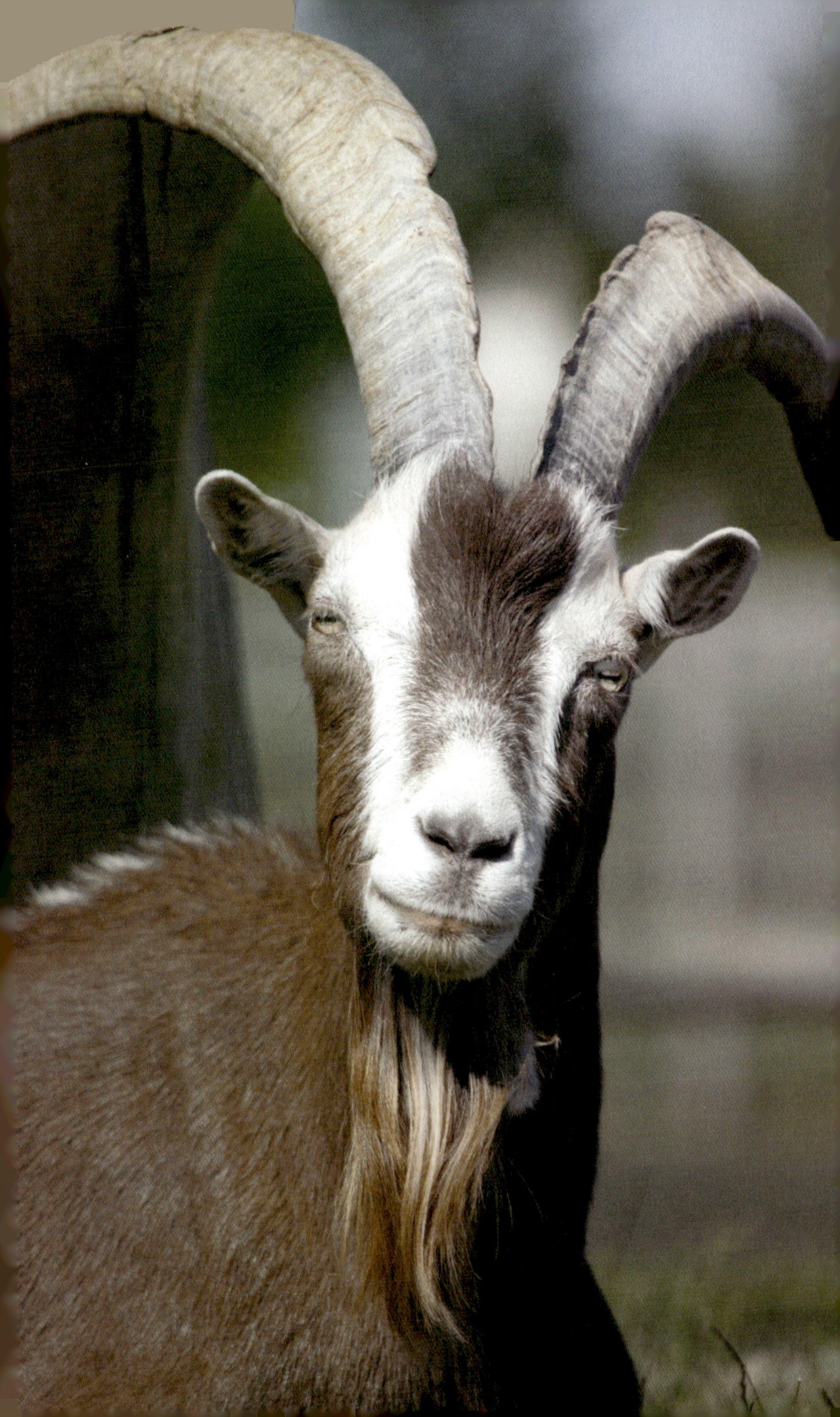

I am in your soul
as power and light.

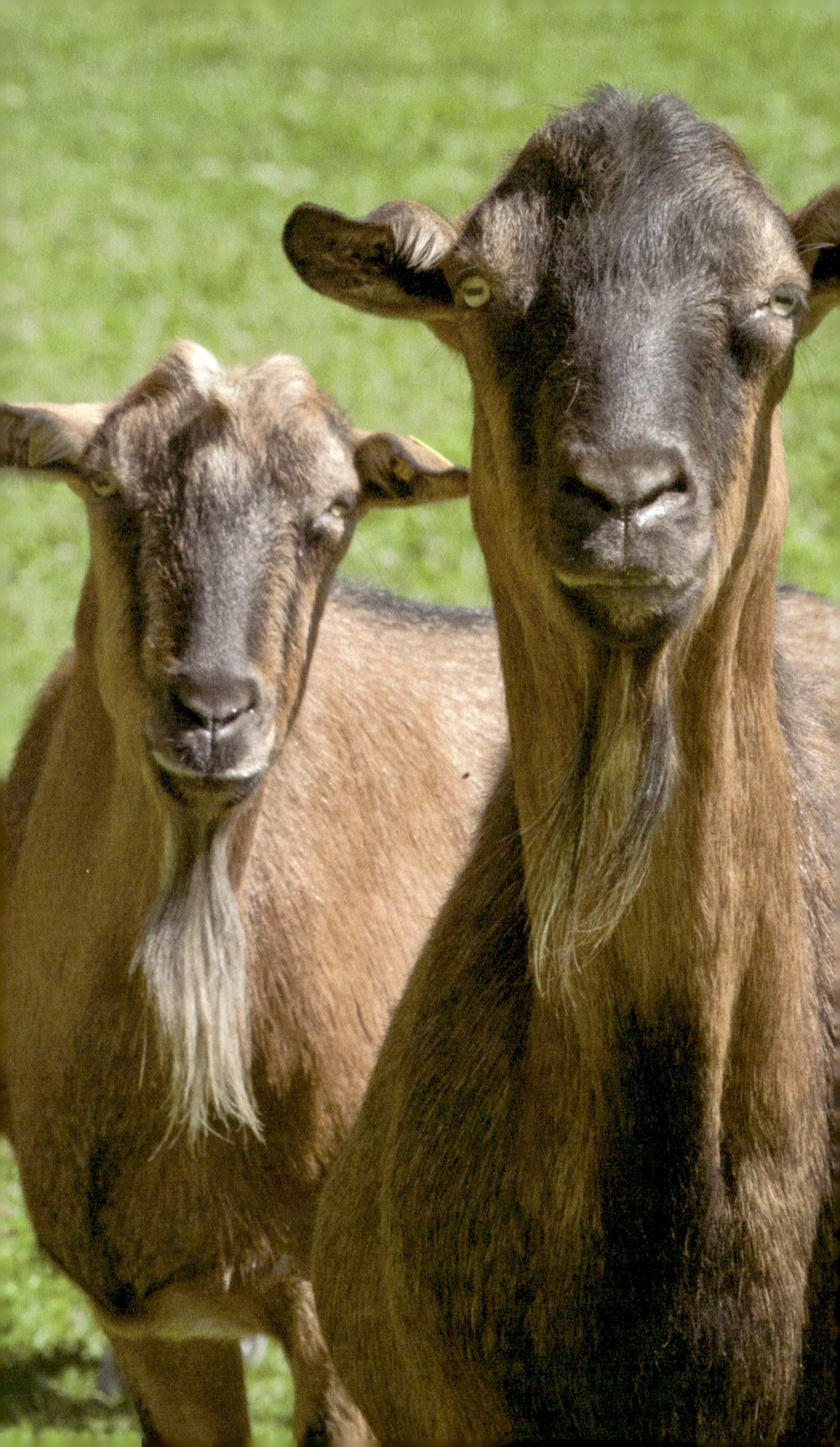

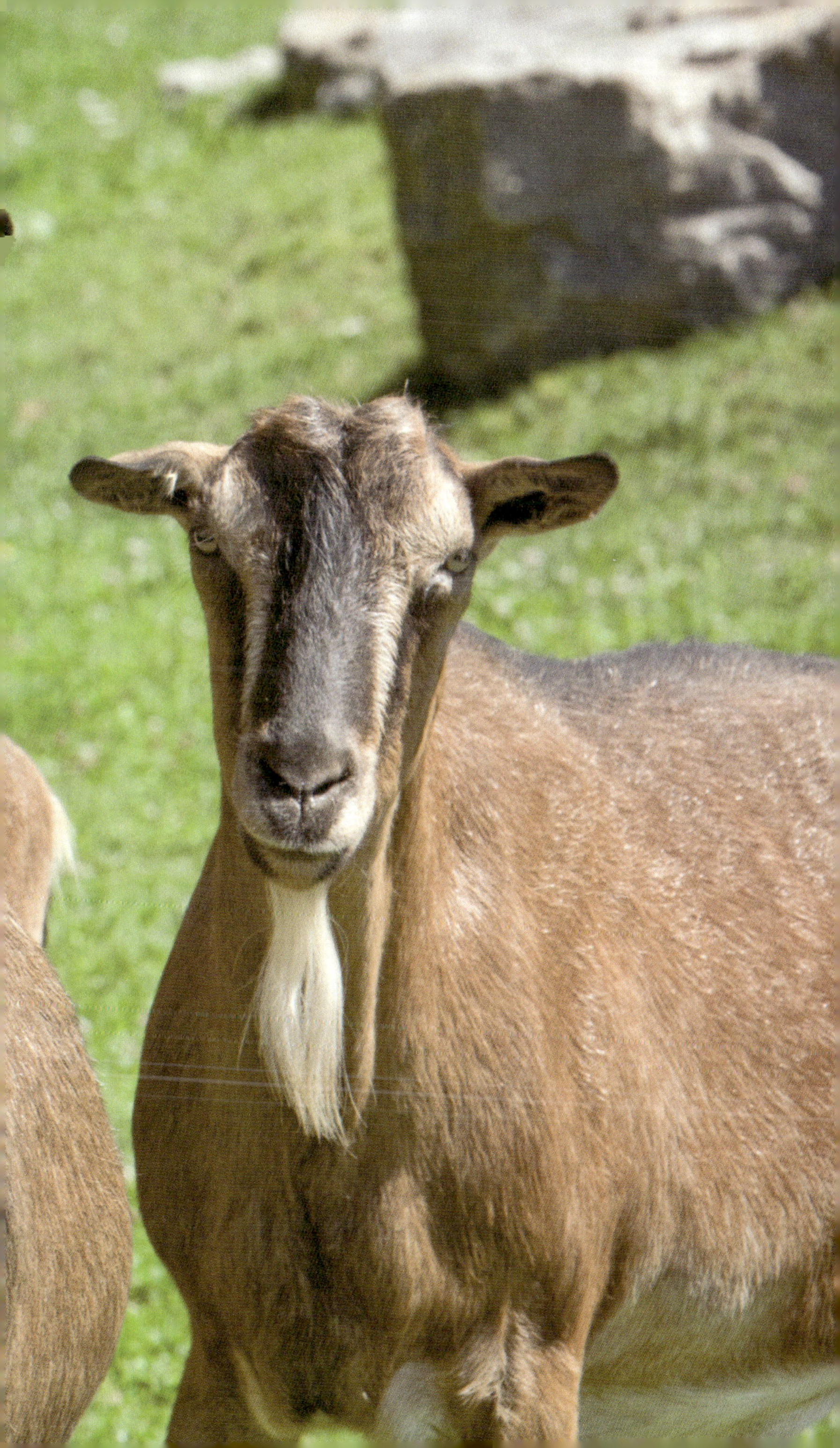

I am in your soul
as power and light.

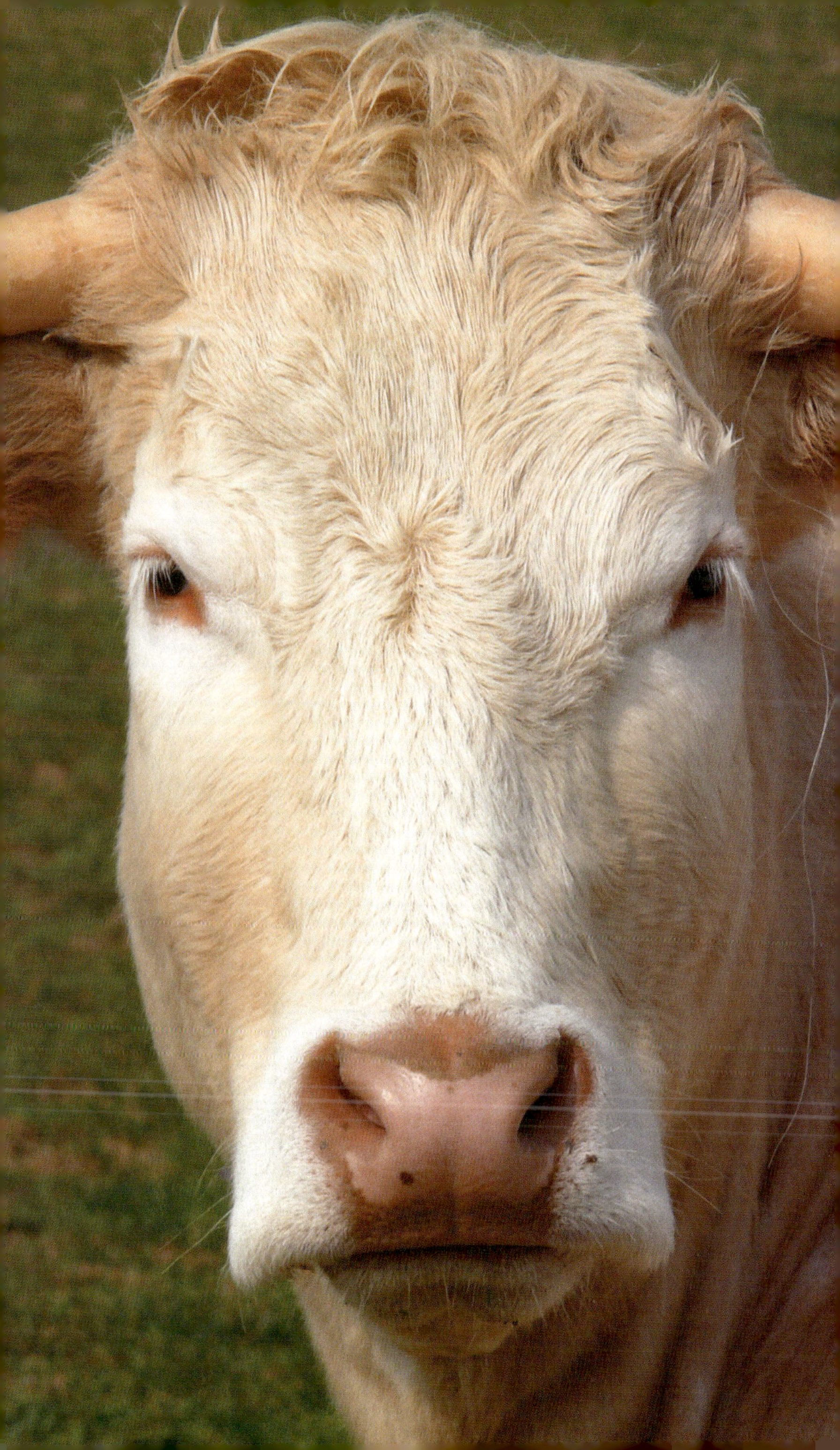

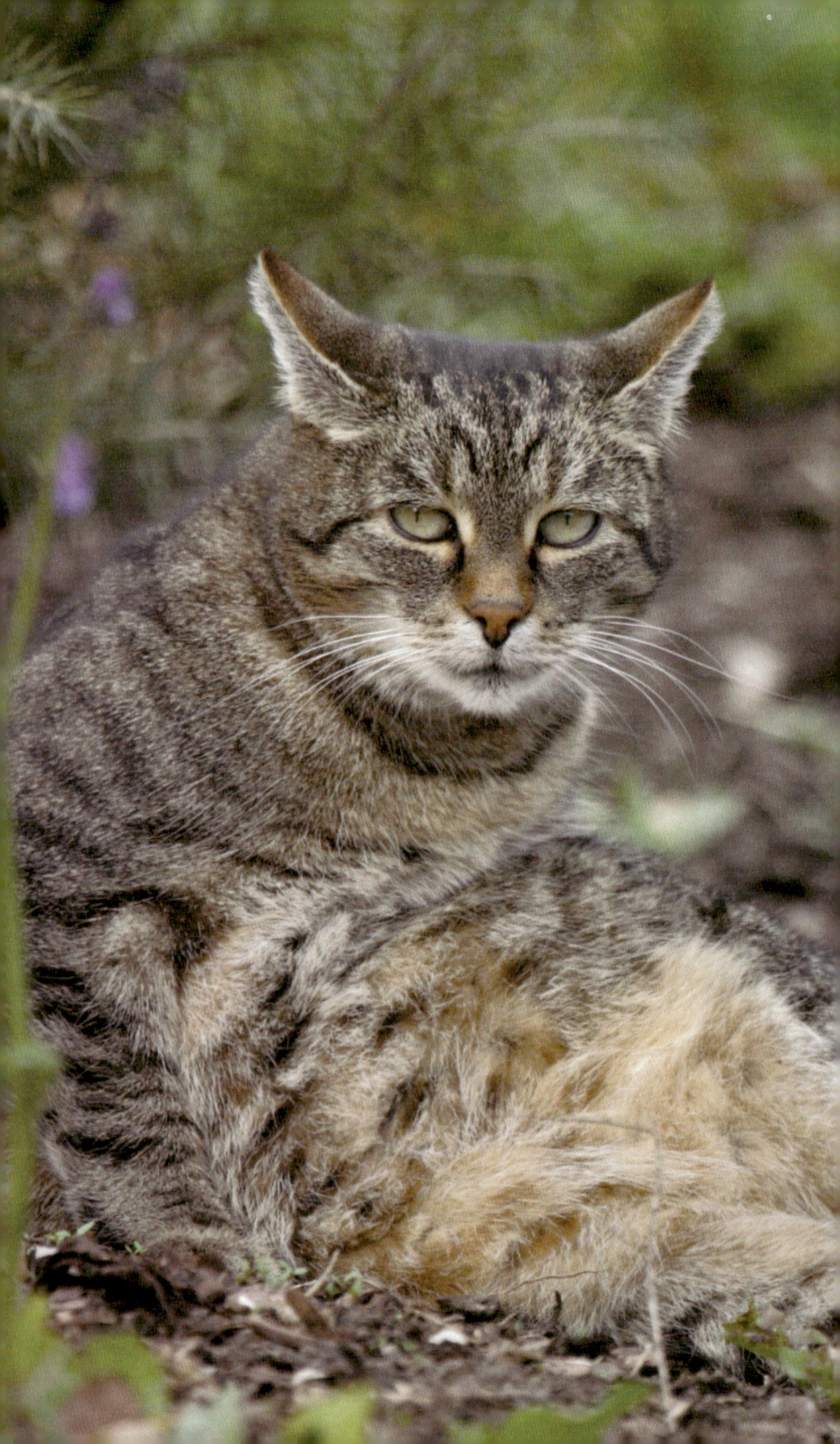

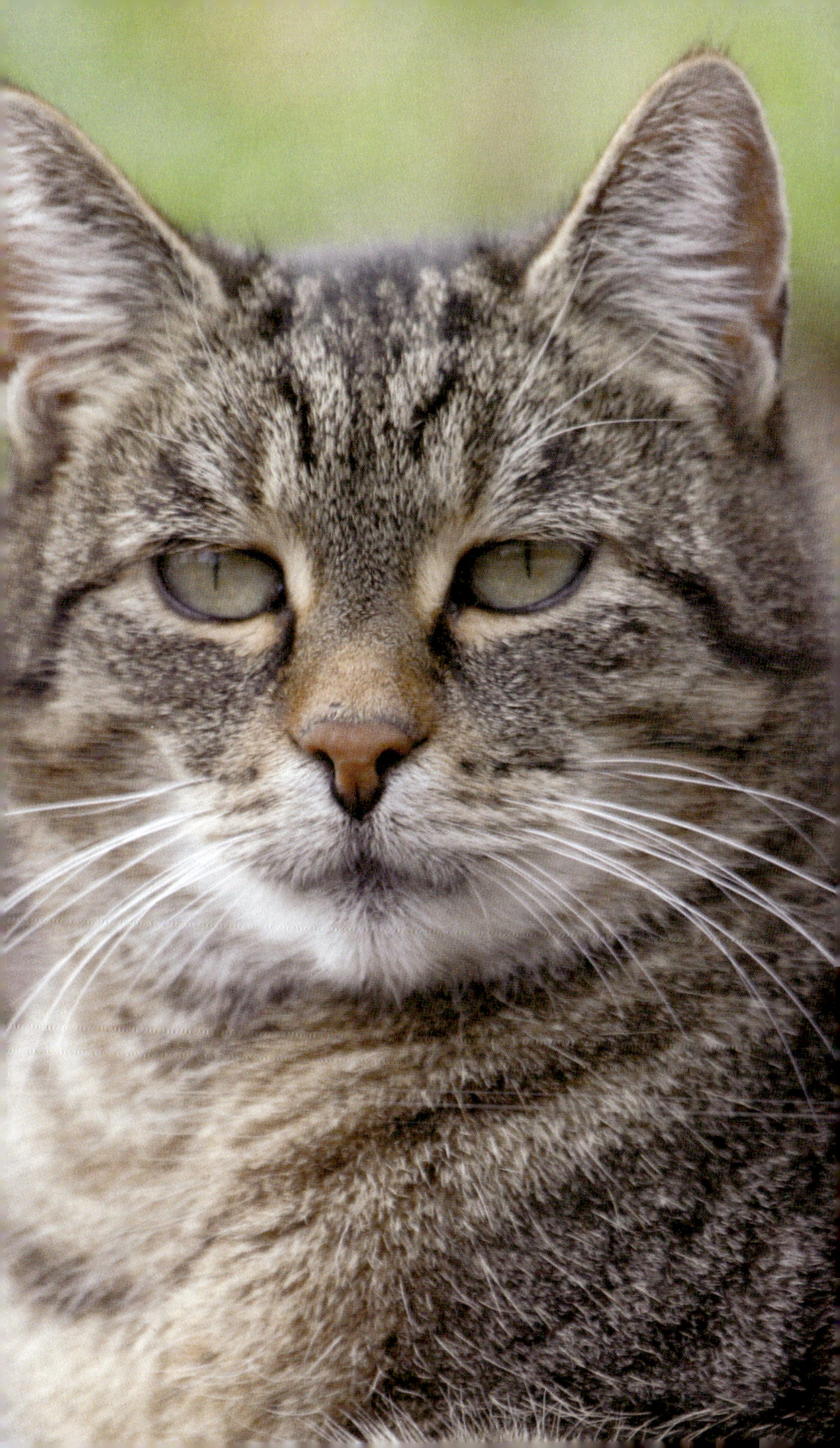

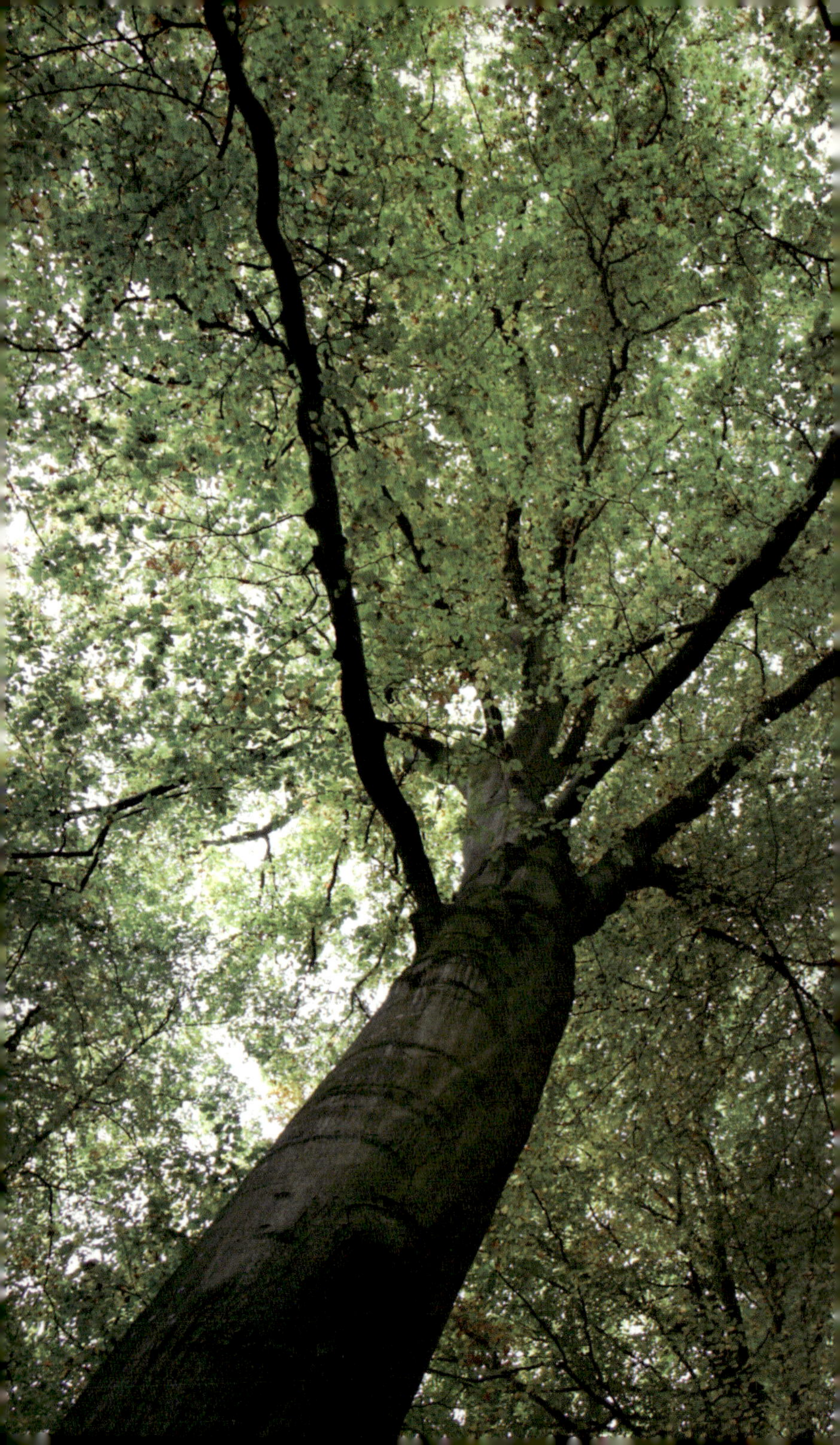

I am in your soul
as power and light.

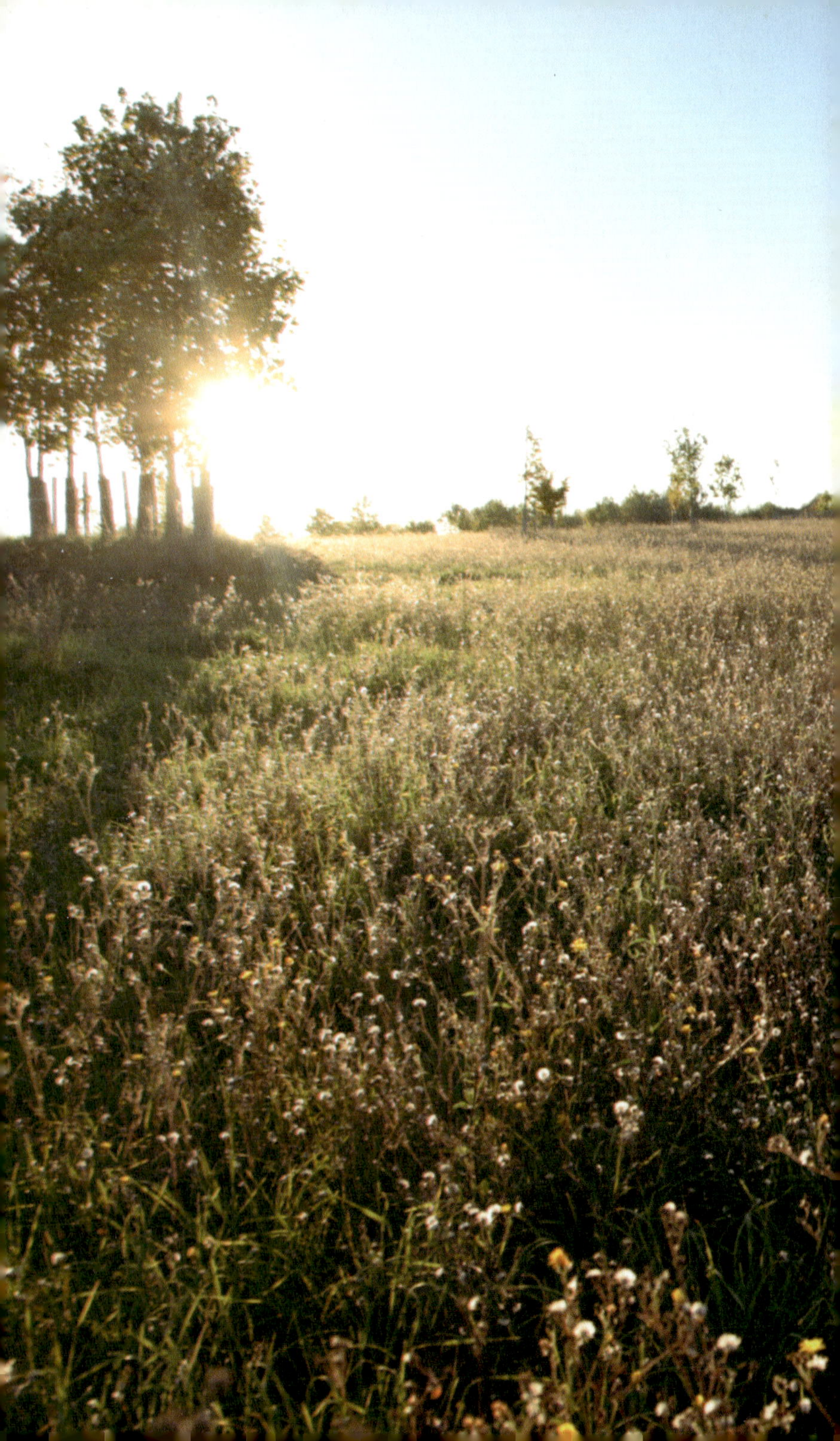

I am in your soul
as light and power.

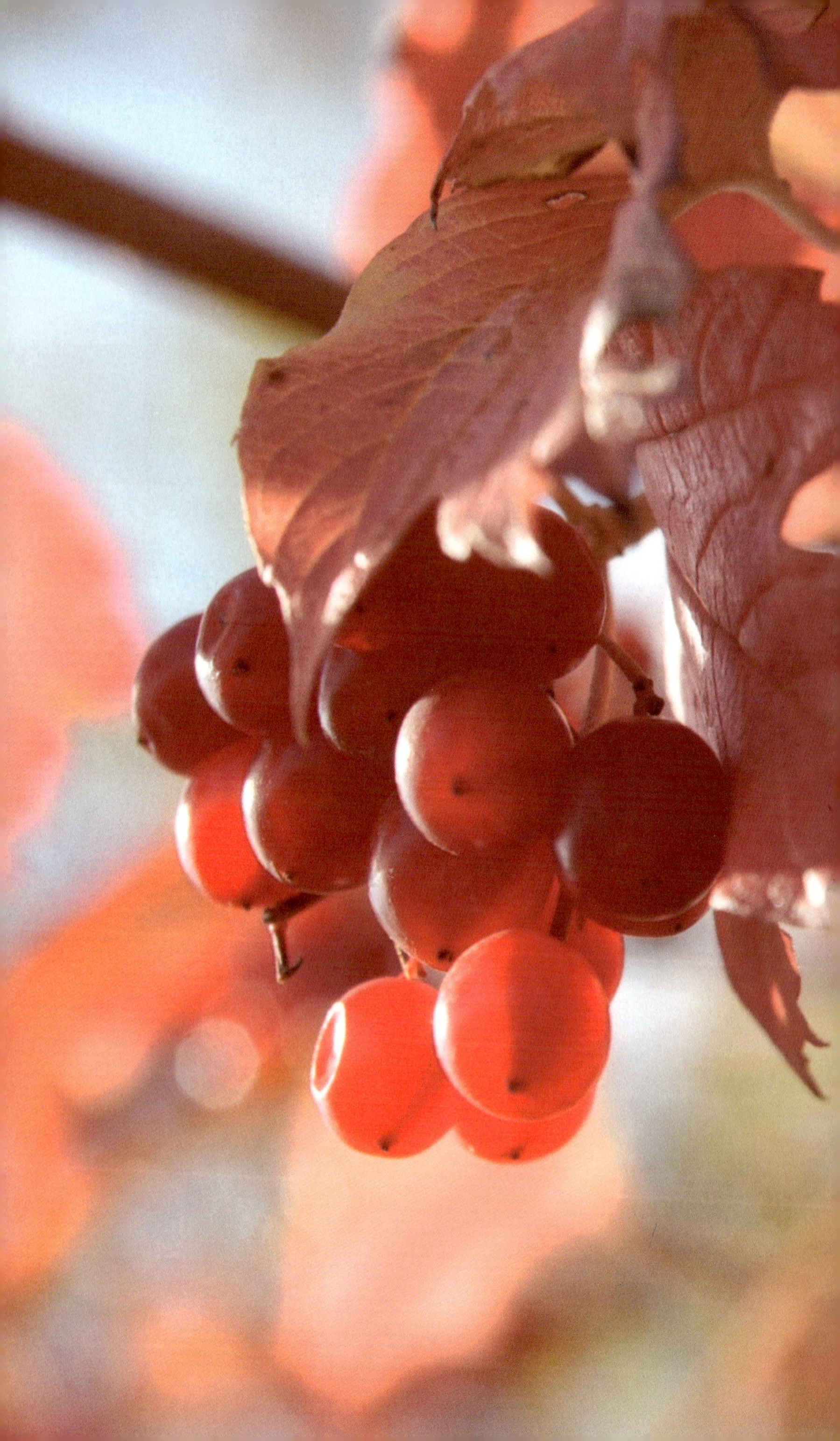

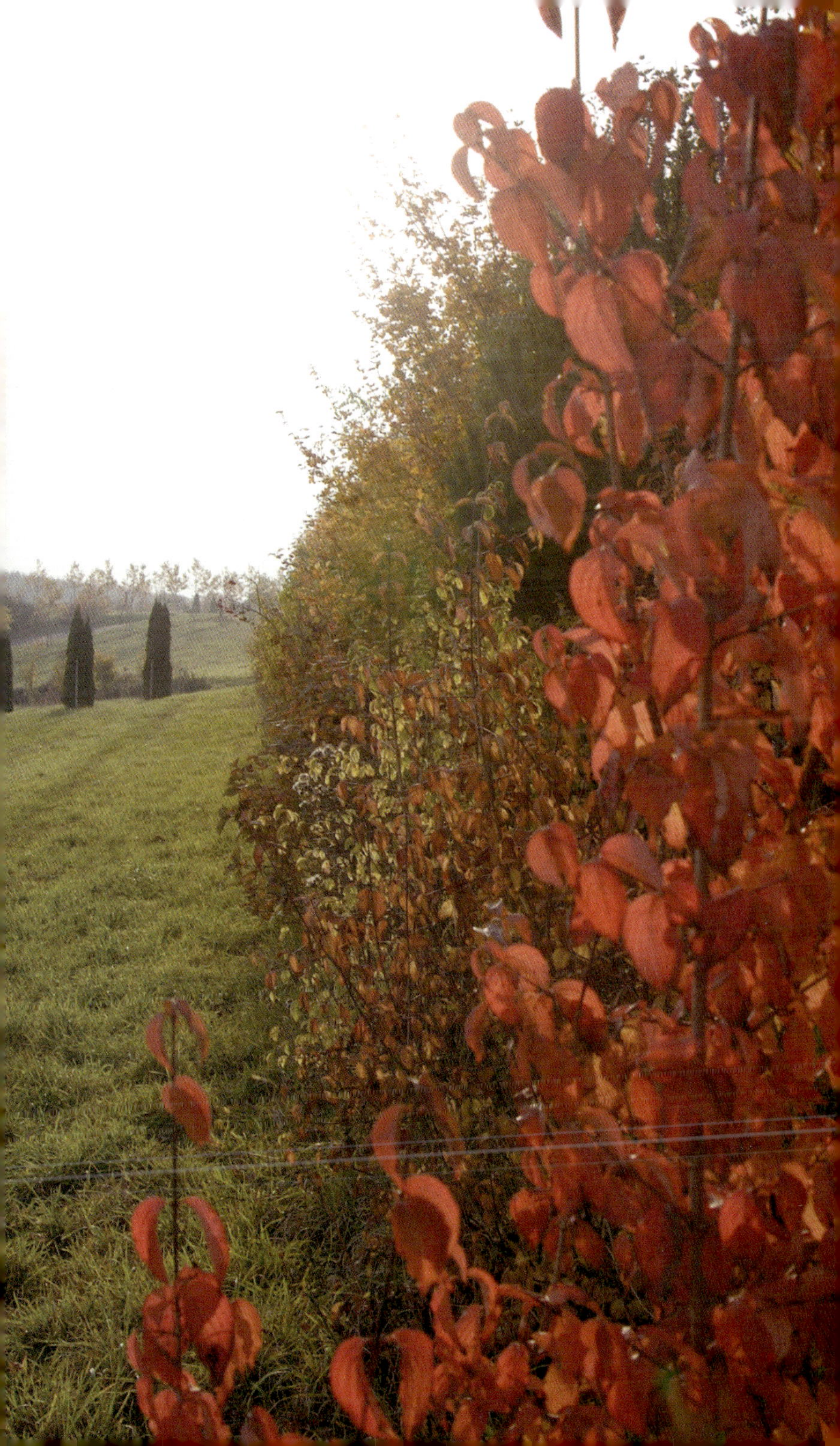

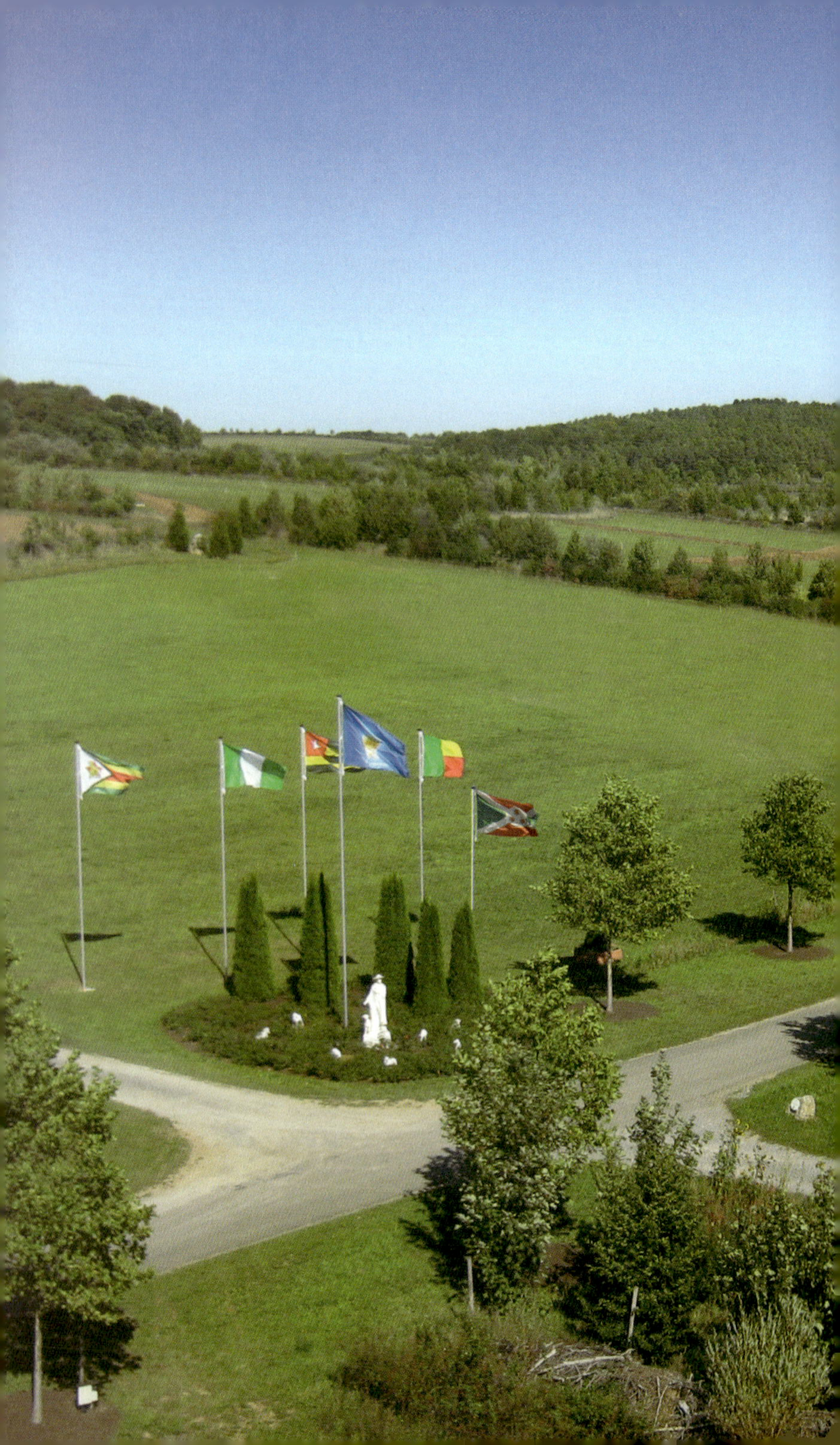

INTERNATIONALE

GABRIELE-STIFTUNG

The International Gabriele-Foundation

The Symbiosis of Man, Nature and Animals

Man has brought much suffering over the Earth and its inhabitants, the animals – through exploitation and poisoning of the soils, through barbaric animal testing and not lastly, through his eating habits. Billions of animals fall victim every year to man's lusts of the palate. The International Gabriele Foundation, founded by Gabriele, the prophetess and emissary of God in our time, is counteracting this suffering and is active worldwide making amends to nature and animals.

The Land of Peace

On the Land of Peace, which the International Gabriele Foundation is developing in the heart of Germany, animals and people have the same right to life. Sheep, cattle or geese may grow old in dignity. Free-living animals such as deer, hares or birds are getting back their original habitats. In just a few years, a connective biotope system of overwhelming beauty has emerged: woods, wetland biotopes, pastures and meadows with scattered fruit trees lie picturesquely in a rolling landscape, linked via kilometers of hedgerows, in which wild animals find protection and food. According to the Golden Rule of Jesus of Nazareth, "Do to others as you would have them do to you," animals are rescued from the butcher, to make a life of dignity possible for them. For just as dogs and cats can develop a close and deep friendship with us humans, all animals want to live in peace and unity with us.

The Beginning of a New Era!

The Land of Peace is still small and many animals are waiting to move in. People from all over the world who have a heart for animals are helping, so that the Land of Peace, the symbiosis of man, nature and animals, can continue growing. During past years, many facilities could be created through the help of many sponsors, for example, an animal infirmary, as well as the senior paradise "Helping Hands for Animals," in which elderly animals can spend their remaining years in dignity.

The example of the Land of Peace continues to spread. In many countries of the Earth, especially in Africa, people are beginning to practice a new way of treating nature and the animals, according to the role model of the Land of Peace in Germany. It is the dawn of a New Era!

Will You Help? The Animals Thank You!

We will gladly send you a comprehensive illustrated brochure on the goals and activities of the International Gabriele Foundation, as well as on the possibilities to assume animal sponsorships.

INTERNATIONAL GABRIELE FOUNDATION
THE SAMMLINIC WORK
OF NEIGHBORLY LOVE
THE SYMBIOSIS OF MAN,
NATURE AND ANIMALS
THE LAND OF PEACE

INTERNATIONAL GABRIELE-FOUNDATION
Max-Braun-Str. 2, 97828 Marktheidenfeld, Tel. +49(0)9393/504-427
Donations: Volksbank Main-Tauber, Account No: 20.62.88
Bank Routing No: 673-900-00
IBAN: DE 37 6739 0000 0000 2062 88 - BIC/SWIFT: GENODE61WTH
www.gabriele-foundation.org

The Center of the Free Spirit

The Sophia Library

For All Cultures Worldwide
The Word in Written, Audio and Visual Form

An Information Center
for all Spheres of Life

Take some time and enjoy
the unique atmosphere of the Sophia Library
to inform yourself about the word
of the Free Spirit.

Books, CDs and DVDs are available
in many languages.

Sophia Library

THE CENTER OF THE FREE SPIRIT
THE SOPHIA LIBRARY
FOR ALL CULTURES WORLDWIDE
THE WORD IN WRITTEN, AUDIO AND
VISUAL FORM

In the Sophia Library - the Center of the Free Spirit - you gain a comprehensive look into Gabriele's life's work, the prophetess and emissary of God in our time.

At numerous information isles, you have the possibility to inform yourself about all spheres of life in many languages: in written, audio and visual form.

A bookstore of new and secondhand books, and a lending library are integrated in the Sophia Library.

Concerts and other events also regularly take place here.

More information: Tel. +49(0)9391/504137.

Open Daily.

97828 Marktheidenfeld, Industrial Area Altfeld
Max-Braun-Str. 2
Below the Shopping Center

Read also ...

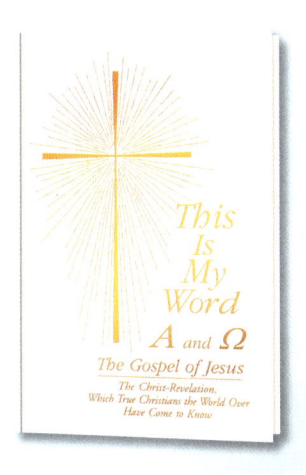

This Is My Word
A and Ω
The Gospel of Jesus

The Christ-Revelation, which True Christians the World Over Have Come to Know

Much that Jesus taught remained hidden from the people, for the present-day Bible contains only what Jerome (383) was allowed to include in the gospels. In the divine work of revelation "This Is My Word," we read from Christ Himself the truth about His life, thinking and working – much that is lacking in the traditional scriptures or passed on ambiguously. A promising and shaking message!

Content:

The childhood and youth of Jesus • The falsification of the teachings of Jesus of Nazareth during the past 2000 years • Purpose and meaning of life on Earth • Jesus taught the law of sowing and reaping • Prerequisites for healing the body • Jesus teaches about marriage • The Sermon on the Mount • About the nature of God • God does not get angry or punish • The teaching of "eternal damnation" is a mockery of God • Jesus exposes the scribes and Pharisees as hypocrites • Jesus loved the animals and always stood up for them • About death, reincarnation and life • Equality of men and women • The true meaning of the Redeemer-deed of Christ ... and much, much more.

With a brief autobiography of Gabriele,
including a charcoal drawing of her.
1069 pages, paperback,
Order No. S007en. ISBN 978-1-890841-38-6. $15.00

Read also ...

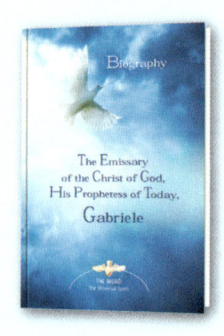

A biography by Matthias Holzbauer

The Emissary of the Christ of God, His Prophetess of the Present Time, Gabriele

"I have yet many things to say to you, but you cannot bear them now. When the Spirit of truth comes, he will guide you into all the truth."

Gabriele is the living proof that God, the universal Spirit, does not allow Himself to be silenced, even today, in our time, for the free Spirit blows where it will. She is the proof that God, the Father of us all, loves His children. For He never forsakes us – not even in a time of upheavals and disasters, into which we human beings have maneuvered ourselves.

Read the biography about a woman of the people, to whom the call of God went out to serve Him as the interpreter of His word, as His prophetess.

Each book includes 2 CDs:
CD1: "Deep Breathing" and "Abide in You" – 2 meditations
CD2: "You Spurn the One God and Believe in Eternal Damnation. I Am the God of Love" – Revelation from God

264 pp., paperback, Order No. S550en, ISBN 978-1-890841-73-7. $16.00

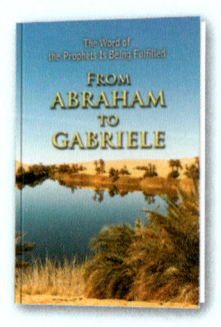

Martin Kübli

The Word of the Prophets Is Being Fulfilled

From Abraham to Gabriele

In a great span, the author sheds light on the word of God, which, uninterrupted throughout the millennia, lets us recognize God's great plan: The return of all fallen beings to the eternal Father's house – from Abraham about 4000 years ago to Gabriele today. The word of the prophets is being fulfilled – despite all hostilities from the priestly religions.

Content: Through Isaiah, the Eternal raised his voice mightily against animal sacrifice and idolatry • Isaiah announced the coming of the Messiah and the Kingdom of Peace • Jesus, the Christ, taught the free Spirit – without dogmas, cults, ceremonies • The Eternal announced a covenant with the animals – the institutional churches continue to sacrifice His creatures • His word through the emissary of God – Gabriele • "On Earth as it is in heaven" – the concept of unity for a new humanity • and much more.

80 pp, paperback, Order No. S465en. ISBN 978-1-890841-34-8. $7.00

Message From the All
God's Prophecy Today - Not the Word of the Bible

The message from the All contains answer to man's fundamental questions: about the meaning and purpose of life on Earth, about the immortality of the soul and its reincarnations in several lives on Earth; it also speaks about the disasters that will hit a mankind that continues to violate Mother Earth, that maltreats nature and animals and wages war with one another. God gave warning in time ... Read for yourself the Message from the All, given through Gabriele, the prophetess and emissary of God in our time.

187 pages, softbound, Order No. S137en. ISBN 978-1-890841-36-2. $15.00

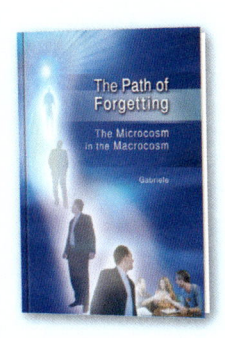

Gabriele
The Path of Forgetting
The Microcosm in the Macrocosm

The soul lives in another dimension, which is finer-material, but it retains the habits it acquired as human being for a long time. Every action is energy and is stored in the macrocosm. Everything that is part of being a human being is taken by the soul into the other world, into the beyond – and it must be discarded on the path of forgetting. This work by Gabriele explains correlations and processes of life that are mostly still unknown, yet decisive for shaping our days on Earth.

112 pages, paperback, Order No. S348en. ISBN 978-1-890841-68-3. $8.00

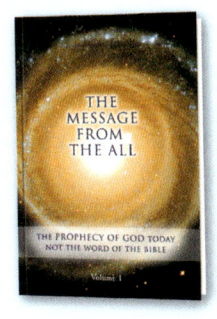

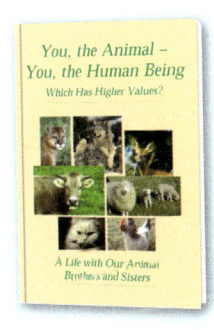

The Life of Our Animal Brothers and Sisters
You, the Animal - You, the Human Being
Which Has Higher Values?

A fundamental divine work of revelation about the right way to treat animals. In addition, it is about the communication of animals and beings with each other; about the possibilities to communicate as a human being with animals; about the invisible helpers on the Earth – the nature beings; about the background to why an animal attacks us; advice for feeding animals and the organization of the course of their day; about the New Era, a new life in connection with animals, plants and minerals, and much more...

108 pages, Order No. S133en. ISBN 978-1-890841- 25-0. $10.00

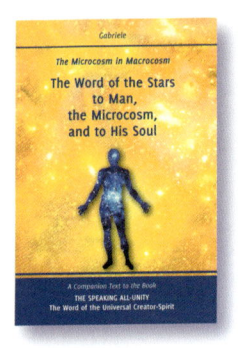

The Microcosm in the Macrocosm
The Word of the Stars to Man, the Microcosm, and to His Soul

Why is there a material cosmos with all its countless stars and planetary constellations - and what does all this have to do with a human being and his soul? Read an explanation on the cosmic correlations of all life, given by Gabriele as a companion text to the book, "The Speaking All-Unity, the Word of the Universal Creator-Spirit."

44 pp., Softbound, Order No. S175 en. ISBN: 978-2-890841-82-9, $3.50.

Free Booklets:

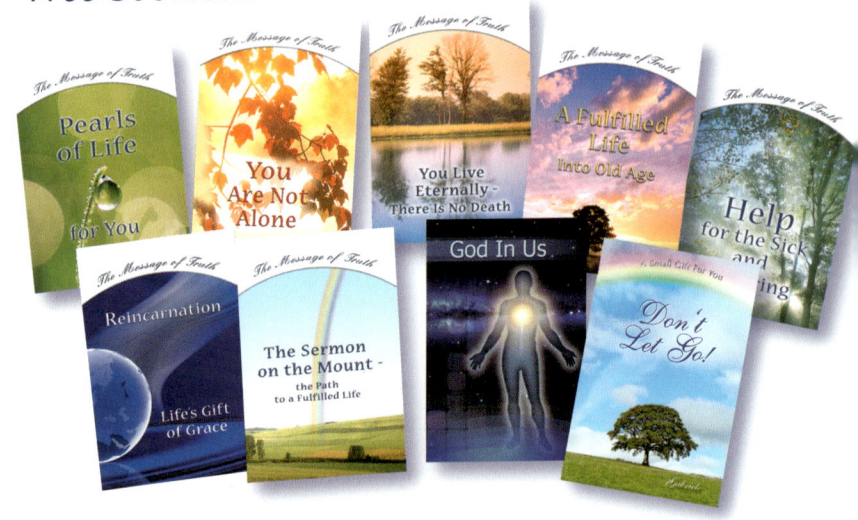

* Pearls of Life For You
* You Are Not Alone
* You Live Eternally - there Is No Death
* A Fulfilled Life Into Old Age
* Help for the Sick and Suffering

* Reincarnation, Life's Gift of Grace
* The Sermon on the Mount - the Path to a Fulfilled Life
* God In Us
* Don't Let Go

We will be happy to send you our catalog of books, CDs and DVDs, as well as our free brochures and reading samples to various topics.

THE WORD - THE UNIVERSAL SPIRIT
P.O. Box 3549, Woodbridge, CT 06525
www.Universal-Spirit.org